Police Integrity Management in Australia

Global Lessons for Combating Police Misconduct

Advances in Police Theory and Practice Series

Series Editor: Dilip K. Das

Police Integrity Management in Australia:
Global Lessons for Combating Police Misconduct
Louise Porter and Tim Prenzler

The Crime Numbers Game: Management by Manipulation
John A. Eterno and Eli B. Silverman

The International Trafficking of Human Organs:
A Multidisciplinary Perspective
Leonard Territo and Rande Matteson

Police Reform in China
Kam C. Wong

Mission-Based Policing
John P. Crank, Dawn M. Irlbeck, Rebecca K. Murray, Mark Sundermeier

The New Khaki: The Evolving Nature of Policing in India
Arvind Verma

Cold Cases: An Evaluation Model with Follow-up Strategies for Investigators
James M. Adcock and Sarah L. Stein

Policing Organized Crime: Intelligence Strategy Implementation
Petter Gottschalk

Security in Post-Conflict Africa: The Role of Nonstate Policing
Bruce Baker

Community Policing and Peacekeeping
Peter Grabosky

Community Policing: International Patterns and Comparative Perspectives
Dominique Wisler and Ihekwoaba D. Onwudiwe

Police Corruption: Preventing Misconduct and Maintaining Integrity
Tim Prenzler

Police Integrity Management in Australia

Global Lessons for Combating Police Misconduct

Louise Porter
Tim Prenzler

CRC Press
Taylor & Francis Group
Boca Raton London New York

CRC Press is an imprint of the
Taylor & Francis Group, an **informa** business

CRC Press
Taylor & Francis Group
6000 Broken Sound Parkway NW, Suite 300
Boca Raton, FL 33487-2742

First issued in paperback 2019

ISBN-13: 978-1-4398-9598-6 (hbk)
ISBN-13: 978-0-367-86694-5 (pbk)

Library of Congress Cataloging-in-Publication Data

Porter, Louise.
Police Integrity Management in Australia : global lessons for combating police misconduct / Louise Porter and Timothy Prenzler.
p. cm. -- (Advances in police theory and practice ; 12)
Includes bibliographical references and index.
ISBN 978-1-4398-9598-6
1. Police administration--Australia. 2. Police corruption--Australia--Prevention. 3. Police ethics--Australia. I. Prenzler, Tim. II. Title.

HV8280.A3.P67 2012
363.2'2--dc23 2011046206

Visit the Taylor & Francis Web site at
http://www.taylorandfrancis.com

and the CRC Press Web site at
http://www.crcpress.com

Contents

Series Preface

While the literature on police and allied subjects is growing exponentially, its impact on day-to-day policing remains small. The two worlds of research and practice of policing remain disconnected even though cooperation between the two is growing. A major reason is that the two groups speak in different languages. The research work is published in hard-to-access journals and presented in a manner that is difficult to comprehend for a lay person. On the other hand, the police practitioners tend not to mix with researchers and remain secretive about their work. Consequently, there is little dialogue between the two and almost no attempt to learn from one another. Dialogue across the globe, amongst researchers and practitioners situated in different continents, is, of course, even more limited.

I attempted to address this problem by starting the International Police Executive Symposium (IPES) (www.ipes.info) where a common platform has brought the two together. IPES is now in its 15th year. The annual meetings that constitute most major annual events of the organization have been hosted in all parts of the world. Several publications have come out of these deliberations and a new collaborative community of scholars and police officers has been created whose membership runs into several hundreds.

Another attempt was to begin a new journal, aptly called *Police Practice and Research: An International Journal* (*PPR*), that has opened the gate to practitioners to share their work and experiences. The journal has attempted to focus on issues that help bring the two onto a single platform. *PPR* completed its 10th year in 2009. It is certainly evidence of the growing collaboration between police research and practice that *PPR*, which began with four issues a year, expanded into five issues in its fourth year, and it is now published six times a year.

Clearly, these attempts, despite their success, remain limited. Conferences and journal publications do help create a body of knowledge and an association of police activists, but cannot address substantial issues in depth. The limitations of time and space preclude larger discussions and more authoritative expositions that can provide stronger and broader linkages between the two worlds.

It is this realization of the increasing dialogue between police research and practice that has encouraged many of us—my close colleagues and I who are connected closely with IPES and *PPR* across the world—to conceive and implement a book series, *Advances in Police Theory and Practice*, that seeks to attract writers from all parts of the world. Further, the attempt is to find practitioner contributors. The objective is to make the series a serious contribution to our knowledge of the police as well as to improve police practices. The focus is not only in work that describes the best and most successful police practices, but also one that challenges current paradigms and breaks new ground to prepare police for the 21st century. The series seeks for comparative analysis that highlights achievements in distant parts of the world as well as one that encourages an in-depth examination of specific problems confronting a particular police force.

Police corruption and misconduct are, unfortunately, universal problems. It seems that no police department is immune from allegations or exposés of corruption, brutality, or other abuses of authority. Around the world, inquiries and scandals continue to sully the police image and detract from public confidence in the police. The problem is not just to the detriment of communities. All hard working and honest police, who risk their lives to protect and serve their communities, suffer from the effects of workplace deviance. While a good deal is known about the nature of the problem and many of its causes, the science of misconduct prevention – or integrity management – is still developing. One useful way to advance knowledge in this area is by in-depth studies of how different jurisdictions have dealt with different types of conduct issues. Comparative studies, including those carried out within one country, provide a mechanism for analyzing complex issues in the field and the impacts of different strategies designed to identify and prevent unethical behavior.

With these issues in mind, I am pleased to introduce the latest release in the CRC Press/Taylor & Francis Advances in Police Theory and Practice Series. *Police Integrity Management in Australia: Lessons for Combating Police Misconduct*, by Louise Porter and Tim Prenzler, is a study of contemporary police integrity management across the eight police jurisdictions in Australia, involving the work of 18 separate agencies, based primarily on practitioner interviews. The first chapter of the book introduces the reader to the complex problem of police misconduct from historical and global perspectives. Subsequent chapters provide detailed analyses of current and emerging ethical challenges, and the highly diverse integrity management strategies in each police department in Australia. The final chapter draws out the implications of these findings for police managers and oversight agencies, with an emphasis on generalizable lessons for improved systems. The book continues the work of the CRC Press series in advancing knowledge about problems and challenges for police, with a focus on best practice principles and effective practices, including advancing productive dialogue between researchers and practitioners.

It is hoped that through this series it will be possible to accelerate the process of building knowledge about policing and help bridge the gap between the two worlds—the world of police research and the world of police practice. This is an invitation to police scholars and practitioners across the world to come and join in this venture.

Dilip K. Das
Founding President,
International Police Executive Symposium, IPES, www.ipes.info

Founding Editor-in-Chief
Police Practice and Research: An International Journal, PPR,
www.tandf.co.uk/journals

Preface

Australia has been the site of major police misconduct scandals and inquiries in the past two decades, and these have stimulated reform programs at the cutting edge of police integrity management practices. This book reports on a stocktake study of these strategies and systems in Australia, conducted in 2008 to 2010 via interviews with key informants and analysis of key documents. It provides a rare national overview and critique of a full suite of policies, institutions, and strategies adopted to combat the diverse and complex forms of misconduct that occur in policing.

Police integrity management is now very much on the political agenda in many countries. Police departments are increasingly required to have well-informed corruption prevention plans in place and be able to account for the exercise of powers using meaningful measures of ethical conduct. These requirements entail major challenges for police managers who need to demonstrate knowledge of current best practice and international standards. However, despite significant advances in knowledge, a large number of questions remain about the most effective and fair methods of both dealing with police misconduct after it has occurred and preventing misconduct.

The aim of the stocktake study was to learn about the present picture of police integrity systems in Australia, particularly regarding effective strategies and emerging issues and challenges. This was designed to enable comparisons of practices and experiences across regions and organizations as well as provide a resource for international counterparts and to enhance knowledge sharing. The study sought to tap into the experiences of two primary groups: (a) agencies delivering policing services, and (b) agencies involved in police oversight. To this end, we contacted relevant agencies nationally and the response was overwhelmingly positive from all. We met with key personnel around Australia who generously shared their knowledge and ideas, as well as their concerns, and it is these insights and the wealth of experience of those individuals that this book represents. Without the help of those people, the book would be considerably slimmer and much less interesting or informative.

Whilst the stocktake study produced a long and systematic report of the information collected, we have tried to present that information here in a more accessible way. The book begins with an introductory chapter to set the scene, explain the contexts, and provide details of the methodology that produced the information presented in the remainder of the book. The chapter outlines the global problem of police misconduct and the corrosive effects it has on victims and on human rights and democratic processes. The chapter includes a summary of current knowledge about best practice in the field and then introduces the reader to the Australian experience of police corruption and the reform agenda that has driven major change and experimentation across the country.

Chapter 2 to Chapter 9 present the set of integrity strategies in place in each jurisdiction in Australia, covering rationales, evidence of effectiveness, and difficulties. The chapters cover the work of both police professional standards departments and oversight agencies, and cover a diverse and interesting range of techniques and issues including undercover stings, drug and alcohol testing, mediation of complaints, ethics training, and regulating police use of force. These chapters organise the material logically by jurisdiction, agency, and strategy with liberal use of subheadings for ease of navigation. Those with particular interests, or those short on time, will hopefully find this aids their search for information. Each chapter also contains an "emerging issues" section. This serves to highlight some of the more promising and/or innovative integrity strategies as well as emerging concerns and emerging ethical issues.

The final chapter provides an overall evaluation of the data presented in the body of the book, assessing the strengths and weaknesses of the Australian system and the implications for adoption of these strategies in other police departments around the world. This chapter draws out and discusses the main themes of shared experience across the agencies and aims to embed these in the international literature. Indeed, most issues experienced by these Australian agencies will resonate with their international counterparts, and we have endeavoured to draw explicit comparisons in the introduction and conclusion chapters.

We would like to express our sincere thanks to all participating agencies and their representatives for their openness and willingness to engage throughout this research. Thank you for making yourselves available for interviews and providing your insights as well as providing information and feedback for early drafts.

We also acknowledge Kirsty Martin and Kristy Meszaros for their research assistance on the project. Finally, we thank our funders, the Australian Research Council Centre of Excellence in Policing and Security and Griffith University.

Louise Porter
Tim Prenzler

About the Authors

Louise Porter is a research fellow in the Australian Research Council Centre of Excellence in Policing and Security (CEPS) based at Griffith University, Brisbane. She has a BSC (Hons) from the University of Leicester, UK, and an MSC. and PhD in Psychology from the University of Liverpool, UK. She is a British Psychological Society Chartered Psychologist and formerly a lecturer in forensic psychology in the United Kingdom. Her research interests centre on interpersonal processes, specifically leadership and peer influence in forensic contexts. Dr. Porter has explored social and organizational features of group crime and, most recently, police corruption and misconduct. Her work on police misconduct has focused on types of misconduct behaviour, its causes, and the systems in place to address such behaviour. She is also interested in police–citizen interactions, police use of force, and police-related deaths.

Tim Prenzler is a chief investigator in the Australian Research Council Centre of Excellence in Policing and Security (CEPS) and a professor in the School of Criminology and Criminal Justice, Griffith University, Brisbane. He holds a PhD, MA, and BA (Hons). In CEPS, he manages the Integrity Systems Project, which is focused on advancing knowledge about effective integrity management strategies in policing and security. In 1991, Prenzler was a foundation member of the School of Criminology and Criminal Justice, where he developed and taught courses in situational crime prevention, security management, criminal justice ethics, social justice, and police studies. He has contributed to a number of textbooks and co-edited (with Hennessey Hayes) *An Introduction to Crime and Criminology* (Pearson, 2009). He is the author of *Police Corruption: Preventing Misconduct and Maintaining Integrity* (CRC Press/Taylor & Francis, 2009), *Ethics and Accountability in Criminal Justice* (Australian Academic Press, 2009), and co-author (with Rick Sarre) of *The Law of Private Security in Australia,* 2nd edition (Thomson Lawbook Co., 2009). Apart from integrity research, his current work includes studies on police and security officer safety, security industry regulation, reducing welfare fraud, and improving the integration of women police.

Introduction

Police Misconduct and Integrity, International and Australian Perspectives

1

The first part of this chapter provides a global perspective on the problem of police misconduct, including analyses of the causes of misconduct and strategies designed to optimize integrity. Knowledge about both the causes and the remedies for unethical policing has grown out of painful processes of inquiry and review often triggered by major public scandals. The chapter provides a brief history of the police corruption problem, including attention to recent high profile cases in the United Kingdom, United States, and Canada. While there is good baseline knowledge about effective anticorruption strategies, there is a need for more advanced knowledge. The persistence of misconduct cases, even in police departments with quite sophisticated integrity systems, evidences the need for development in this area. With that goal in mind, the second part of the chapter provides a rationale for a close examination of the contemporary Australian experience with police integrity systems, given the size of the historical misconduct problem in Australian policing and the range of anticorruption initiatives that have been introduced in the past few decades.

Historical Background

Modern policing as we know it developed in the 19th century following the establishment of the London Metropolitan Police in 1829. British Home Secretary Robert Peel sought to place police on a professional footing, with uniforms, salaries, selection criteria, a formal organization of tasks, a hierarchy of command and supervision, and detachment from politics. The "New Police" were preceded by forms of law enforcement and crime prevention that variously involved village watchmen, parish constables with customary duties, militia, and private prosecution or "thief taker" societies (Johnston, 1991). These ad hoc forms of policing were generally ineffective, often capricious and violent, and frequently corrupt. The fact that policing duties were unpaid or poorly paid was one factor in a financial trade in justice that favoured those able and willing to pay for preferential treatment (Critchley, 1967; Kappeler, Sluder, & Alpert, 1998).

The professional model of policing, which has been adopted from the London model around the world, was, in theory, designed to make policing a broad public service, impartial, free of corruption, with a commitment to crime prevention and minimal use of force (Critchley, 1967, p. 51). However, the fledgling forces in Britain faced many internal problems, including officers being found drunk on duty and numerous cases of neglect of duty and acceptance of bribes. These problems also manifested themselves in many colonial and postcolonial police forces, including in the United States and Australia. Here the challenges of supervision, and the many pressures and temptations on police, were exacerbated by problems of distance, rapid population growth, and frequent lawlessness and frontier violence. In colonial societies:

> Police became enmeshed in crooked local politics; in the racist, sometimes genocidal, policies of the time; in the brutal suppression of labour strikes; and in organised protection rackets involving alcohol, gambling, prostitution, and abortion. The beating and torture of suspects became a routine way of administering justice for minor crimes and extracting confessions for serious crimes (Prenzler, 2009b, p. 2).

While the development of more settled middle class societies in the latter part of the 19th century allowed for improvements in policing, in many countries, notably the United States, the professional movement was undermined in the prohibition period in the 1920s and 1930s with the growth of alcohol-related organised crime. The protection of illegal liquor and vice outlets, and the unjustified use of force, remained common features of many police departments until well into the 1970s (Kappeler et al., 1998).

The 19th and 20th centuries also saw the growth of more sinister forms of aberrant policing in the form of "security police" or "secret police" operating in "police states" (Prados, 1986; Prenzler, 2009b). Initially, secret police organisations were formed to protect monarchies from revolutionary movements, but the models were adopted by left- and right-wing dictatorships in the 20th century, first in Europe and Russia, then in South and Central America, Africa, and Asia and the Middle East. State security police in autocratic regimes act against their own populations through systematic human rights abuses. Their work is characterised by close surveillance, kidnappings, torture, mock trials, and executions, and, in some cases, by the deployment of death squads. They generate a climate of fear and constant uncertainty, and often coercively recruit citizens into their extensive networks of spies and informants.

The latter part of the 20th century saw a variety of dramatic exposés of police misconduct through the instrument of the well-resourced and legally empowered judicial inquiry (Prenzler, 2009b). The most famous of these was the Knapp Commission of Inquiry in New York City from 1970 to 1972. The Knapp (1972) Report exposed a highly organised system of payments to police for the protection of illegal parking as well as vice, illicit gambling, and drug dealing. Police also operated an extortionate system of gratuities against café and bar owners. They engaged in theft of money and valuables from crime scenes, and there was widespread abuse of the department's overtime and sickness benefit schemes. There was also a major problem with the fabrication and manipulation of evidence, and bribery of lawyers by police (Daley, 1978).

The Knapp Commission established a benchmark for inquiring into police conduct issues. Subsequent enquiries have made good use of the suite of investigative tools developed by the Commission, including compelling testimony, providing indemnities to witnesses, covert surveillance, and stings. Many prominent police forces have been subject to inquiries or reviews that have exposed systemic problems of financial corruption, legal process corruption, violence, racial and sexual discrimination, and neglect of duty. The 1991 Christopher Commission, which followed the beating of African American Rodney King, identified a culture of excessive force and brutality in the Los Angeles Police Department (Christopher, 1991). The later "Rampart Scandal" in 1997–1998 involved serious crimes by a small number of officers, including armed robbery, theft of drugs, assaults on detainees, and fabrication of evidence (Board of Inquiry, 2000). In the United Kingdom, the 1981 Scarman Inquiry, which followed the Brixton riots, revealed police harassment of racial minorities by London Metropolitan Police officers (Scarman, 1986). The 1999 MacPherson Inquiry into the investigation by Metropolitan Police of the murder of a Black teenager again sparked revelations of racism in English forces (MacPherson, 1999). The 1982 McDonald Commission into the Royal Canadian Mounted Police Security Service exposed a "dirty tricks" campaign against separatist groups, including arson, burglaries, interference with mail, and data theft (Royal Commission, 1981).

Inquiries and research in many democracies in the later decades of the 20th century revealed similar problems of entrenched and diverse forms of police misconduct (Prenzler, 2009b). The 1990s represented a major turning point in the conditions necessary for democratic policing with the collapse of the Soviet Union and the liberation of the Eastern Bloc countries. However, reform of the Russian police has been particularly problematic, with ongoing problems of opportunistic graft and extortion, police involvement with organised crime groups, politicized prosecutions, and widespread denials of human rights (Beck & Robertson, 2009). Recent research involving interviews and surveys of members of the public has led to the conclusion that:

> ...in Russia, it appears that torture by state law enforcement officials is an entrenched and systematic problem. Torture is carried out for multiple purposes, including as extra-legal punishment, and in order to fabricate evidence by eliciting false confessions and false testimony. This then corrupts the whole legal process. However, it appears that the official policy is to either deny or deliberately ignore the problem. This means that corrupt police can act with confidence that they have impunity from investigation, prosecution, and accountability. (Gilinskiy, 2011, pp. 169–170)

Reform of police in postcommunist Eastern Europe has been particularly challenging where civil war has broken out (in areas such as the former Yugoslavia) where police have been heavily militarized with little in the way of accountability to civil society (Vejnovic & Lalic, 2005). The world's most populous country—The People's Republic of China—remains a communist police state, with no democratic lines of accountability to curb police abuses (Wong, 2011). Following the 9/11 terror attacks, an international coalition, led by the United States, sought to impose democracy on Afghanistan and Iraq. A key challenge in these emerging democracies, with ongoing major ethnic and religious conflict, has been the creation of apolitical police forces, free of personal and tribal loyalties, and free of the reflex to coerce confessions and fabricate evidence (Wilson & Grammich, 2011). The recent democratic revolutions in Tunisia, Egypt, and Libya all now face major challenges in converting their police forces from malevolent instruments of state power and terror to virtuous servants of the people.

Recent Cases

In the 21st century, unreconstructed police forces remain a major obstacle to the advancement of democracy and enjoyment of human rights. What is of particular concern in established democracies is that while (a) there is a substantial body of knowledge about the causes and prevention of police misconduct, (b) policing remains plagued by scandals, largely as a result of the failure to implement ethical standards and best practice methods of corruption detection and prevention.

A recent case in point concerns police involvement in the "phone hacking scandal" in Britain. In 2011, the Commissioner and Assistant Commissioner of the London Metropolitan Police Service resigned over the police role in the affair in which tabloid journalists accessed the phone messages of celebrities, politicians, and crime victims. Police failed to investigate repeated allegations despite probative evidence, and were also compromised by improper associations with newspaper executives and reporters, including through hospitality, lunches, gifts, and a partial "revolving door" of staff appointments (van

Natta Jr, 2011). An investigation is also underway into police selling confidential information to journalists. The scandal overlapped with widespread rioting in August 2011, allegedly triggered by a police shooting of a Black man (Muir & Taylor, 2011).

Recent assessments of corruption in British policing by Transparency International UK (2011a, 2011b) found that anticorruption systems appeared to be robust, especially given the presence of the Independent Police Complaints Commission (IPCC) in England and Wales, but that there was insufficient detail in official data to obtain an accurate picture of the nature and extent of police involvement in unethical practices. One report pointed to the lack of accountability of individual officers in high-profile cases, including the 2005 shooting death of illegal immigrant Jean Charles de Menezes in the London Underground in a counterterrorism operation, and the 2009 death of Ian Tomlinson after he was knocked to the ground by an officer during G20 protests (Transparency International UK, 2011b). Another of the Transparency International reports emphasised emerging corruption threats:

> The rise of personal IT use through social networking, online dating, and so on, has opened new opportunities for corruptors to approach members of the police. It also enables corruptors to access higher levels of personal information than was once possible. New subcultures have emerged, particularly involving bodybuilding and weightlifting, forging new associations between criminals and members of the police force. All of these factors have contributed to increased risks of exposure to corruptors for potential police targets (Transparency International, 2011a, p. 16).

The report also provided some detail on selected serious cases of malpractice (2011a, p. 16):

> In March 2010, former Detective Chief Superintendent Phil Jones was jailed for 18 months for misconduct in a public office and conspiracy to commit fraud by false representation. Jones persuaded former colleague David Lloyd to pass him information from police computer systems and also employed freelance investigator Christopher Barnett, 37, to illegally pose as a customer to gain information from government and private institutions. Lloyd also had been supplying police information to Robert Morgan, a known criminal involved in drug dealing, and when Lloyd was arrested he was found to be concealing more than £200,000 of Morgan's money in his attic.

In 2010, Metropolitan Police Commander Ali Dizaei was sentenced to 4 years in prison for misconduct in a public office and perverting the course of justice. Dizaei was a former president of the Metropolitan Black Police Association, and had 24 years experience as a serving officer. He had previously been investigated for a number of allegations. One investigation examined claims of corruption, fraud, and dishonesty and involved a multi-million-pound undercover operation. Dizaei had been accused of spending more than £5,000 on clothes and perfume during a trip to the United States, but an inquiry by Dorset Chief Constable Martin Baker found no evidence of wrongdoing.

In November 2010, Police Constable (PC) Stephen Mitchell, of Northumbria Police, was convicted of two charges of rape and three indecent assaults and was also found guilty of six counts of misconduct in a public office. Mitchell was able to become a police officer despite being accused of a serious sexual offence before applying to join. During his trial, it emerged that he had been disciplined when it was discovered he had sex with a woman he had met as part of his duties. Mitchell also had previously been disciplined for looking up his wife's new friends on the police computer after the couple had separated, and was fined three days wages.

Contemporary policing in the United States is also plagued by recurring scandals and allegations of misconduct. The Civil Rights Division of the Federal Department of Justice is engaged in an ongoing process of investigation and attempted reform of police departments that evidence patterns of abuse. In September 2011, the Division had 17 investigations underway (Savage & Alvarez, 2011). A March 2011 report on the New Orleans Police Department found that:

> …for too long, the Department has been largely indifferent to widespread violations of law and policy by its officers. NOPD does not have in place the basic systems known to improve public safety, ensure constitutional practices, and promote public confidence. We found that the deficiencies that lead to constitutional violations span the operation of the entire Department, from how officers are recruited, trained, supervised, and held accountable, to the operation of Paid Details [an overtime scheme]. In the absence of mechanisms to protect and promote civil rights, officers too frequently use excessive force and conduct illegal stops, searches, and arrests with impunity. In addition, the Department's culture tolerates and encourages under-enforcement and under-investigation of violence against women. The Department has failed to take meaningful steps to counteract and eradicate bias based on race, ethnicity, and LGBT [lesbian, gay, bisexual, and transgender] status in its policing practices, and has failed to provide critical policing services to language minority communities (United States Department of Justice, 2011a, p. v).

The New Orleans Police Department had received international attention over police shootings of civilians in the aftermath of Hurricane Katrina in 2005. In 2011, four officers were convicted in relation to the fatal shootings of two civilians and the wounding of four others on the Danziger Bridge (Usborne, 2011). The officers' supervisor was also convicted in relation to the cover-up of the event. Also in 2011, a New Orleans police officer was convicted for kicking and beating a man to death, while his partner was convicted in relation to inaction and covering up the attack (McCarthy, 2011).

The U.S. Department of Justice Civil Rights Division also produced a damning report on the Puerto Rico Police Department in 2011. It stated:

> …Based on our extensive investigation, we find reasonable cause to believe that PRPD officers engage in a pattern and practice of:
>
> - excessive force in violation of the Fourth Amendment (related to searches and seizures);
> - unreasonable force and other misconduct designed to suppress the exercise of protected First Amendment rights (related to rights of assembly and free speech); and
> - unlawful searches and seizures in violation of the Fourth Amendment. In addition to these findings, our investigation uncovered other deficiencies of serious concern. In particular, there is troubling evidence that the PRPD frequently fails to police sex crimes and incidents of domestic violence (United States Department of Justice, 2011b, p. 2).

The report also identified a particular problem with police race-based discrimination against persons of Dominican descent and failure to enforce the law against officers who commit domestic assault. Furthermore, the report also strongly implied that police misconduct was part of the problem of escalating crime, including violent crime, in Puerto Rico.

The Royal Canadian Mounted Police (RCMP) in the 2000s provides another example of a police force embroiled in controversy over misconduct allegations. The RCMP has had a long-standing reputation for integrity. It was "arguably the most revered and iconic of Canadian institutions," but has "come under extreme criticism in recent years, leaving its future existence in question" (Perrott & Kelloway, 2011, p. 120). A shift in policy away from community-based policing to a more security-oriented role is alleged to have alienated the Mounties from their public constituency and initiated a more politicised management culture that allowed ethical standards and responsibility to slide. Perrott and Kelloway (2011) identify four major scandals that illustrate the nature of these problems and turned public opinion strongly against the organization. The first was the exposure of "the pension scandal," involving embezzlement, persecution of whistleblowers, and the inevitable cover-up. Second, "the Maher Arar Affair" involved the arrest of Canadian citizen Maher Arar by U.S. authorities at JFK airport on a flight from Tunisia to Canada. His arrest was allegedly based on information supplied by the RCMP implicating him in the Al-Qaeda terrorist organization. After his arrest, he was flown to Syria, where he was held captive for a year and tortured under the U.S.'s "extraordinary rendition" program of offshore processing of terror suspects. He was later exonerated by the Canadian government. Third, "the Mayerthorpe murders" involved the ambush and murder of four junior RCMP officers in a drug raid due to lack of proper planning and risk management. The fourth scandal involved the death of Robert Dziekanski after he was repeatedly Tasered by RCMP officers after an airport altercation. Video of the incident released on YouTube revealed that the officers over-reacted to disruptive but nonthreatening conduct by the man.

Impacts

Cases of police misconduct undermine the rule of law and often have a serious negative impact upon public attitudes toward the police. This is often especially the case with ethnic and racial minorities (Kaariainen, 2007; Weitzer, 2002, 2004). This negativity reduces public cooperation and impedes police effectiveness. In the New Orleans and Puerto Rico cases (above), the U.S. Department of Justice reports (2011a, 2011b) noted that systematic violations of civil rights had alienated communities to the extent that police could not engage local communities in problem-solving and partnership approaches to crime prevention. Public mistrust and resistance is also particularly damaging in the present environment of terrorist threats, with increasing concerns about threats to public safety from terrorist attacks, as well as increased police powers under new counterterrorism legislation that engender added risks for suspects who may be held without charge and subjected to investigative misconduct. Police themselves acknowledge that effective counterterrorism policing is dependent on information from the public, and often this information is held by ethnic minorities who are easily alienated by police discrimination or neglect (Murray, 2005).

Police corruption also directly contributes to criminal victimisation, especially through graft and protection of organised crime (Prenzler, 2009b). Police involvement in the drug trade contributes to the misery of drug addiction and the violence associated with the drug trade. Police protection rackets also frequently involve illegal gambling, which can lead to severe debt and poverty—and prostitution—which can involve human trafficking, sex slavery, and even child prostitution. More generally, when police are collecting payments, sleeping on the job, or drinking on duty, they are neglecting crime and victims of crime (Knapp, 1972, p. 146). Inaction by police, along with distrust of police, has been identified as a factor in wealthy persons turning to private security and the enactment of vigilante justice (Commonwealth Human Rights Initiative, 2005). Repressive policing, especially race-based harassment, can trigger riots involving extensive property damage and loss of life (Perez, Berg, & Myers, 2003).

Another major consequence of police misconduct is miscarriages of justice, where police fail to prosecute offenders and innocent people are wrongfully convicted. Wrongful convictions have resulted in many innocent persons spending decades in prison or even being executed (Prenzler, 2009a, Chapter 6). Miscarriages of justice almost invariably begin with police investigative misconduct, which feeds through the entire criminal justice system, reducing public trust in the impartiality and reliability of the system.

Unethical policing is also a major drain on the public purse through successful litigation by aggrieved citizens. Rodney King won US$3.8 million from the City of Los Angeles after he was beaten by police officers (BBC News, 2002). In a notorious case in New York City, Abner Louimas settled with the City Council for US$8.75 million after he was assaulted and anally raped with a drain plunger handle while in police custody (Matthews, 2007). In the 5 years to the end of 2009, it was estimated that police actions were costing New York City US$117.6 million per annum in payments to litigants (Dwyer, 2009). More recently, in Minneapolis, police actions cost the city US$3.3 million in the first 7 months of 2011 (McKinney & Mitchell, 2011). Judicial inquiries and anticorruption systems also come at great cost to taxpayers.

Large numbers of complaints are another by-product of police misconduct, entailing a cumbersome and expensive administrative burden on police and oversight agencies. In England and Wales, with approximately 143,000 police, in 2009–2010, there were 33,854 complaints, representing an 8% increase over the previous year, including 58,399 separate allegations (Home Office, 2010; Independent Police Complaints Commission, 2010). The complaints involved 35,557 police officers and there were also 5,584 appeals against decisions, representing a 21% increase on the previous year. In New York City in 2010, with approximately 34,500 police (New York Police Department, 2011), the Civilian Complaint Review Board (2010) received 17,024 complaints, although in this case the number represented an 11% fall from the previous year. Police complaints often trend upward or are fairly stable at high volumes over the long term, while documented cases of major reductions in complaints are extremely rare (Porter, Prenzler, & Fleming, 2011). Only a small proportion of complaints against police are usually substantiated, and the majority often involve lower level "customer service" issues, but all allegations signify a problematic police–citizen relationship. Complaints also typically represent only the "tip of the iceberg" of public dissatisfaction. Surveys indicate that as many as 90% of people who have felt they wanted to complain about police did not do so because they felt it would not achieve anything or because they could not be bothered or they were afraid of repercussions (Maguire & Corbett, 1991, pp. 53–55; Criminal Justice Commission, 2000).

Police misconduct has numerous other negative and, at times, devastating effects (Prenzler, 2009b, pp. 17–20). Excessive force results in a spectrum of physical and psychological injuries, including death, disability, and Post Traumatic Stress Disorder. Investigations into corrupt conduct can destroy the careers and families of police, and lead to the suicide of accused officers. Misconduct also often undermines harmonious working relations between police, and can involve intense persecution of nonparticipants or informants.

Causes of Police Misconduct

Efforts to counter the tendency toward misconduct in policing need to be based on an informed understanding of the causes of, or influences affecting, officer conduct, which might present vulnerabilities that agencies can assess and address. Proponents of the "bad apple" theory of corruption and misconduct (Punch, 2003) assert individual level factors to be primarily responsible for poor behaviour, such as personality, attitudes, or personal circumstances, thus placing blame with the individual subject officer. Bad apples, therefore, require screening out at the recruitment stage, or adequate support, education, and training so that they can perform to the required standard. However, individual members are also affected by their environment, which consists of the organisation that they are part of (the police) and the work that they do (general and specific duties), as well as other people that they come into contact with. Porter (2005) summarised these influences as "organisational" and "social" influences, and drew on psychological literature to explain the potential effects of each on police misconduct. Organizational influences, or obstacles to good performance, included an organisational culture that values the ends rather than the means (e.g., crime clear-up rates rather than professional standards); inadequate policies and rules; poor or absent leadership; available opportunities, and; a lack of investigative capacity or consequences for misconduct. Social influences that can encourage misconduct were described as a social culture that is closed to external scrutiny, hostile to those who report misconduct, and supportive of members who engage in misconduct (or turn a blind eye); colleagues, including superiors, who do not uphold ethical values; and external influences from associations with criminals, informants, or others who may encourage inappropriate behaviour in members.

Porter (2005) argued that strategies to prevent misconduct should address both organisational and social influences. Table 1.1 summarises many of the contributing individual, social, and organisational factors highlighted in the literature, and potential focuses for prevention. These explanations are picked up in different ways by inquiries and reviews. As one example, the U.S. Department of Justice report on misconduct in the Puerto Rico police, cited above, explained the extensive problems it identified in terms of a "profoundly broken" system for making police accountable. The primary factors

Table 1.1 Summary of Contributing Factors to Misconduct and Corruption and Associated Prevention Possibilities

Contributing Factors		Prevention
	Individual	
Personality/attitudes/ coping mechanisms	Attitudes that support misconduct; personal problems (e.g., financial, drug/alcohol dependence/ stress); lack of knowledge/ skills/confidence	Recruit screening Staff support
	Organisational	
Organisational culture	Emphasis on performance and clear-up rates	Emphasis on professional standards
Policy/rules	Lack of consistent policies or unworkable rules	Clear rules with definitions and working examples Communication of rules and ethics training from external personnel on risks and implications of corruption
Leadership	Lack of supervisory presence	Visible leadership, fair and consistent appraisal and feedback; transformational leadership
Opportunities	Undercover work, informant handling, special squads (e.g., drugs)	Vetting, rotation, procedural controls (e.g., levels of access to data)
Ineffective investigation/ consequences	Knowledge of difficulties in proving and convicting for corrupt acts	Encourage reporting (help lines) Openness and fairness of investigations External oversight Speedy and fair discipline process
	Social	
Social culture	Solidarity and silence, pressure not to report, negative toward investigators and those who cooperate	Intolerance to harassment—peer protection
Colleague influence	Influence from peers to conform, influence of observing supervisor's bad example	Use solidarity to encourage integrity Good leadership (set good example)
External influence	Pressure from family/ friends or criminals	Combination of above, particularly those associated with policy and opportunities

contributing to misconduct were analysed under the following headings (2011b, pp. 5–7):

1. Policies fail to guide officers on lawful policing practices.
2. Preservice field training is insufficient.
3. In-service training is virtually nonexistent.
4. No external oversight of officer stands and training.
5. Tactical units have been allowed to develop violent subcultures.
6. Supervision is lacking.
7. Internal investigations take years to complete.
8. Discipline is seriously deficient.
9. Inoperable risk management system.

The Evolution of Police Integrity Management

During the 20th century many democracies were characterized by cycles of failed police reform (Henry, 1994). Cases of police abuses would be brought to light by the actions of courageous journalists, police whistleblowers, civil rights workers, and others, which would force reluctant governments to establish judicial inquiries. These inquiries struggled against a wall of silence and intimidation of whistleblowers, but they often indicated there was a problem of systemic misconduct and recommended a raft of reforms. Some attempts at reform might eventuate, although with little commitment to making real changes in police governance and accountability. Police abuses would resurface and escalate, fresh scandal would ensue, and the inquiry and reform process would repeat itself. However, since the Knapp Commission of Inquiry in New York City, from 1970 to 1972, which forcefully articulated the problem of reform cycles, there has been a much stronger commitment discernable in many jurisdictions to embedding probity in policing (Henry, 1994).

Integrity management in policing has been marked by incremental change. Systems can be categorised in different ways, but a simple division between "basic" and "advanced" systems is one way to think productively about the field. In democracies, basic systems begin with accountability to the public through elected officials, often through a designated elected individual, such as a police minister or mayor. Police also need to be "accountable to the law" (Sarre, 1989). This has a number of meanings, but a key implication is that police should not be immune from prosecution for criminal offences, such as assault, and that officers or departments can also be sued civilly for wrongful actions, with accountability through damages payable as a partial remedy to the successful plaintiff, and punitive damages to deter future misconduct. Accountability to the law should also involve the scrutiny of police conduct through the prosecution process, where prosecutors and judges assess the nature of evidence acquired by police and exclude material illegally obtained. Basic systems also include supervision of officers within the police hierarchy, complaints investigation and discipline, training in law and ethics, and applicant screening (e.g., through criminal history checks). Larger police departments have sought to standardise disciplinary procedures and develop department-wide misconduct prevention systems through the creation of dedicated professional standards units. Since the 1950s, various forms of civilian oversight have been added to the basic model, with these agencies usually limited to paper-based reviews of police handling of complaints and disciplinary decisions (Finn, 2001). There have also been advances in areas, such as applicant screening, with the addition of psychological tests designed to screen out applicants with a predisposition toward violence or deceit.

The history of police misconduct has shown that the basic model, including various refinements, has been entirely inadequate to either prevent misconduct or bring corrupt officers to justice. In response to this problem, a range of advanced strategies have been developed. It is not necessarily the case that all police departments should have these in place, but a mix is likely to be necessary subject to the specific history and risk profile of departments. The use of covert methods is an important addition (Marx, 1992). These can include telephone intercepts, other listening devices, undercover operatives, and "stings" or "integrity tests" (simulated corruption opportunities). These methods have proved to be successful in exposing hidden corruption where conventional investigative methods have failed. The use of overt recording devices—including closed-circuit television (CCTV) in police stations/cells and body-worn video—is an emerging tool to both deter and identify misconduct, and to help dismiss false allegations against police. Video recording of interviews, especially in-station interviews with suspects, is an extremely valuable counter against false confessions (Dixon, 2006). The introduction of drug and alcohol testing has also been valuable in minimising the problem of police drinking or being under the influence of alcohol while on duty (Prenzler & Ronken, 2001). Drug testing is also seen as a valuable tool to reduce drug use by police (Mieczkowski & Lersch, 2002).

Many of these strategies entail a "get tough" approach to detecting and deterring misconduct, and are based in part on generating fear in officers. However, a large body of research in social psychology and organisational psychology shows that behavioural change through internalisation of values (e.g., "transformational") is much more effective on a number of levels than behavioural change through fear of punishment or desire for rewards (e.g., "transactional") (see Judge & Piccolo, 2004, for a meta-analysis). Girodo (2003) also noted the difference between "values-based" and "compliance-based" approaches to integrity management. In that regard, complaints profiling and early intervention to address problem behaviour by police has emerged in the international policing literature as a promising technique for reducing complaints through behaviour correction (Walker, 2003, 2007). Early intervention systems are aimed at the early detection of potentially escalating problems (utilising a number of warning indicators) and addressing the problem through interventions to correct the behaviour. Typically, interventions are aimed at officer learning; recognizing that poor performance can be due to "honest mistakes" rather than malicious intent.

Early intervention systems also tend to overlap with a trend toward various forms of nonpunitive resolution of complaints, including through apologies, explanations, and mediation. These can provide a relatively inexpensive and efficient way of managing complaints in ways that are also satisfactory to both complainants and the subject officers (Ede & Barnes, 2002; Prenzler, 2009b, pp. 97–112). However, evaluation studies also show that aspects of the management of complaints resolution need service delivery level improvements, and, to date, there has been no consistent and comprehensive mainstreaming of these procedures. There are also questions about which categories of complaints are best suited to dispute resolution, which agency should manage the process, and how resolution procedures should feed into primary and secondary misconduct prevention techniques.

The advanced model has also included a shift to closer oversight of police by external agencies with powers to conduct independent investigations, obtain evidence and testimony, and input disciplinary decisions. This approach is based on findings of internal cover-ups and lack of appropriate discipline by police professional standards units. Surveys of complainants whose matters are dealt with by police through a traditional investigate and prosecute approach normally show very high dissatisfaction rates, averaging around 70 to 95% (Brown, 1987; Hayes, 1997). A common finding is that dissatisfaction is linked to the lack of independence in complaints systems. Complainants feel that investigations are not sufficiently rigorous and that investigators favour the version of events given by the responding police officer. Complainants are also often dissatisfied due to poor communication, not being kept up-to-date with the progress of their matter, and not being given opportunities to meet with the subject officers and discuss the matter through a mediator (Prenzler, 2009b, pp. 97–112; Prenzler, Allard, Curry, & Macintyre, 2010).

Generally, there would appear to be a consensus that external agencies should have the power to conduct their own investigations as well as review or supervise police internal investigations. However, oversight agencies have been created with differing models and powers, which are also evolving rather than static (although subject to legislation and resources) (Seneviratne, 2004; Walker, 2001). Each agency involved in preventing and responding to incidents of alleged police misconduct, therefore, has its own methods and its own measures of performance.

The Australian Experience

Police Misconduct

Early policing in Australia, following European settlement in 1788, was characterised by the same problems described above in 18th- and 19th-century Britain and colonial societies, such as the United States. General police duties were initially inappropriately assigned to militia, creating confusion between the guarding of convicts and general law enforcement and crime prevention responsibilities (Bryett, Harrison, & Shaw, 1997). The marines both avoided their policing duties and exploited their position by committing opportunistic crimes. The New South Wales Corps, established in 1795, was quick to profit from an illicit trade in spirits, hence, the sobriquet "The Rum Corps." Efforts to improve policing included converting reformed convicts into constables, but this tended to generate further conflicts (Prenzler, 2010).

It was virtually impossible to implement the New Police model in the colonial environment, despite the influx of free settlers in the 19th century. Police tended to maintain a paramilitary form as they struggled with problems of bushranging and disorder exacerbated by the gold rushes in the mid-19th century (O'Malley, 1979). One of the darkest chapters in Australian policing history involved the actions of the "Native Police" who acted as flying squads against displaced indigenous tribes who threatened settlers. The force consisted of native troopers under the command of White officers. Although officially intended to follow due process to arrest suspects, in reality the strategy devolved into punitive expeditions that included shooting suspects and "dispersing" native groups by charging and firing at them (Richards, 2008).

The expansion of colonial self-government, from the mid-19th century, involved attempts to put police on a more professional footing. The 1833 Sydney Police Act placed police under the control of magistrates. However, police continued to be held in low regard by many sections of the community (Bryett et al., 1997). By federation in 1901, the system of state-based police departments was firmly entrenched (absent local police departments), with a small commonwealth force established in 1917. Police worked long hours for low pay under difficult conditions. Discipline could be harsh, although police discretion was difficult to supervise in the dispersed policing environment, and there were recurring allegations of corruption (Finnane, 1999). Prohibitions or restrictions on gambling, alcohol, and prostitution generated police protection rackets that continued in various forms well into the latter half of the 20th century.

Judicial inquiries into police conduct in the 20th century were often inconclusive, partly due to inadequate powers, but they also generally failed to dispel presumptions of widespread misconduct. The first inquiry to systematically expose misconduct was the Fitzgerald Commission in Queensland. The Fitzgerald (1989) Report lifted the lid on longstanding police protection of organised crime and the management practices that fostered corruption.

> The Queensland Police Force is debilitated by misconduct, inefficiency, incompetence, and deficient leadership. The situation is compounded by poor organisation and administration, inadequate resources, and insufficiently developed techniques and skills for the task of law enforcement in a modern complex society. Lack of discipline, cynicism, disinterest, frustration, anger, and low self-esteem are the result. The culture which shares responsibility for and is supported by this grossly unsatisfactory situation includes contempt for the criminal justice system, disdain for the law and rejection of its application to police, disregard for the truth, and abuse of authority (Fitzgerald, 1989, p. 200).

The Fitzgerald Inquiry was followed by the Wood Royal Commission in New South Wales, from 1994 to 1997. Sydney had been seen as the most corrupt city in Australia, with police protection rings that included politicians, and police involvement in armed robberies and drug trafficking. The Wood Commission identified a diminution in these practices, partly due to the regulation of vice, but revealed numerous groups of police involved in ongoing organised protection and graft, along with process corruption in the form of fabrication of evidence, as well as assaults on suspects, extortionate gratuities, opportunistic thefts, and continuing police involvement in the drug trade (Wood, 1997). In Western Australia, the Kennedy (2004) Inquiry also revealed "the full range of criminal conduct from stealing to assaults, perjury, drug dealing and the improper disclosure of confidential information" (p. 1).

Australia's other major police force, Victoria, escaped a top-to-bottom inquiry, but has been plagued by continuous allegations and exposés of misconduct. One of the most notorious scams ran for two decades, across the 1970s and 1980s, involving kickbacks for preferential notifications by police to emergency security hardware installers. Disciplinary charges were brought against 550 officers (Ombudsman of Victoria, 1998). Victoria Police have also been entangled in controversies over shootings of mentally ill persons, "payback" shootings of criminals, political surveillance, sexual harassment and discrimination against women police, harassment of police whistleblowers, systematic abuse of strip searching, theft and on-selling of drugs, and leaking of information to criminals (Office of Police Integrity, 2007a). More recently, the Victorian Office of Police Integrity revealed the regular practice of violence against suspects by the Armed Offenders Squad, and exposed a high level plot to replace the police commissioner (Office of Police Integrity, 2009a). In 2011, the Chief Commissioner was forced to resign over allegations that the Victoria Police released misleading crime data in order to support the government during an election (Stewart, 2011).

There has also been a wider critique of police practices in Australia, consistent with international trends from the 1960s. Police were criticised for neglecting victims of hidden crimes, such as domestic violence and sexual assault (Hatty, 1989). The 1991 report of the Royal Commission into Aboriginal Deaths in Custody was highly critical of reactive arrest practices carried out by police when dealing with problems of disorder and crime amongst indigenous Australians (Johnston, 1991). There have been repeated criticisms, as well, of police behaviour in relation to high-speed pursuits, excessive force against public demonstrators, and the over-use of arrest (Prenzler, 2010).

Police Reform and Civilian Oversight

Reform of policing in Australia has followed a tortuous path (Lewis, 1999). Considerable resistance to improved accountability was mounted by police management and police unions, and by politicians who felt it was better to have police on their side than to alienate them with intrusive anticorruption measures. For many decades in the post-World War II period, most police departments had only the simple integrity infrastructure, or less, described in the section titled The Evolution of Police Integrity Management under "basic systems." There were few or no measures to preemptively detect or prevent misconduct. Very limited, often tokenistic, oversight was introduced from the 1970s, mainly in the form of ombudsmen (Lewis & Prenzler, 1999). However, repeated scandals and commissions of inquiry drove major structural change. The 1990s saw a shift away from ombudsman-style bodies toward commissions, with significant powers to conduct independent investigations; compel testimony and seize evidence; and develop programs of research, education, and prevention. The Independent Commission Against Corruption was established in New South Wales in 1989, with its police role taken over by the Police Integrity Commission in 1996 as a consequence of the Wood Commission. In Queensland, the Criminal Justice Commission was established in 1990 in response to the Fitzgerald Inquiry recommendations. The Victorian Office of Police Integrity took over from the Ombudsman in 2004. In the same year, the Western Australian Anti-Corruption Commission (est. 1996) was replaced with a more powerful Crime and Corruption Commission as a result of the Kennedy Inquiry. An Integrity Commission was established in Tasmania in 2010. One notable feature of developments in a number of Australian jurisdictions is the inclusion of police within a public sector-wide, anticorruption commission in response to scandals that included politicians and public servants, indicating a common risk profile for misconduct.

The commissions of inquiry into police corruption also drove the introduction of other advanced integrity strategies. The Wood Commission made extensive use of undercover tactics, including stings and hidden cameras, and was responsible for placing these tactics on the integrity management agenda. A 1999 survey of the eight main police departments found a patchwork of advanced strategies: two employed covert surveillance; two used targeted integrity testing and drug and alcohol testing, with another two planning their introduction; three had a form of complaint profiling and early warning; and three had introduced complaints resolution (Prenzler & Ronken, 2003). Overall, there was only a very limited uptake of proactive or "smart" strategies. The work of the new external integrity agencies has been similarly mixed (Prenzler, 2011; Ross, 2007). While most now have access to inquisitorial and covert powers, these tend to be applied to very few cases. The large majority of complaints are still dealt with by police, and oversight agencies lack adjudicative powers. The limited use of independent authority has generated ongoing dissatisfaction amongst complainants as well as journalists, civil libertarians, and academics. While there is a broad consensus view that these reforms have assisted in eliminating the more blatant and organised forms of police process corruption and financial corruption, there are concerns with ongoing problems of excessive force and poor client service standards. Each year, police in Australia are prosecuted and convicted over a very wide range of offences (see, for example, Sandy & Baskin, 2011). These convictions provide testimony to the commitment and vigour of the contemporary integrity systems, but they also place a question mark over the preventive value of the systems. High volumes of complaints against police also remain a feature of the police landscape (Porter et al., 2011).

A National Stocktake Study

The past 40 to 50 years of inquiry and research into police misconduct has led to the establishment of a strong knowledge base about the nature, causes, and prevention of misconduct. Nonetheless, the question of "what works in police corruption prevention and integrity management" remains one of urgency, with a wide opportunity for further research and for improved practice. Australia has been the site of numerous "natural experiments" in police integrity management in response to findings of significant and diverse forms of misconduct. There would appear to be a great deal to learn from the Australian experience, both its successes and failures. The last two decades in particular, since the time of the Fitzgerald Inquiry in Queensland, have seen considerable innovation in techniques designed to address misconduct risks. Indeed, one of the most salient features of contemporary policing in Australia is the large infrastructure dedicated to supporting integrity. However, different jurisdictions have adopted different frameworks and strategies, and are at different stages of evolution. While there are numerous jurisdictionally specific reports on reform, and some evaluations of specific integrity strategies, there has, to date, been no national study comparing integrity strategies across the eight main policing jurisdictions, including both police departments and oversight agencies.

With this situation in mind, the authors set out to conduct a "national stocktake" of police integrity strategies in operation in Australia. Comparative studies have the advantage of highlighting overlaps in practices of agencies working to common goals, as well as highlighting gaps in provision or, indeed, innovative strategies that are currently in operation in one or just a few locations. The study was designed to contribute to the international scientific body of knowledge about police integrity management. It was also designed to enhance knowledge sharing and advance best practice within Australian policing, while also recognising that a "one size fits all" model may not be appropriate in many cases, given different jurisdictional governance, laws, resources, and experiences. In summary, the project aim was to provide a comprehensive picture of current and emerging police integrity strategies at a national level in Australia. Specifically, the project aimed to present information on:

- current jurisdictional and national practices;
- innovative integrity strategies;
- experiences and evaluation (positive and/or negative) of integrity strategies; and
- opinions as to new and emerging issues in ethical policing that require attention.

Eighteen agencies were selected for inclusion in the study, reflecting all the state and territory police forces and their primary oversight and/or anti-corruption bodies. Crime commissions and security agencies were omitted due to the nature of their work presenting very different risks to state/territory policing. Table 1.2 lists the agencies, and departments, that participated in the research. As noted above, policing in Australia is state- and territory-based, with no local or regional police departments. The departments range enormously in size (see Table 1.3). At the time of study, in 2009, the Australian Federal Police consisted of approximately 3,000 sworn officers, while the New South Wales Police Force had the largest number of sworn officers (around 15,000), and the Northern Territory, with the smallest population, had the smallest number of sworn officers (approximately 1,000). Tasmania, being geographically the smallest state, had a similarly small number of sworn officers (approximately 1,200).

The research was carried out through two methods: searches of public documents and interviews with agency representatives. Systematic searches,

Table 1.2 Participating Agencies

Jurisdiction	Police	Oversight
ACT/ Commonwealth	Australian Federal Police Professional Standards	Australian Commission for Law Enforcement Integrity Commonwealth Ombudsman
NSW	New South Wales Police Force Professional Standards Command	Police Integrity Commission NSW Ombudsman
NT	Northern Territory Police Ethical and Professional Standards Command	Northern Territory Ombudsman
QLD	Queensland Police Ethical Standards Command	Crime and Misconduct Commission
SA	South Australia Police Ethical and Professional Standards Branch/ Internal Investigations Section	Police Complaints Authority
TAS	Tasmania Police Internal Investigations Unit/Police Academy	Tasmania Ombudsman
VIC	Victoria Police Ethical Standards Department	Office for Police Integrity
WA	Western Australia Police Complaints Administration Centre	Corruption and Crime Commission

Table 1.3 Sworn Officers by Jurisdiction, Australia 2008–2009

New South Wales	15,394
Victoria	11,028
Queensland	10,124
South Australia	4,209
Western Australia	5,522
Tasmania	1,212
Northern Territory	1,024
Commonwealth*	2,842

Source: Australian Federal Police, 2009, p. 190; Productivity Commission 2010, Tables 6A.1-6A.8.

* The Australian Crime Commission (2009, pp. 80 & 168) had 418 staff, many of whom are seconded from other policing agencies.

primarily using online resources, were conducted of reports and policy documents by (and concerning) the above agencies to identify measures aimed directly or indirectly at preventing and responding to police misconduct or enhancing police integrity, and associated performance indicators. Publicly available reports were collected between 2008 and 2010, inclusive, and agencies were also asked to provide any further documents or information appropriate for inclusion in the research (e.g., policies, training materials, complaints statistics, or data). Examples of reports utilised included agencies' annual reports, investigation reports, training materials, commissions of inquiry or reviews of agencies, legislation, and also agency-specific policy documents.

Follow-up interviews were conducted between November 2008 and December 2009 with key personnel in each agency to develop a detailed map of current integrity practices and challenges encountered. Interviews were tape recorded and transcribed. Each agency was asked to nominate a person (or appropriate selection of people) to participate in an interview lasting between 1 and 3 hours. Interviewees were presented with a list of integrity strategies as prompts, and were asked about their agencies' current strategies and their opinions as to how effective these were. They were also asked to share their experiences of particularly innovative and successful strategies as well as emerging ethical concerns or issues. Interviews were, therefore, semistructured and led by the interviewees to a certain extent, and different agencies provided a different emphasis on topics, dependent on their functions and experiences. Agencies were provided with a draft summary of the findings regarding their jurisdiction and provided comments, clarification, and updates where necessary.

The approach of the research was to offer a detailed picture of police integrity frameworks and strategies in Australia during the period of study. Practices and issues in this field are evolving as new issues are highlighted and new practices explored and shared. The information reported here, therefore, provides an overview of practices at the time of study that can serve as both a platform to aid further change and, eventually, an historical resource for tracking the extent of this change.

Conclusion

This chapter outlined key dimensions of the complex and continuing problem of police misconduct. Research shows that unethical policing has a corrosive effect on society, undermining the system of democratic authority and threatening the security of ordinary citizens. It fosters organised crime, government waste, public disaffection, victimisation, resistance to authority, and noncooperation with police. Ensuring ethical conduct by police remains an ongoing challenge for advanced democracies and a significant challenge for emerging democracies. Australia is an advanced liberal democracy that has not been immune from the problem of police misconduct. Malpractice has occurred across a wide range of types, with many victims and the development over time of a large infrastructure to combat the problem. The remainder of this book provides an in-depth examination of Australia's police integrity system, with evaluations about the value of different strategies and numerous lessons for any government or community concerned to ensure their policing is the best it can be.

Commonwealth 2

The Australian Federal Police was established in 1979, and was subject to very limited oversight by the Commonwealth Ombudsman. This situation continued until 2006, despite a number of Australian Law Reform Commission reports calling for an oversight agency with an enlarged role in police corruption prevention and complaints investigation (Prenzler, 2011). One 1995 report argued that asking police to investigate police "places them in a hopeless conflict of interest position" that produces inevitable pressures to disbelieve the complainant and support the officer (Australian Law Reform Commission, 1995, p. 149). The case for reform was strengthened by the Wood Royal Commission into the New South Wales Police, which found evidence of past corruption involving Australian Federal Police (AFP) officers within a narcotics joint task force (Wood, 1997, p. 15). The Harrison Inquiry of 1997 was established to follow up on the Wood Commission findings in relation to the AFP. Several officers were subject to dismissal proceedings over minor isolated incidents and there was some internal restructuring and changes to processes, including evidence handling, informant management, and whistleblower protection (Prenzler, 2011). The issue of enlarged oversight was sustained by changes in other jurisdictions and intermittent allegations of federal police misconduct. In response to this situation, in 2006, oversight was restructured and shared between the Commonwealth Ombudsman, responsible for lower level complaints, and the new Australian Commission for Law Enforcement Integrity (ACLEI), which was responsible for investigating and preventing corruption. The Commission has the power to conduct telecommunications intercepts and covert surveillance, along with a range of other significant investigative powers (Australian Commission for Law Enforcement Integrity, 2008, p. 12). Internally, conduct matters are handled by the AFP's Professional Standards Unit.

Australian Federal Police

The AFP Professional Standards Unit, within the Human Resources portfolio, is responsible for developing and maintaining professional standards throughout the organisation. The standards expected of AFP members are supported by the core values (integrity, commitment, excellence, accountability, fairness, and trust) and the code of conduct, both of which are available on the AFP Web site. Professional Standards works within a framework of three essential areas of activity: prevention, detection, and response. Professional Standards is responsible for the oversight and investigation of complaints about members of the AFP, and so involves an Investigations Unit as well as an Operations Monitoring Centre and an Integrity Assurance area.

Complaint Handling

Complaints can be made to the AFP about the conduct or actions of an AFP member as well as about policies, procedures, or practices of the organisation. The AFP receives complaints in writing (including letter, e-mail, and fax), by telephone, and in person at any AFP office or station. If a complaint is given orally, the AFP must reduce it to writing or can request that the complainant do so. The AFP can decline to act further on a complaint until such a request is completed. The AFP publishes information on how to make a complaint on its Web site. This information includes the fact that AFP members are obliged to record all complaints received by them, including those where they may be the subject of the grievance, and also that AFP members must identify themselves if asked, including providing their names, identification numbers, and work locations.

AFP annual reports show that in 2008–2009 and 2009–2010 over a third of complaints were received internally and just under two thirds from members of the public (the remaining small percentage were self-reported or anonymous) (Australian Federal Police, 2009, 2010). This is an increase from only 19% internal complaints in 2006–2007, but a slight drop from the 41% received internally in 2007–2008 (Australian Federal Police, 2008). Numbers of complaints from the public have decreased in recent years, from 668 in 2006–2007 to 509 in 2008–2009 and 447 in 2009–2010 (Australian Federal Police, 2007, 2009, 2010). Anonymous complaints are accepted, but the AFP makes it clear that this prevents follow-up inquiries for the purpose of clarifying details as well as future contact regarding the outcome of the matter. The AFP encourages complainants to provide as much specific detail as possible as well as indicating a desired outcome.

Complaint Categorisation

The AFP introduced a new complaints management model at the end of 2006 that utilises a managerial model in terms of addressing and rectifying complaints. In relation to this, a four-tier complaints categorisation model was introduced on January 1, 2007. Category 1 matters are minor matters relating to customer service; category 2 involves less serious or minor misconduct; and category 3 includes serious misconduct matters (not including corruption) that could lead to termination or criminal charges as well as serious neglect of duty; the fourth tier involves corrupt conduct. The model covers all AFP members, both sworn and unsworn.

The AFP has a central Complaint Coordination Team (within the Operations Monitoring Centre of Professional Standards) as well as 16 regional Complaint Management Teams who locally manage category 1 and category 2 conduct issues. The Complaint Coordination Team is responsible for advising the regional Complaint Management Teams and Investigating Officers. The Team also has administrative responsibility for, and provides advice regarding, the electronic Complaints Recording and Management System (CRAMS) as well as managing the complaints hotline. The Team also provides quality assurance of complaint handling for category 1 and 2 complaints and provides a liaison point for the Ombudsman's oversight and review role.

When complaints are received onto CRAMS, they are automatically categorised within the four-tier model and the response is dependent upon that categorisation. The model refocuses Professional Standards to dealing with more serious matters, while responsibility for dealing with minor matters is devolved to local managers (and overseen by Professional Standards) with a focus on changing behaviour rather than punishing individuals. The management areas are viewed as having a better understanding of local issues than a centralised office and are able to utilise the information to better identify complaint trends within their local context.

Thus, category 1 and 2 matters are allocated to Complaints Management Teams within the appropriate functional area or state-based offices. The Complaint Management Teams use the electronic CRAMS to manage complaints, assign investigators, review categorisation of matters, manage timeliness of investigations, review investigation reports, determine findings, apply outcomes, and finalise matters. Professional Standards is able to provide advice to the Complaints Management Teams on matters as necessary. The primary objective of the CMTs is resolution of workplace conduct issues, with a focus on early intervention for behaviour before it escalates to more serious misconduct.

While generally anyone in the AFP who receives a complaint is obligated to record that complaint, Section 40SC(2) of the AFP Act 1979 provides for discretion in specified circumstances on the understanding that minor matters may be easily resolved through communication with the complainant, for example, to provide an explanation for behaviour. Where (a) a complaint relates to a category 1 matter or AFP practices issue and (b) the recipient is satisfied that the complaint arises due to a misunderstanding of the facts, law, or practices, or is appropriate for informal resolution in some other way, and (c) the recipient is satisfied that an explanation or other action will likely resolve the issue, and (d) the recipient is satisfied that such an action can be provided within a reasonable time period (48 hours), the Act allows for the recipient to attempt to informally resolve the complaint without recording the information into CRAMS. However, that member must make a diary or notebook entry of the details. If this resolution fails to resolve the matter, the recipient must then record the matter and deal with it through the appropriate categorisation procedures.

More serious (category 3) matters are investigated centrally by Professional Standards and must also be reported to the Ombudsman. During 2009–2010, the AFP established a Professional Standards Adjudication Panel to improve the timeliness of dealing with category 3 matters. The panel considers category 3 issues and adjudicates on the recommendations of the investigators and may recommend outcomes. Complaint issues are deemed either established or not established. Category 4 (corruption) matters are forwarded to the Australian Commission for Law Enforcement Integrity (ACLEI) to decide what action should take place. All category 3 and 4 matters, while being recorded in CRAMS, are also referenced to a Professional Standards case in PROMIS (Police Real-Time Online Management Information System).

In response to the Ombudsman's review of AFP complaint handling in 2007 and 2008 (Commonwealth Ombudsman, 2008a), it is now mandatory for a complaint investigator to record whether the complaint involves an AFP practices issue or a conduct issue. The Ombudsman highlighted the importance of identifying practices issues in order to analyse trends that may have wider implications for the organisation beyond the individual complaint.

Mediation

While the complaint-handling model encourages resolution of complaint matters, formal mediation was not described by the AFP as a likely response to complaints. However, less formal resolution is possible between the complaint investigator and the complainant with regard to providing an explanation for the conduct or explaining the outcome of an investigation. Further, in the course of such a resolution, the complaint investigator may visit the complainant personally to talk through the issues. All parties, however, would not be brought together formally for mediation.

Complaint Investigation

For complaints that warrant investigation, the internal investigations section of Professional Standards has investigation teams in Canberra, Brisbane, Sydney, Melbourne, and Honiara, Solomon Islands. The internal investigation teams investigate category 3 matters, which include serious misconduct matters, criminal misconduct, criminal conduct that is not corruption; misuse of power, fraud, and also failure to report a breach of the code of conduct.

The AFP explained that there are prescribed time frames around completion or resolution of matters to ensure timeliness standards of investigations.

For example, category 1 matters are aimed to be finalised within 21 days, category 2 complaints within 45 days, and category 3 and corruption complaints finalised within 180 days.

AFP investigators of category 3 matters (or corruption issues that ACLEI have referred back to be investigated by the AFP) have the power to enter and search any AFP premises at any time, and examine, remove, or take copies of documents or things found on those premises that are relevant to the enquiry. Where a criminal matter is being investigated, the member subject to that allegation will be given the opportunity to participate in an interview under criminal caution. Where the allegation involves misconduct, then the member can be interviewed under direction. The directed interview was described by the AFP as one of the core investigative tools for internal investigations (not involving criminal matters) as it compels members to answer. A member interviewed under direction is provided with a written copy of the legislative document to sign in order to confirm that he/she understands the direction. The document outlines the complaint and also states a secrecy provision that the subject member is not permitted to discuss the matter with anyone other than for welfare, including victimisation, purposes. The directed interview has the benefit of compelling members to answer questions put to them, where noncompliance with the direction (including refusing to answer or providing false or misleading statements) amounts to a further, serious, conduct issue. However, given that the information obtained in such an interview is done so under compulsion, any evidence obtained is not legally admissible in court against that member and so cannot be used against the subject member for criminal charges (for that complaint).

Covert/Controlled Operations

The AFP has the ability to conduct controlled operations for the purposes of investigating police misconduct if the need arises. However, the AFP noted that such operations were most likely to be necessary in the most serious matters, which are typically investigated externally by ACLEI, or jointly between ACLEI and AFP. Professional Standards Investigations has the same resources available as any other investigations area in the AFP. The AFP's use of telecommunications interceptions and surveillance devices is reported to, and reviewed by, the Commonwealth Ombudsman who has previously made recommendations regarding deficiencies observed regarding the AFP's recordkeeping (Commonwealth Ombudsman, 2007a). The Commonwealth Ombudsman's Annual Report (2008b) notes that the recommendations were generally accepted by the AFP and that a range of improvement measures have been implemented. Subsequently, the Ombudsman's 2009–2010 Annual Report (2010) states that compliance with the Telecommunications (Interception and Access) Act 1979 (TIA Act) is generally very high and that "there is a good understanding by agencies of the legislative requirements" (Commonwealth Ombudsman, 2010, p. 85).

Integrity Testing

The AFP is considering developing an integrity testing program; however, a decision as to the final model to be implemented and when has not been made. AFP Professional Standards is examining the issues associated with developing a targeted integrity-testing capability to further strengthen the AFP's ability to detect serious misconduct and corruption. The AFP is also a member of the Integrity Testing Practitioners Committee, which was endorsed by the Board of the Australia New Zealand Policing Advisory Agency (ANZPAA) as a subcommittee of the Police Integrity Forum.

The AFP noted that, while there is no evidence to indicate that there is systemic misconduct or corruption within the AFP, the implementation of AFP integrity testing would support and complement a number of existing proactive strategies under the AFP's Integrity Framework. ACLEI acknowledged that, while integrity testing would be a very valuable tool, it could also be controversial and resource intensive. ACLEI noted that integrity testing needs to be properly directed and applied in the right circumstances to be an effective deterrent.

Discipline and Other Outcomes

The AFP has adopted a managerial model of complaint handling aimed toward correcting poor behaviour rather than centring on a punitive response. Minor matters are dealt with via training and development of members, including coaching, mentoring, and increased supervision. Or, for slightly more serious (category 2) matters, the option of remedial action, such as counselling by a supervisor, reprimand, a formal warning, or requiring the employee to adopt particular improvement strategies. Remedial action is defined in the AFP Act 1979 as action aimed at improving behaviour; structured changes to a member's employment (such as changing or restricting shifts or duties, reassigning duties, or transferring the member); or recording an adverse finding against the member. The performance of a member subject to a complaint, therefore, can be managed beyond the resolution of that complaint.

Established category 3 and corruption matters can result in the above outcomes for the subject member, with the addition of options of termination and criminal charges. Category 3 and corruption matters are provided a natural justice approach, whereby subject members are given a report of matters established against them and provided the right of reply and appeal against an outcome. Members involved in category 1 and 2 matters cannot appeal to the same level, but have the right to request review of an outcome by the Manager of Professional Standards and, if still dissatisfied, can seek review by the Commonwealth Ombudsman.

Where a case suggests criminal behaviour by members, a brief of evidence can be handed to the Director of Public Prosecutions (DPP), who chooses whether to pursue charges. The appropriate DPP (either Australian Capital Territory [ACT] or Commonwealth) will be consulted by the AFP in this process, as will the AFP's own legal officers, to improve the likelihood of successful prosecution.

Witness Support

The AFP Act 1979 asserts that complainants (to the AFP) are to be kept informed regarding the AFP's response to their complaint, including updates during the course of any investigation and the outcome in relation to the member concerned. Those who give evidence in relation to serious organised crime and corruption are provided with the National Witness Protection Program as well.

The AFP Act 1979 makes it an offence to victimise any person for making a complaint, and members who are subject to complaints are reminded of that offence when the complaint is put to them. This includes the subject officer signing that he/she understands the victimisation offence provision. Thus, it is not simply written in the legislation, but officers are reminded of this at the time that they go through the complaints process.

The AFP operates the Confidant Network to provide support and information to members on reporting misconduct. The Confidant Network is also recognised as a formal reporting channel, thus reporting to a Confidant is considered fulfilling the mandatory reporting requirement. The Confidant Network can be used, as well, by employees who have workplace issues or grievances, so it is based in the Human Resources area. The Confidant Network comprises over 200 Confidants throughout Australia as well as overseas. The AFP 2009–2010 Annual Report states that the Confidant Network received 131 referrals in the reporting period; 25 of these were integrity-related (Australian Federal Police, 2010). Confidants are voluntary, trained within the AFP (including in communication and conflict resolution), and located throughout the AFP workplaces so that they can be accessed by all employees. Information sessions are provided to recruits and also at various geographical locations to promote awareness and enhance the accessibility of the Network. In addition to providing advice or information, Confidants can also be present with a member during a Professional Standards interview.

The Confidant Network uses an independent secure database to record referrals. However, they are obligated to report any matters alleging misconduct to Professional Standards. While this can be done while maintaining the anonymity of the reporting member for noncriminal matters, Professional Standards may compel the Network to identify the member, for example, where Professional Standards needs to contact the reporting member for further information. However, given that this may create some anxiety in members, or reduced confidence in the Network, the AFP explained that Confidants are clear with reporting members that:

> . they will do everything in their power to maintain their anonymity if they have a good reason for wanting to be anonymous, but they do tell them that there are certain circumstances, like a criminal conduct matter or other special circumstances, where they may have to be identified. People are told that up front.

Thus, breaking anonymity is limited to necessary circumstances, and those using the Network are informed of this in advance. The AFP produces a National Guideline on the Confidant Network for internal reporting of conduct issues. A change in AFP Commissioner Orders now also allows AFP members to fulfil their reporting obligations by reporting direct to ACLEI.

Early Intervention/Complaint Profiling

The AFP Annual Report for 2009–2010 states that the AFP is continuing to develop an early intervention system to identify individuals and work areas vulnerable to conduct and corruption issues. The system is described as "examining behaviours that may lead to misconduct rather than relying on the early warning of conduct that is already occurring" (Australian Federal Police, 2010, p. 152).

The AFP utilises information to highlight trends and patterns of behaviour or issues and Professional Standards (PRS) offers an intelligence capability for detection and prevention of conduct issues. PRS established a system of Integrity Reports, specifically for reporting exposure to integrity risks so that these risks can be assessed and managed. During the 2009–2010 reporting period, 872 integrity reports were received and assessed (Australian Federal Police, 2010).

The AFP highlighted that local complaint management also aids local areas in recognising their own patterns of complaints. In respect to the early identification of corruption issues, ACLEI agreed that police members at the local level are best placed to identify problems, stating that "police agencies themselves are best placed to discover wrongdoing because they are the ones who are supervising their staff, are on the ground, and know their risks." Managers were described by ACLEI as being at the frontline of corruption control and, therefore, needing knowledge of corruption indicators and the tools to recognise and respond to corrupt conduct.

The AFP mentioned in an interview that there was a possibility of adding enhancements to the CRAMS system to raise flags in predefined cases, thus, systematically identifying patterns or problems. The AFP 2009–2010 Annual Report states that, during the reporting year, the functionality of CRAMS was enhanced to significantly improve its capability to produce reports on a number of professional standards issues (Australian Federal Police, 2010). This is said to have improved the ability to analyse behavioural and other trends.

Information on serious complaints is held in a database managed by PRS. This database, PRS PROMIS (Police Real-Time Online Management Information System), records the complaint as well as the investigation and outcome and the relevant reports. Thus, an individual member's history can be checked in this system where a new issue is highlighted.

Assessments can also be conducted in relation to particular individuals or areas. For example, in January 2007, the AFP instigated a joint review with the Commonwealth Ombudsman to assess Watch House operations in the ACT, which made recommendations regarding governance, detainee health and well-being, and use of force (Commonwealth Ombudsman, 2007b). The AFP implemented all of the recommendations that were within its power, including improved use of force training and amendments to the use of force policy.

Risk Management

The AFP has a Fraud Control and Anticorruption plan that is reassessed every 2 years. The current Fraud Control and Anticorruption Plan (2009–2011) incorporates fraud and corruption risks for the AFP, including ACT policing. The plan aims to ensure that emerging risks are identified and that risk management strategies are assessed for their effectiveness. Progress regarding the identification of risks and the implementation of risk treatments identified within the plan is reported on each year to the Attorney General's department. The plan is revised every 2 years to ensure updated risk assessment.

While the Fraud Control and Anticorruption plan is a corporate level strategy, it also requires each business area to assess its own risks. This ensures that each area has a tailored risk management strategy, recognising potentially unique risks associated with specific work functions. Thus, responsibility and accountability for ethical standards sits throughout all levels of the organisation and not just at the corporate level. If specific issues are identified, then strategies, measures, and outcomes must be implemented through the business area plans.

The risk assessment process is the responsibility of the Policy and Governance area. Information from the risk assessment process is provided to Professional Standards members, who quality assure the assessments and ensure that the risks identified are appropriate in relation to the intelligence that they hold for complaints and conduct issues. The associated tools and templates for the risk assessment process are based on the current Australian and New Zealand standard on risk management and incorporate a mix of standard categories that each area must comment on, for example, compliance with financial regulations, security, the integrity of staff, and also issues specific for each area. The tools are maintained by the Strategic Risk Management Team within Policy and Governance, who also provide risk management training and advisory services for the agency.

Procedural Controls

Regarding procedural measures put in place to address risks, the AFP has a governance framework that incorporates guidelines for a variety of activities, such as handling property seizures, interviewing, and collecting evidence. Many activities are also regulated by specific legislation. The purpose of the governance framework is, therefore, to ensure that the legislative requirements are met as well as the expectations of the community and the government. The AFP pointed out that the legislation in place that governs its interviewing procedures is different to other jurisdictions in that it is provided with a shorter time frame to hold a person in custody and interview them without charge (for nonterrorism-related criminal offences); that period being a maximum of 4 hours.

Traffic officers in the ACT have in-car video cameras with audio recording. Most vehicles were also said to have GPS (global positioning system), allowing patrol cars to be tracked.

Other strategies in place to protect the integrity of AFP members and the organisation include a secondary employment policy that requires written approval for secondary employment activities, declarable association reporting, an obligation to complete a use-of-force report in all cases when force is used, recorded access to databases, rules regarding the use of IT systems presented at login, and the AFP values as the computer screen saver.

Drug and Alcohol Testing

Learning from the Royal Commissions into policing in other jurisdictions of Australia, the AFP introduced the drug-free workplace model, including a drug-testing regime. This was initially voluntary, but now is legislated and, thus, compulsory.

The AFP utilises three forms of drug testing: targeted, random, and certain incident testing. Areas designated as higher risk are likely to be subject to more testing over certain periods of time. The AFP 2008–2009 Annual Report states that 6,367 mandatory targeted drug tests were conducted (the AFP had 6,332 total employees as of 30 June 2009), and that Mandatory Targeted Tests accounted for 92.41% of the total tests conducted during the reporting period (Australian Federal Police, 2009). Drug testing decreased somewhat over the 2009–2010 period, with the Annual Report (Australian

Federal Police, 2010) showing 5,307 mandatory targeted tests conducted (while total employees increased to 6,715 at 30 June 2010).

Members can also be targeted for a drug test on the basis of suspicion of drug use. Members can be subject, as well, to an alcohol screening test if they are on duty and a manager reasonably suspects that they are under the influence of alcohol. If the screening test is positive, they may be directed to undergo a breath test and must comply with such a direction, and, if the breath test is positive for alcohol, they may supply a specimen of blood for a test.

Successful employment applicants and contractors are also subject to mandatory drug testing, as are members involved in specific critical incidents. Critical incidents are defined in the Act 1979 as any "certain" incident where a person is killed or seriously injured as a result of driving a motor vehicle or a death in custody or if a person is killed or seriously injured by discharging a firearm or use of force. Critical incident testing involves providing a breath test for alcohol and a urine test for drugs.

Where a member is selected for a drug test, he/she is served with a direction to attend and supply a bodily sample (e.g., blood or urine) for a test. Failure or refusal to comply with a test is typically considered a category 3 misconduct matter. There are, however, safeguards built in to ensure that members who are lawfully on medication that does not impair performance are not disadvantaged by the drug testing. For example, members are asked to declare if they are taking medication, and medical history can be checked and a doctor's certificate supplied to support a case. Further, the AFP has a medical doctor review each positive test result and assess the substance, levels and context, etc., before it is referred as a conduct issue. Thus, members are given a chance to explain positive test results and have experts review them.

The AFP is currently reviewing and strengthening its drug testing policy and is consulting with ACLEI on the matter. The AFP stated that it monitors development in drug testing best practice with a view to identifying improvements in methodologies and technology.

Staff Screening

Applicants to the AFP undergo a variety of checks, including those set by the Commonwealth for each level of security clearance (up to top secret negative vetting). Checks include character and security checks, criminal history and criminal association checks, fingerprint checking, former employer references, credit history checks, psychological testing, and also a test for illicit drugs. The AFP explained that the aim of the screening process is to identify potential security risks posed to the organisation and whether these risks can be managed or mitigated.

Psychological testing is also used to assess the well-being of members in identified high risk areas, such as child protection, over the course of their employment in that area. Security clearances are reviewed periodically. Currently, security clearances are valid for 5 years at all levels. The AFP stated that it has a robust employment framework that requires all AFP appointees to maintain integrity and employment standards. It is also the responsibility of all AFP members to notify of any change of circumstances. A range of reporting and auditing mechanisms are in place to identify potential issues for security clearance holders and invoke a review process to ensure any threat or vulnerability is addressed. Where a significant issue is identified, security clearance can be revoked. However, less serious issues may result in an "after-care" program for the individual, whereby certain restrictions or compliance agreements are placed on the individual for a time period and monitored by AFP Security. For example, a person could be asked to provide financial statements after a further 6 months. While this function used to be a part of Professional Standards, it has now been moved to the Security Portfolio of the AFP.

Members seeking promotions, selected transfers, awards, and overseas deployments are screened with respect to their Professional Standards history and information held on CRAMS in relation to complaints. Information relating to the member's credibility and reliability as a witness is disclosed for any member giving evidence in a Commonwealth prosecution, so his/her integrity can be assessed. Thus, complaints and conduct issues can be problematic for members and the cases in which they are involved. In this context, the seriousness of lying to Professional Standards during the investigation of a complaint matter can subsequently affect that member's credibility in providing evidence in court. Integrity checks are also required for confidants engaged in the Confidant Network.

Ethics Training and Education

AFP Professional Standards delivers a number of proactive programs under its education and awareness strategy. This strategy is designed to help maintain and support the values and code of conduct, which are the foundations of its organisational integrity. This strategy involves collaborative partnerships between AFP Professional Standards and other internal stakeholders within the Human Resource portfolio, including Well-Being Services, Confidant Network (internal "whistleblowers" network) and Learning and Development.

The principal aim of these programs is to raise AFP appointees' awareness of their responsibilities under the professional standards framework throughout all stages and levels of their career with the AFP. The key success of these programs was described by the AFP as "the practical application of the professional standards framework, combined with a contextual, holistic approach of information based on case studies."

AFP Professional Standards has had a prominent role in the development and delivery of the AFP Respectful Workplace Strategy, which is currently being implemented throughout the organisation. This strategy aims to raise awareness about behaviour that reflects respectful workplace practices and avenues of support available to AFP appointees who experience behaviour that may be perceived as inappropriate and/or unacceptable.

Additionally, various internal information technology strategies are employed to raise AFP members' awareness of their responsibilities concerning the professional standards. These include the publications of case studies with learning outcomes, "In Focus" bulletins advising of updated governance, survey questions regarding integrity-based questions, and IT (information technology) screen savers currently promoting the organisational code of conduct.

Professional Standards provides training and awareness sessions as part of its marketing strategies regarding expected conduct and obligations of members of the AFP as well as promoting professional standards best practice. For example, Professional Standards has a close partnership with Learning and Development Units in order to deliver awareness modules on all major AFP training programs, including recruit training, induction sessions, and ethics and integrity sessions at the request of business areas. Professional Standards has also engaged with leadership programs and forums, specifically around issues of managing staff performance and conduct and preventing issues from escalating to complaints. Sessions are delivered across geographical locations and also target deployment branches including international, protective services, airport police, and air security.

The AFP reports that 211 professional standards awareness and prevention programs were delivered during the 2009–2010 reporting period (Australian Federal Police Annual Report, 2010) in capital cities and regional locations. Further, since 2008, Professional Standards has delivered week-long Interagency Integrity Investigators Programs annually. The programs cover contemporary and emerging issues within the integrity environment and are attended by national and international integrity investigators from law enforcement agencies and oversight bodies.

Professional Standards sessions are run by team members and investigators who are experienced in the area so that they can offer real practical examples and answer questions. The mandatory reporting obligations (of members' conduct that is not in line with the AFP values) are a particular concentration of the sessions, including the Confidant Network. Sessions also educate as to possible risks or circumstances in which they need to report or seek advice from Professional Standards. Indeed, the AFP highlighted that these sessions encourage contact with Professional Standards for advice in integrity-related matters. However, there is also a general ethos of integrity being every member's responsibility; as the AFP noted, "You're not to rely on Professional Standards to maintain integrity, it's your responsibility, you're the organisation, you must report it, you must look after it, you must know what your standards are, and you must make the judgement." So, while advice is available and accessible to members, it was stated that it was important for Professional Standards to encourage the members to talk through the issues, in relation to the standards of the organisation, and make their own decision, rather than Professional Standards simply prescribing an answer.

The AFP spoke in the interview about surveying members regarding integrity-related issues. This had largely taken the form of surveying members' knowledge of particular policies, practices, or available resources (such as the Confidant Network), but ethical culture questions were raised as a way forward. Particularly, work surveying members' views of the seriousness of particular examples of conduct and their preparedness to report, was raised as a possibility for future surveys. The aim of the survey is to identify needs for improvement in ethical health as well as identifying particular gaps or failures in training or strategy provision for enhancing integrity.

The AFP reported that data previously gathered "in-house" identified that most AFP members have an understanding of expected values and expectations regarding ethical behaviours and corruption, they are aware of the consequences, they know the operational procedures for reporting corruption or unethical behaviour, and they are mostly willing to report corruption.

The AFP publishes case studies on its intranet of de-identified internal investigation cases. The case studies are actual events involving AFP appointees, which raise issues of significance concerning safeguarding the AFP's integrity. The case studies ensure that privacy and legal requirements around identifying particular appointees have been considered and are protected. ACLEI supported the use of such material for awareness-raising and noted that such cases may also "demonstrate that disciplinary decisions are taken fairly, which is a key factor in the preparedness of individuals to report wrongdoing in the future."

Australian Commission for Law Enforcement Integrity

The Australian Commission for Law Enforcement Integrity (ACLEI) was established by the Law Enforcement Integrity Commissioner Act 2006 (the LEIC Act) and commenced operations in 2007. ACLEI consists of approximately 24 staff members, led by the Integrity Commissioner, and

> ... is responsible for preventing, detecting, and investigating serious and systemic corruption issues in the Australian Crime Commission and the

> Australian Federal Police. From January 2011, the Australian Customs and Border Protection Service is also subject to the Integrity Commissioner's independent scrutiny, in respect of that agency's law enforcement functions.*

The ACLEI Annual Report for 2007–2008 states that "ACLEI was not established in the context of crisis or doubt about the integrity of Australian government law enforcement agencies. Rather, ACLEI was established so that there could be added confidence in their integrity, based on independent scrutiny" (Australian Commission for Law Enforcement Integrity, 2008, p. 4). Thus, ACLEI was established in a context of no known serious corruption problem in either the Australian Federal Police (AFP) or the Australian Crime Commission (ACC) and no known systemic issues, but as a precautionary approach, due to the high corruption risks in the type of work that the AFP and ACC undertake, and to create an independent organisation that has visibility of all corruption issues.

The LEIC Act is premised on those agency heads taking responsibility for the integrity of their agencies. Therefore, ACLEI is intended to provide an additional independent assurance to the public and the Minister about the integrity of these agencies, by detecting, investigating, and preventing corrupt conduct. This report will focus on ACLEI's role in relation to the AFP.

Receiving Information About Corruption

The focus of ACLEI is on serious and systemic corruption, thus any information that raises a corruption-related issue regarding the AFP can be reported to ACLEI. Under the LEIC Act, the AFP Commissioner is obliged to notify all category 4 (corruption) matters that come to his/her attention to ACLEI. Under the Ombudsman Act 1976 the Commonwealth Ombudsman must also report to ACLEI any information that, in the Ombudsman's opinion, raises a significant corruption issue. Other government agencies may also refer corruption issues to ACLEI. ACLEI, therefore, receives such notifications from a variety of agencies as well as the general public from whom it can also receive information anonymously. ACLEI recently introduced a "hotline" to increase access for reporting corruption matters, and also provides an online form for reporting, which asks for details of the matter and whether the person would like to be notified of the outcome of his/her complaint. The LEIC Act provides that a person who has reported a possible corruption issue can elect to be informed of the progress and outcome of the matter. In practice, however, the sensitivity and complexity of corruption investigations often prevents the provision of regular progress reports or updates.

* ACLEI Web site at http://www.aclei.gov.au/ (accessed 15 February 2011).

ACLEI stated in interview that, given its role to provide independent assurance to government that Commonwealth law enforcement agencies and their staff act with integrity, ACLEI does not view reports of possible corruption issues as "complaints," but as information or intelligence that may be the starting point for an investigation. Thus, while some people do approach ACLEI with a particular complaint for which they retain an interest in the outcome, investigations are not a service to the complainant and are not specifically oriented to providing restitution (although that may be one outcome of an investigation).

Investigation

Matters received by ALCEI enter into a triage process of assessment. For example, the information is assessed regarding credibility, susceptibility to investigation, and seriousness of the matter. Based on this assessment, ACLEI has a number of response options available, including deciding that the matter should not be investigated. Where investigation is deemed warranted, the Integrity Commissioner can choose to investigate the matter using ACLEI's own resources, can refer the matter to the subject agency (AFP) to investigate, or can choose to refer the matter to another external agency to investigate. For example, where the matter involves a seconded member from a state agency, ACLEI may refer the matter to an agency of that state (state police or state anticorruption body). Where ACLEI hands the matter back to the AFP to investigate, ACLEI can oversee, manage, or review the AFP investigation. ACLEI can also choose to conduct a joint investigation with another agency. For example, ACLEI can conduct joint investigations with the AFP into matters concerning AFP employees. This arrangement was seen as particularly beneficial for reinforcing the relationship between ACLEI and the AFP and for providing an independent perspective. As ACLEI stated, "We may well be able to see things in a different light to them, because we're several steps removed and can bring a dispassionate viewpoint to the matter."

Under the LEIC Act, the Integrity Commissioner must focus on serious and systemic corruption, and has the option of referring matters back to the agency for investigation, with or without management or review by ACLEI. In practice then, ACLEI investigates relatively few of the matters that come before it. The Annual Report for 2009–2010 reports that, of the 130 matters that comprised its workload, it began or continued 22 investigations during that year, including 10 investigations conducted jointly with other agencies (Australian Commission for Law Enforcement Integrity, 2010).

While ACLEI retains an independent investigative function over the AFP, ACLEI also has described its work with the AFP as an "integrity partnership." More recently, ACLEI has recognised that this partnership could extend beyond ACLEI's work with AFP Professional Standards to other areas of AFP core business that link to corruption, particularly organised crime.

The Integrity Commissioner has termed the relationship between organised crime and corrupt law enforcement officials as the "corruption handshake," and has suggested that ACLEI and the AFP can assist one another by sharing information in this area.

Powers

Aside from responding to information notifications and referrals, ACLEI has the power to conduct its own motion investigations. This allows a proactive approach regarding matters that are in the public interest and ACLEI has identified risks associated with organised crime, mentioned above, in much of its casework.

Also available to ACLEI to support its investigative function are a variety of information-gathering powers, including the power to enter the premises of a law enforcement agency without prior warning and to seize articles; apply for and execute warrants for searches, arrests, and passport seizure, e.g., where a person is attempting to evade giving evidence; and the power to access financial transaction records. ACLEI also has the authority to conduct controlled operations and utilise assumed identities, telecommunications interception, and data access as well as electronic and physical surveillance. ACLEI was established with a "building block" approach, which has seen its capabilities and its use of powers grow over the years of operation. ACLEI has only recently acquired the authority to obtain search and telecommunications interception warrants, having "developed the expertise and specialised facilities that are prerequisites for the use of these significant powers" (ACLEI Annual Report 2010, p. 4). The health and safety issues of invoking the arrest power, with regard to use of force, were highlighted as an issue and it was stated that the ability to second law enforcement officers from other agencies to carry out work in relation to coercive powers was a beneficial option. Other powers that were stated as valuable included the power to covertly scrutinise financial transactions, the use of listening devices, and also the use of covert human information sources (informants) and whistleblowers.

ACLEI also has the power to conduct coercive hearings in public or private. The hearing power includes being able to summon a person to give evidence or produce documents or other items. It is, therefore, an offence to fail to attend a hearing or fail to comply with a direction to give evidence, even where that evidence may be self-incriminatory. However, given that such evidence is obtained under duress, it is inadmissible for criminal proceedings against the individual regarding that matter. ACLEI has an in-house legal practice that assists with matters relating to hearings, warrants, notices, and summons to ensure accountability and that lawful practices are followed.

Outcomes

While the power to compel answers to questions was highlighted as a valuable tool and a key deterrence mechanism, the tension regarding the inadmissibility for criminal proceedings of the evidence gained was noted. The issue was discussed in relation to the purpose of independent integrity agencies, for example, whether the important aspect of activity was in finding the truth, creating a deterrent for corrupt behaviour, removing unsuitable members of the police, or "locking people up." As ACLEI explained, "On the one hand, we want to have confidence in our police forces, but for some people that means we don't want them to 'get away with it,' so there's always this tension." The tension was described by ACLEI as one between targeting an individual versus understanding and deterring corrupt conduct. While ACLEI stated that it is sometimes possible to do both, ACLEI's higher purpose was described as to strengthen the integrity system, for example, through systemic change, even where evidence is not available to provide proof to the criminal standard (required by prosecutions).

Evidence gained through coercive hearings, however, can be used for disciplinary purposes and in proceedings under proceeds of crime legislation. While ACLEI does not have the power to discipline members of the AFP, it can pass on information to the AFP in relation to disciplinary matters. In ACLEI investigation reports, the Integrity Commissioner can also recommend disciplinary action of AFP members, including action related to improving performance as well as termination of employment.

During the course of an investigation, ACLEI may uncover information that poses a present risk to the operations of a law enforcement agency. In appropriate circumstances, the Integrity Commissioner disseminates such information to the heads of law enforcement agencies to allow them to manage the immediate integrity risks to their operations.

ACLEI investigation reports can also include other recommendations, for example, regarding the policies or practices of the agency that may have contributed to, allowed, or failed to detect the conduct/incident. Where recommendations are made, the Integrity Commissioner can request that the AFP Commissioner provide a response regarding any action to be taken in respect of the recommendations, and that request must be complied with. Where the Integrity Commissioner is not satisfied with the response, matters can be referred to the Minister.

In relation to criminal conduct, where such evidence is uncovered during an investigation, ACLEI may refer the matter to the DPP. Thus, decisions over prosecuting cases of police corruption arising from ACLEI investigations are made independently of ACLEI and the AFP.

Outcomes of investigations must be reported to the person who referred the corruption issue, if they chose to be kept informed. However, ACLEI can choose not to do this if doing so is likely to prejudice an investigation or any action taken as a result of the investigation.

Witness Support

ACLEI's legislation contains provisions to protect whistleblowers and internal witnesses. The LEIC Act 2006 provides that ACLEI can protect any person making a complaint or providing information to ACLEI, who may be subject to intimidation, harassment, or compromised safety. Protection can extend to physical security, relocation, or provision of a new identity.

Early Detection/Profiling

While the ACLEI does not have an early detection system for flagging problems in the AFP, it has live access to AFP Professional Standards databases, allowing visibility of trends. ACLEI also has functions that relate to proactive identification of trends and issues. For example, ACLEI must report annually on any patterns or trends identified regarding corruption matters. In 2009, ACLEI established an organisational unit (Strategic Support) that is tasked with identifying emerging corruption risks and conducting research into the treatment and prevention of corruption. It also has the task of keeping up to date with anticorruption best practice from other jurisdictions and learning lessons from their experiences. In addition, ACLEI has implemented a case management and intelligence system to enable storing and retrieval of investigation and intelligence data.

Risk Management

ACLEI provides advice on potential risks to the AFP in the area of corruption as well as recommendations for improvements in risk management. ACLEI conducted a review of the AFP's (and ACC's) anticorruption arrangements (Australian Commission for Law Enforcement Integrity, 2009a) toward this aim. The review highlighted the potential risks faced by the AFP, in light of the nature of its work. It provided a largely positive assessment of the AFP's integrity framework, while noting that planned new integrity initiatives (such as integrity testing) that could strengthen the framework might need consideration of available resources. The report also recommended a stock-take to identify areas of corruption risk, for example, the report (Australian Commission for Law Enforcement Integrity, 2009a, p. 11) noted some areas of the work of the AFP are more susceptible than others (e.g., community policing, information management, drug handling, and international deployment).

Further, ACLEI has observed specific changes in the corruption risk environment in relation to organised crime. ACLEI outlines in its 2009–2010 Annual Report that it has specifically targeted the threat of organised crime, the models of law enforcement to combat organised crime (particularly calls for interoperability and information sharing), as well as changes to the "corruption-deterrence regime," as creating new risks for corruption that must be addressed (Australian Commission for Law Enforcement Integrity, 2010).

Education and Prevention

Early 2009 saw a recommendation by the Parliamentary Joint Committee on ACLEI that it add corruption prevention and education to its functions. ACLEI already makes targeted presentations a number of times each year to raise awareness about corruption and the integrity framework. The aim of this awareness-raising activity is to build corruption resistance, particularly in terms of staff recognition of what constitutes corrupt behaviour and how it should be reported. As a result, ACLEI awareness-raising sessions are strategically directed and are generally embedded within other agency-run activities, such as ethics or recruit training. Tailored presentations are given to AFP members in a variety of organisational groups at locations around Australia, including to recruits, middle managers, and senior executives. ACLEI stated that it recognises that managers and supervisors are the front line of corruption control, best placed to recognise and act on corrupt behaviour. Accordingly, presentations to managers focus on raising their awareness of corruption indicators.

ACLEI's 2008–2009 Annual Report states that these sessions have resulted in immediate effects where "on occasions, these presentations resulted in information about corruption issues being provided to ACLEI or to the agency concerned" (Australian Commission for Law Enforcement Integrity, 2009b, p. 20). ACLEI also participates in the AFP's Inter-Agency Integrity Investigators Program, which is attended by investigators from national and international police and oversight agencies.

Commonwealth Ombudsman

The Commonwealth Ombudsman is also the ACT Ombudsman and the Law Enforcement Ombudsman. The Ombudsman fulfils five key functions: complaint handling and investigation, own motion investigations (see below under Powers), compliance auditing, monitoring or oversight of agency functions, and promoting good administration.

Complaint Handling

The Ombudsman can receive complaints about actions of AFP members as well as more general agency policies, practices, and procedures. Complaints can be made in person, over the telephone, or in writing (letter, fax, or using an online complaint form available through the Ombudsman's Web site). However, the Ombudsman encourages complaints to be made directly to the agency concerned in the first instance, to try to resolve matters, with the option of complaining to the Ombudsman if the agency does not handle the complaint satisfactorily. This is particularly the case for lower category complaints where complainants will be asked when making a complaint if they have tried to resolve the issue with the AFP, and sometimes told to do so before a complaint will be taken by the Ombudsman. Among the issues most commonly received are complaints of discourtesy, typically for ACT policing, issues around treatment during arrest or execution of search warrants, and also, somewhat common were complaints of unfair treatment in relation to suspicion of terrorism offences.

In many cases, complaints received by the Ombudsman will be referred back to the AFP to handle in the first instance where the Ombudsman has confidence that the matter can be handled internally. Indeed, while the Ombudsman receives close to 350 approaches regarding the AFP a year, around half of these individuals are referred to the AFP. Complainants can return to the Ombudsman if they are unhappy with the outcome or method of handling. In some cases, the Ombudsman may choose to investigate the matter directly, without referring to the AFP, or may choose to supervise the AFP investigation. For example, there may be particular matters that the Ombudsman retains an interest in, particularly after a review, such as the review of Watchhouse practices (Commonwealth Ombudsman, 2007b). Where matters of serious corruption are alleged, the Ombudsman is obliged to refer the matter to ACLEI to handle. The Ombudsman also has discretion to refer other matters to ACLEI that may entail less serious corruption or indicate systemic corruption.

Complaint Investigation

Commonwealth legislation has changed the way in which complaints against the AFP are handled. Previously, the AFP investigated all complaints against them, with the Ombudsman only providing an oversight role to that investigation. This oversight role would comprise only the receiving of a report on the investigation and providing comment. In rare cases, the Ombudsman's Office could conduct its own investigation if unsatisfied with the AFP's handling of the matter, but those investigations could only be conducted under the Complaints (Australian Federal Police) Act 1981 as the Ombudsman Act did not provide for investigations of complaints against police. The Ombudsman Act 1976 (Cth.) now provides for investigations of police complaints, which provides the Ombudsman with powers previously unavailable for this area. The 2008–2009 Annual Report states that, during that reporting period, 39 complaint investigations were completed and 52 complaints oversighted (Commonwealth Ombudsman, 2009). In 2009–2010, 53 investigations were completed (Commonwealth Ombudsman, 2010).

The Ombudsman continues to oversight the AFP's investigations of category 3 matters (serious conduct issues). These matters are reported to the Ombudsman when they are received by the AFP, but are investigated by the AFP Professional Standards area. Oversight by the Ombudsman includes receiving reports on the progress and outcome of the complaint. The Commonwealth Ombudsman may also conduct investigations jointly with the AFP for category 3 matters or AFP practices issues, such as the joint (with the AFP) Review of ACT Policing's Watchhouse Operations (Commonwealth Ombudsman, 2007b), or can have police officers assist with investigations.

Powers

The Ombudsman has an own motion investigation power that can be used to initiate an Ombudsman investigation into a matter that has not risen out of an individual complaint, but that has come to its attention through insights gained from handling a number of related complaints or through other means. An example of the latter is that the AFP may ask the Ombudsman's Office to investigate a matter in the interest of demonstrating public accountability and independence of the investigation and enhancing public confidence in the outcome.

In the course of an investigation, the Ombudsman has the power to enter premises occupied by the AFP and can require a person to provide information, including answering questions and producing documents or other records that the Ombudsman believes would assist in the investigation. Where such information may incriminate the person, the Ombudsman Act 1976 states that this is not admissible against the person in criminal proceedings.

Outcomes

Primarily the outcomes of Ombudsman investigations, reviews, or oversight involve recommendations to the AFP, typically regarding improvements to policies, practices, or systems. The AFP is not obliged to accept recommendations, but can be asked to provide a response to the recommendations including steps taken to implement or reasons why recommendations will not be accepted. The representative for the Ombudsman's Office at interview discussed the process of implementing recommendations and highlighted that the office is conscious that some recommendations may be difficult to implement, impractical, or not cost-effective, and that it is mindful of the feasibility of recommendations when making them. Generally, though, it was highlighted that the uptake of recommendations was good and that draft reports are provided and recommendations will be discussed between the two agencies. As the Ombudsman's representative stated:

> We might say "change your systems to provide this kind of information" and they'll say that their system can't do that and it can't be changed to do that. So, we might change a recommendation to say they should invest in a new system or something like that. There's no point in making a recommendation that's impossible to implement or we've got it wrong because we haven't understood, which is why we send them a draft of the report.

If the Ombudsman is not satisfied with the AFP's response over implementation of recommendations, a public report can be released that identifies the AFP's lack of response and the Ombudsman may inform the Prime Minister in writing. However, before any report that is critical of the AFP is released, the Ombudsman must allow the AFP the chance to comment.

The representative of the Ombudsman's Office explained, however, that where complainants are concerned, often the outcome that is most sought after to resolve the matter is an explanation and an apology by the AFP. This was seen as often difficult due to agencies' apprehension over admitting blame. However, the Ombudsman's representative explained that apologies did not have to equate to blame in the sense of civil litigation: "You can say you're sorry when you've done the wrong thing and admit that you've done the wrong thing and it doesn't mean that you're going to be sued." Where the Ombudsman believes that there is evidence that an AFP member is guilty of misconduct or a breach of duty, the Ombudsman is obliged to inform the AFP.

Early Intervention/Complaint Profiling

While the Ombudsman's Office does not have an early intervention system, the aim of its inspections and reviews is to intervene in, and rectify, problems before they escalate, or identify potential system failures that may lead to misconduct. The Ombudsman's representative at interview stated that dealing with misconduct in an effective and timely manner lessens the risk of corruption "because corruption doesn't emerge fully formed in an organisation ... it always starts off as misconduct, minor misconduct that is tolerated by the system that leads to corruption. So, we see our role as really important at that stage before it gets up to something that's really wrong, before it gets to corruption."

The Ombudsman's Office also records the issues that concern each complaint. These "issues strings" allow trend analysis to link issues rather than individual complaints. Such trends can inform decision making, for example, whether a particular issue trend warrants an own motion investigation.

Ethics Training and Education

At the time of interview, the Ombudsman did not play a role in the training or education of AFP members. However, it was recognised in interview that members might benefit from presentations regarding the role of the Ombudsman in police complaints. Further, it was also stated in interview that AFP members could benefit from specialised complaint handling training as opposed to complaint investigations training.

Audit/Review

The Commonwealth Ombudsman has two main audit and inspection functions: inspection of the AFP's complaint handling system and compliance auditing regarding legislative requirements of certain activities. Inspection of the AFP's complaint handling system generally includes post hoc reviews of how complaints have been handled by the AFP, such as timeliness and appropriate categorisation and referral practices. Inspections are legislated to take place at least once a year, but in practice typically occur twice a year, and reports are provided to the AFP and then aggregated into an annual report to Parliament on the efficiency and effectiveness of the complaint handling system. The inspection involves reviewing a random selection of complaints (approximately 25%) regardless of how they were received. Complaints are inspected in detail, but the focus is on systemic issues and general practices, rather than individual complaint issues.

The Commonwealth Ombudsman also conducts compliance audits, through records inspections, to check AFP compliance with its legislative obligations regarding certain activities. For example, under the Telecommunications (Interception and Access) Act 1979, the Ombudsman audits compliance with recordkeeping and reporting requirements regarding conducting telephone interceptions. The Commonwealth Ombudsman also audits access by both federal and state agencies to stored communications under the TIA Act and use of surveillance devices under the Surveillance Devices Act 2004. The Ombudsman also audits the AFP in relation to controlled operations and also the ACT child protection register. As the representative of the Ombudsman's Office stated at interview:

> We look at: (a) whether they are complying with their requirements under the act; and (b) best practice, that something maybe isn't a compliance issue, but indicates that if they keep this up they will end up having a compliance issue; a weakness in their system.

Commonwealth Emerging Issues

The Commonwealth has seen a number of changes in the past 5 years that have enhanced its police integrity framework, including the introduction of ACLEI to prevent and respond to high-level corruption matters as well as new legislation to support the Commonwealth Ombudsman's oversight role of the AFP. The AFP itself has also seen an overhaul of its complaints-handling framework and associated performance and discipline focus; the focus being on early resolution, local responsibility, and correction of behaviour rather than punishment.

During recent years, ACLEI has also aligned the focus of its work with an emerging environment around risks associated with organised crime, as well as the potential for ACLEI to work in partnership with the AFP (and other relevant agencies) to combat the relationship between organised crime and corruption. ACLEI noted that the 2008 National Security Statement of Former Prime Minister Kevin Rudd (Rudd, 2008) recognised a new threat to Australia from serious and organised crime and changed the operating environment of law enforcement agencies. Subsequently, the 2009 Commonwealth Organised Crime Strategic Framework (Attorney General, 2009) highlighted the possibility of criminal networks infiltrating law enforcement, and outlined a multiagency response plan that included sharing of intelligence data.

ACLEI's casework and experience was said to correlate with the notion of organised crime responding to increased deterrents through displacement to softer targets (e.g., nontraditional partners engaged with task forces). Further, ACLEI's Annual Report for 2009–1010 notes an increase in the number of corruption issues with links to organised crime, which it states provides some validation to the notion that organised crime is "fighting back" using methods of infiltration of law enforcement (Australian Commission for Law Enforcement Integrity, 2010). Thus, ACLEI has changed its policy basis from a reassurance and precautionary model to matching the integrity measure to the risk (of organised crime). This has included the addition of Customs and Border Protection to the LEIC Act jurisdiction from January 2011. Further, ACLEI's integrity partnership with professional standards areas of agencies, such as the AFP, has extended to sharing of information with other core business areas—intelligence collected by law enforcement on organised crime can provide insights about corrupt conduct and corruption risk, while ACLEI's integrity investigations can yield new information about the activities of criminal groups.

Innovative Strategies

Risk Assessment

Noted above, ACLEI have moved to a model of assessing environmental risks in a precautionary approach rather than responding to evidence of corruption. The Integrity Commissioner stated in a 2009 speech (Moss, 2009) that:

> … through investigation, research, and analysis, we identify and understand more fully the challenges. It can only be through taking an informed approach that we may assess our corruption risks accurately and be sure that we craft our measures to match.

ACLEI noted that an area of important focus is the notion of broadening corruption investigations beyond the behaviour of an individual to the context within which the behaviour was able to occur. This was seen as a risk management focus, to identify the potential gaps in management systems or practices that enabled the behaviour. ACLEI stated that, traditionally, corruption investigations are focused on "who's involved and what they're doing, but the broader context is why are they doing it, how are they doing it, how did it emerge, what was the gap in the market if you like, what's the niche that they are filling, what is the opportunity that they've seized?"

Accordingly, ACLEI's investigations are aimed at strengthening the integrity system, including detection and deterrence: "When we know their risks, it informs [us] where we should best deploy our resources." The Ombudsman's representative also mentioned the importance of focusing on systemic issues over individual complaint issues in their oversight of the AFP complaint handling system.

Reporting

The AFP has in place several strategies that support the mandatory reporting of misconduct, which were viewed as both innovative and successful. The Confidant Network provides a system of support and advice for members as well as representing an official reporting channel. The Complaints Reporting and Management System (CRAMS) also provides a networked electronic reporting capability for members (to report conduct they have witnessed or to record complaints made to them by citizens). This was seen as particularly beneficial in that it was accessible to all members and allowed "instant" reporting rather than a paper-based system that could be intercepted.

At a further level, the Integrity Reports provide a channel for reporting incidents that may constitute potential risks, described in interview as "that grey area of things that don't seem right, but there's nothing obvious to say there's something wrong." Examples were given that included off-duty contact with persons of interest, and off-duty receiving of fines or infringement notices. Thus, the reporting system enables self-reporting and reporting of others for any incident that may impact on integrity. Integrity Reports are assessed and reviewed for trends that indicate a particular emerging issue that needs to be addressed.

Successful Strategies

Drug Testing

The AFP strongly enforces its drug-free policy through its drug testing regime. This offers not only a random program of drug testing in relation to when employees will be tested, but also a mandatory program of testing that is designed to increase the deterrence effect. The AFP viewed their drug policy and annual testing program as effective at communicating both to the workforce and the general public that the AFP is a drug-free organisation. This was said to both increase public perception of the AFP as well as discouraging unsuitable people from applying. The number of tests conducted, together with the small number of positive tests yielded, was taken as a positive sign that the policy is working.

Education/Marketing

The AFP noted that Professional Standards education sessions were successful at informing employees of their ethical obligations and raising awareness of reporting requirements and channels. It was noted that spikes in complaints had been recorded in areas after receiving an integrity presentation, which was taken to be a positive sign that the presentation had increased reporting behaviour.

Public Hearing and Reporting Powers

ACLEI stated that its powers to conduct public hearings and release public reports (as well as reports to the Minister) were important. The powers were seen as beneficial for a number of reasons including investigative, deterrent, and persuasive.

Broad Definition of Corruption

ACLEI noted that its legislation (the LEIC Act 2006) included a broad definition of corruption that allows flexibility in the issues that it chooses to investigate. As ACLEI explained, "That gives us a flexibility to look at many things, we focus on serious and systemic corruption, but we can still take an interest in corruption indicators, which might otherwise be treated as individual instances of less serious conduct."

Ombudsman Investigations

The Ombudsman's Office noted that changes to the Ombudsman Act that enabled its office to conduct independent investigations had improved its relationship with the AFP. The Ombudsman's Office representative explained that, under the former regime of the Complaints Act, the Ombudsman could only comment on AFP investigations, which was seen to be a critical and potentially antagonistic role. Under the new Ombudsman Act, they are now able to conduct their own investigations and make recommendations: "I think it takes us out of a relationship that I think wasn't functioning as well, that I think works a lot better now." Particularly, the ability to conclude "administrative deficiency" was noted as helpful because this highlights system failures rather than individual failures and allows recommendations for improvement rather than placing blame.

Emerging Ethical Issues

Each agency was asked during the interviews to highlight any emerging ethical issues that it has identified for its jurisdiction or that might potentially be issues for the future. While some new issues were identified, there was also a feeling that ethical issues tend to rotate and resurface. Jurisdictional trends are a focus of all three of the Commonwealth agencies and the AFP also noted that it scans other law enforcement agencies, nationally and internationally, for emerging issues. Furthermore, members of the AFP meet on a weekly basis to discuss all the category 3 matters and any emerging trends. The Ombudsman's team that deals with AFP complaints also meets on a weekly basis and is able to run reports on their system on an ad hoc basis on specific issues.

Organised Crime

ACLEI identified that new powers and functions for law enforcement agencies, in relation to combating organised crime as well as new non-traditional partners (e.g., banks, Centrelink) working with law enforcement in this area, could lead to new temptations for organised crime in terms of seeking access to new powers and information. ACLEI noted that new partner agencies working with law enforcement could be viewed by organised crime as softer targets providing new potential entry points to law enforcement.

ACLEI also raised the issue that abuse of power is always going to be a concern for law enforcement agencies, particularly with new powers being brought in as well as new staff. As ACLEI stated at interview:

> When additional powers become available, there's always a question of whether that power is taken up with an understanding of the ethical framework, and an appreciation of the tensions involved, and then how that translates into how those powers are exercised.

ACLEI highlighted the importance of accountability and transparency mechanisms for the use of powers.

Multiple Roles

Both the AFP and the Ombudsman's Office noted that the breadth of the work that the AFP is engaged in presents a range of different risks for the organisation. Further, it was noted that recruitment for some of these roles, such as international deployment and airport policing, comes from state police agencies and so this can provide a mix of organisational cultures with different values and understanding of the integrity framework. This was also highlighted as an issue with the recent amalgamation of the protective services role into the AFP.

Ethnic Groups

The representative of the Ombudsman's Office noted that policing ethnic minority communities, or individuals, may create new areas of risk, particularly ethnic groups that may be of interest in relation to terrorism. The Ombudsman's representative stated that the issue was in how police interact with such individuals and, particularly, refugees who may have negative experiences with police and/or are unaware of their rights in Australia: "... people who might be refugees, who might be from an environment where they've escaped persecution, it can be quite difficult for them to encounter a police person, when they are used to being afraid." It was acknowledged that the AFP is working to improve liaison with Islamic communities, but that there are other groups that may need the same level of attention.

DNA Sampling

There has been discussion around mandatory DNA sampling of AFP members and this was raised as presenting an emerging ethical issue. The reasons for collecting DNA samples of members were presented as allowing identification in fatal incidents, excluding members from crime scenes, and background checking of new employees (whether they were linked to any unsolved crimes). There is also the potential for DNA sampling to be a deterrent in criminal and corruption behaviour by members as it may aid investigation. However, a working group is exploring the ethical and human rights issues around having such a policy.

Social Networking Sites

Use of social networking sites, such as Facebook, was highlighted as a new ethical issue that had been picked up both by the AFP and nationally by other agencies.

New Generation

Generational issues of new recruits, in terms of a difference in culture and values, were also highlighted as an emerging issue that was receiving attention from the AFP. The Ombudsman's Office highlighted that recruits to the AFP seemed to be younger in recent years and that youth, coupled with inexperience and increased frontline exposure (e.g., in ACT community policing), might increase complaints regarding police action. As the Ombudsman's representative at interview stated, "If the demographic of your police force is quite young and inexperienced, you are more likely to have issues around intervening, taking too much action as opposed to not taking enough. What happens when you've got young officers is that they think they have to take control of the situation and do something, whereas a more experienced officer might stand back."

Information Access

The AFP highlighted that issues around control of access to information and release of information were always important, but may be a potential future issue particularly in relation to terrorism. While AFP members are bound by the Secrecy Provision both during employment and after employment, there were problems highlighted regarding inadvertent leaks to media, to former members of the AFP, as well as the issue of release of information deemed to be in the public interest.

Relationships with former AFP members were stated by the AFP representative to be potentially problematic as there was a perception of continued culture of police. "Even when a member leaves the AFP, they are still considered to be a part of the inner circle of police. They'll always be police. So, you have to really reinforce the requirement not to discuss things with these networks that people maintain with former members."

Global Financial Crisis

The global financial crisis was raised as a potential influence on corruption where members might feel financial stress and, accordingly, be more motivated to be involved in corrupt activity. While no actual problem had been identified, the possibility of seeing more opportunistic crime for financial gain was noted. So, too, was the possibility that budget reductions could impact on deterrence mechanisms.

New South Wales

3

The police integrity system for New South Wales (NSW) consists of a tripartite model of the internal police Professional Standards Command, the NSW Ombudsman, and the independent anticorruption body the Police Integrity Commission. The NSW Independent Commission Against Corruption also has jurisdiction over a very small number of employees of New South Wales police, namely special constables (e.g., security guards employed under the state constitution and administered by the Police Commissioner). The Ombudsman was given jurisdiction over police in 1979, and the Independent Commission Against Corruption (ICAC) was set up in 1989 after decades of corruption problems in both the police and government. Oversight of serious police corruption cases was taken over by the Police Integrity Commission, established in 1996, after the Wood Commission of Inquiry into the New South Wales Police (1994–1997) identified entrenched abuses that the ICAC had been unable to counter (see Chapter 1, Police Misconduct and Integrity, International and Australian Perspective).

The final *Qualitative and Strategic Audit of the Reform Process (QSARP) of the NSW Police*—required by the Wood Commission Report—was completed in 2002 and criticised police management for focusing on administrative efficiency and crime fighting at the expense of integrity management (HayGroup, 2002). A survey of 40 justice system stakeholders found the majority were highly supportive of the Police Integrity Commission (PIC) in detecting corruption, but just under 90% felt there had been no "real change" in the police culture (pp. 104–106). The report also noted that performance measures on reform were lacking, including complainant satisfaction surveys. The most recent major review, a *Ten Year Review of the Police Oversight System in New South Wales,* by the Parliamentary Committee on the Office of the Ombudsman and the Police Integrity Commission (The Committee, 2006), supported the tripartite system against submissions by police management and the police industrial union that sought to take back more responsibility for complaints. The Committee was highly critical of inefficient internal processing of complaints and failures in addressing problems associated with complaints at the local level. The PIC has also been highly critical of police internal disciplinary processes (e.g., Police Integrity Commission, 2000), but in recent years the New South Wales Police Force has been receiving much more positive reports. For example, in 2009 the PIC and the Ombudsman stated that approximately 90% of police investigations were assessed at a satisfactory standard (New South Wales Ombudsman, 2009, p. 66).

New South Wales Police Force

The New South Wales Police Force (NSWPF) has a Professional Standards Command (PSC) with responsibility for the standards of performance and conduct of the NSWPF. PSC emerged from an amalgamation of functions of Internal Affairs and Human Resources and, thus, has a variety of functions including setting and promoting standards of performance and conduct as well as management practices, identifying and responding to behaviour considered to be high-risk (where misconduct is a factor), and investigating corruption and serious criminal allegations involving police. PSC described this as a "net widening" of responsibilities and functions, moving beyond the previous internal investigations model to a more comprehensive role in supporting the professional standards of the organisation:

> The Professional Standards Command is then offering, at multiple levels, a continuum of interventions, coercive powers, investigative powers; it's responsible both at the individual level and at the corporate level while still recognising the requirement for local discretionary capability to promote an ethical professional standards culture.

The Ombudsman's Office supported this widening of responsibility and role:

> We think professional standards are developed and enforced by positive behaviour and intolerance for bad behaviour and that is not just criminal conduct, it's a whole range of conduct. A professional police force has to have very high standards, in everything from customer service issues to integrity issues and the complaints system really has to capture all of it.

Complaint Handling

Complaints made to the NSWPF must be in writing, but complainants can remain anonymous. The NSWPF has produced a brochure explaining how to make a complaint and also a complaint form that details the information that should be included, if possible, when making a complaint. The complaint form asks for a description of the matter being reported, any evidence such as witnesses, and also asks the complainant to identify what outcome he/she wants or believes would be appropriate. Both the form and information are available on the NSWPF Web site; complaints can also be lodged online through the police Web site.

All complaints received by members of the NSWPF are required to be registered electronically in the complaints management system (C@ts.i), and this fulfils their obligation (under the Police Act 1990) of forwarding the complaint to the Commissioner. The C@ts.i system is shared by the NSWPF, the Ombudsman, and the Police Integrity Commission, who can come to an agreement about what information has to be put on the system. Typically, when a complaint is registered on C@ts.i, the name(s) of the subject officer(s) are identified and registered against that complaint on the system. However, where a complaint is declined and meets the criteria under a Memorandum of Understanding under s128(2) of the Police Act 1990, either the NSWPF or the Ombudsman can seek permission (each can seek permission from the other) for the registration of the complaint without identifying information.

Annual Reports show that each year the NSWPF receives between 5,000 and 6,000 complaints, comprising between 8,000 and 9,300 issues; each year around 50% of issues are classed as local management issues or service delivery. The 2007–2008 Annual Report shows that between 2003–2004 and 2007–2008 around 43% of complaints each year are made internally (New South Wales Police Force, 2008). This shows that a proportion of NSWPF members are willing to report the misconduct of their colleagues, which the Ombudsman's Office noted is an indication of an ethical culture and healthy complaints system.

Under the Police Act 1990, the NSW Ombudsman and the Police Integrity Commission have a Class and Kind agreement as to which complaints are notifiable to the Ombudsman (copies of notifiable complaints must be sent to the Ombudsman). The Commissioner determines whether or not a complaint should be investigated and is responsible for communicating that decision to the complainant as well as to the Ombudsman. However, the Ombudsman can reverse a decision by the Commissioner not to investigate, if in disagreement with that decision.

Resolution/Mediation

The NSWPF has a system of Complaint Management Teams (CMTs) within each command that is overseen by the PSC. CMTs provide advice, supervision, and direction in complaint management to improve the timeliness and effectiveness of local complaint handling. However, the Committee on the Office of the Ombudsman and the Police Integrity Commission recommended in its 10-year review of police oversight in NSW (The Committee, 2006) that the NSWPF should consider ways in which to encourage the informal resolution of minor complaints at the local command level without the involvement of CMTs. During 2008–2009, the NSWPF introduced a new model for complaint handling that was designed to streamline the management of complaints and reduce the time and resources required for complaint investigations. The new model shows a move toward complaint resolution: "It's about trying to resolve matters with complainants rather than simply investigate and say we're right and you're wrong or vice versa."

Indeed, the Police Act 1990 states that "a person conducting an investigation may attempt to resolve a complaint by means of alternative dispute management procedures" (144). Further:

> Statements made by police officers during alternative dispute management procedures cannot be used against the officer in any civil or criminal proceedings for that conduct or as a basis for any reviewable or nonreviewable action against the officer.

Thus, this type of management encourages candidness without repercussions, highlighting the importance of resolving issues to the satisfaction of the parties involved rather than punishing the "guilty."

While not face-to-face mediation between the complainant and the subject officer, PSC highlighted that resolution managers will try to meet with complainants and that face-to-face is the best way to resolve matters. However, for a variety of reasons, this is not always convenient and so resolution was described as most often occurring over the telephone. The Ombudsman noted that resolution was usually conducted as "sort of shuttle diplomacy resolution, so they'll talk to the complainant, then go talk to the officer, then go back to the complainant, and they'll try to look at a resolution."

The NSWPF launched a new Customer Service Charter during 2009, which commits to being accessible, being professional and helpful, taking appropriate action, and keeping the public (e.g., victims and witnesses, as well as communities) informed. The Charter is part of a wider Customer Service Program that aims to improve the quality of service delivery and reduce the number of matters that are notified to the Ombudsman. PSC explained that "those customer service matters are about minor matters, but they are still notifiable to the Ombudsman, oversighted and scrutinised by the Ombudsman." The Customer Service Program aims to improve the ability of the organisation to deal with minor matters, for example, rudeness or incivility, and prevent potential escalation of matters.

> We're moving toward better service and we're moving to resolve those things that are … "an officer was rude when he gave me that ticket or they were rude at the front counter." It just needs to be resolved; it just needs an "are we professional enough to deal with that sort of matter?" A representative from NSWPF stated that, for us, in terms of managing complaints is the next sort of quantum step forward. That would have reduced a lot of the Ombudsman's work.

One identified method of improving service, particularly in the management of complaints, was providing information to complainants and subject officers. This was seen by PSC as a potential method of reducing the number of minor complaints:

> If you actually tell them what you did, what the answer was, most times you never hear from them again. You've sanitised the effect of the complaint by telling people what the actual issue was and what we did about it. That is, to me, a real way to satisfy customers.

The Customer Service Program has introduced a variety of strategies to improve customer service. For example, a mystery shopper program was introduced in February 2009 to test customer service levels. This reportedly achieved "exceptional results. An independent provider rated some police stations as achieving a score of 100% on their customer service measures, while the overall average was 87%" (New South Wales Police Force, 2009).

The Ombudsman's Office was supportive of this strategy:

> We've used mystery shopping quite extensively in the Ombudsman's Office, in the nonpolice area, and found it to be quite a useful tool to highlight deficiencies, particularly in customer service standards … and I think that there is a place for that in the police.

The mystery shopper program is to be extended and all NSW Police Force employees are scheduled to receive customer service training specific to their duties and responsibilities. The NSWPF also has conducted phone surveys with crime victims to assess how well staff are implementing the program. PSC commented that a particular success of the new customer service program is clarity over who are considered "customers:"

> The old customer service program included offenders as a customer. … In the new program, offenders are not classed as customers. Offenders have their own classification … so I think that's a step forward in relation to quantifying that victims and people who come to you for help or inquiries are your customers.

Investigation

Complaints can be investigated within the NSWPF at the local level or by PSC. Indeed, where a local area may not have the technical skills or resources available to deal with matters, they can call on PSC to assist. Further, the Police Act 1990 allows for assistance to be sought in the conduct of investigations from federal and interstate police. In the course of an investigation, officers can be required to furnish a financial statement or integrity statement and explain any matters arising, including satisfying that any assets or income were lawfully gained.

Complaint investigations can extend beyond the particular subject officers to encompass other members, particular areas of the NSWPF, or the NSWPF in general. This allows for systemic issues to be investigated beyond individual officers of complaint. At the conclusion of a complaint investigation, a report is provided to the Ombudsman that includes details on any action taken, or to be taken, as a result of the complaint as well as whether the complainant is satisfied with that outcome.

The Ombudsman's Office explained that "investigation" can mean everything from evidence-based criminal investigation to something that is more outcome and/or resolution focused, which is pursued by way of relatively informal inquiries. Generally, if a complaint is alleging criminal activity or serious misconduct that would warrant reviewable disciplinary action, an evidence-based investigation will be conducted. For less serious issues where the ultimate sanction would be a nonreviewable action, then it will likely be dealt with by less formal means, such as resolution.

However, the Ombudsman commented that the Police Act 1990 provides for the resolution of a complaint by alternative dispute resolution methods at any stage during an investigation, if appropriate. This allows for a change in the course of action, for example, if an investigation reveals a matter to be less serious than first thought, the Act allows for a change to resolution. In reality, the Ombudsman noted that police underuse this provision: "They tend to make an assessment right at the outset about whether something should be pursued by way of evidence-based investigation or by a resolution-focused investigation and they don't tend to mix them up."

Covert Operations/Integrity Testing

NSWPF internal investigations can also involve covert operations. The Covert Investigation Unit, within PSC, has capabilities to conduct targeted integrity testing. This is currently provided to local area commands on a consultancy basis, for example, where a command will identify a need for an integrity test to aid in a misconduct investigation, PSC will assess the matter and conduct the test if deemed appropriate. The results of the test will then be sent to the Local Area Command that is responsible for taking the management action. Targeted integrity testing was introduced in 1996 in response to the Wood Royal Commission interim report (Wood, 1996). Sworn members of the NSWPF can be targeted for a test, with targets selected on the basis of intelligence, including complaint patterns. The Police Act 1990 supports the integrity testing program by providing that actions committed for the purpose of running an integrity test are considered lawful. The legislation states that the tests conducted and their outcomes must be reported on a quarterly basis to the Police Integrity Commission (PIC).

The Ombudsman's Office expressed the opinion that targeted integrity testing is a very important tool for preventing, as well as identifying and exposing, misconduct and corrupt conduct in particular. "You don't need to do a lot of it, the fact that you can do it and you occasionally publicise that you're doing it sends ripples through the system, so it's a bit like mystery shopping methodology." Indeed, NSWPF commented that positive results (charges arising from failed tests) are highly publicised within the organisation due to their deterrence effect. Furthermore, targeted integrity tests were viewed as a useful investigations tool that can help fast-track investigations by way of testing allegations against specific officers. For example, recent tests have identified drug use and sale, as well as police involved in releasing confidential information to organised crime groups. Tests have also quickly resolved issues relating to theft and other forms of misconduct, often clearing officers of any inappropriate or criminal behaviour.

Discipline

NSW police have two discipline systems: one for public servants, and one for police officers. While the public service system was described as driven by procedural fairness, it was commented by PSC that the system for police officers was not quite so procedurally fair. Particularly, it was noted that issues had been raised regarding the procedural fairness for officers who are investigated and "held to account" by the oversight agencies. During 2010, the Lancaster Project was conducted, which examined the way in which the NSWPF applies the provisions of Part 9 (Management of Conduct) of the Police Act. It was decided that improvements could be made, based on the public sector system, which would benefit NSWPF decision makers and could be achieved within the current legislation. The process now provides the subject officer with a copy of the investigation report and supporting documentation and the opportunity to respond, prior to making a sustained finding regarding a complaint (under Part 8A). This process commenced on 1 January 2011.

Also, it was noted by PSC that the police complaints system is punitive and lacks some of the structures that public sector systems have in place for ensuring fairness. PSC has, therefore, moved to a remedial versus dismissal test, rather than the three level punitive model (i.e., nonreviewable low level; reviewable action intermediate and; dismissal is the ultimate sanction). The decision is now whether an officer is suitable for future employment (dismissal test); if yes, then remedial (nonreviewable) actions should be implemented to raise the officer's standards to an acceptable level. Reviewable action is now only considered appropriate in circumstances where there is no nonremedial option that would achieve the results required (e.g., there is no option other than dismissal if the officer remains at his/her current rank, but he/she could be retained at a lower rank). Therefore, while the NSWPF no longer supports the use of reviewable action as a punitive sanction, transfers or demotions are still available where it is necessary to save the officer's employment. The NSW

Ombudsman Annual Report for 2009/2010 (New South Wales Ombudsman, 2010) supports the move to increased use of nonreviewable management actions, stating that this is in line with principles outlined in the Wood Royal Commission (Wood, 1997). However, the Ombudsman report also states that the new procedures will be monitored regarding the risk of treating serious misconduct cases too lightly.

The NSWPF Commissioner has the power to remove police officers under Section 181D of the Police Act 1990 "if the Commissioner does not have confidence in the police officer's suitability to continue as a police officer, having regard to the police officer's competence, integrity, performance, or conduct." Reviewable actions and loss of confidence dismissals can be appealed to the Industrial Relations Commission on the grounds that the action is harsh, unreasonable, or unjust. Further, decisions to impose these sanctions must go through the Internal Review Panel. The Internal Review Panel includes Assistant Commissioners as well as representatives from Human Relations and PSC. An officer of the Ombudsman also observes at these meetings. Further, for Section 181D dismissal cases, typically an external law firm is included on the panel to advise on the case. This was seen as particularly useful in these cases where problems have led to decisions being overturned, for example, due to the standard of paperwork. Cases do get contested and appeals are supported by the Police Association. The Ombudsman noted:

> When Justice Wood recommended it (loss of confidence provision), he saw it as a quick informal way of getting rid of the bad apples, but because of the political reality, the weight of the Association, when they actually enacted it, they put in a number of safeguards, which complicated the process.

The PIC indicated that the removal of officers under Section 181D is often a drawn out and protracted process, despite the intention of the provision being to allow the Commissioner of Police to act expeditiously in removing officers in whom he/she has lost confidence.

Witness/Staff Support

Sworn officers of the NSWPF have specific legislative obligations to report corrupt or unethical conduct. In support of this, protections are offered under the Police Act against reprisals in the form of detrimental action for alleging misconduct. The Protected Disclosures Act 1994 and the Internal Witness Support Policy are also in place to protect those who report misconduct. An Internal Witness Support Unit exists to encourage reporting by building confidence in the support and protections available, and a specialist workplace equity unit was established in 2007 for dealing with harassment and discrimination. The NSWPF also has a corruption hotline—a telephone line that allows anonymous reporting of misconduct and corruption.

Further, the Police Act states that the identity of a complainant must not be disclosed by a member of NSW police (unless under certain circumstances prescribed by the act, for example, where the complainant gives consent, or for the purpose of legal proceedings). However, the Ombudsman's office noted:

> Certainly there are complaints made about police for disclosing names of complainants. It's taken very seriously when it happens, but it's a difficult area. Often it's hard to get enough evidence to prosecute, but certainly it's not something that has been overlooked in New South Wales.

The Ombudsman's Office further noted that there was still a lot of fear of detrimental action for reporting colleagues and that there was "a long way to go" both in terms of dealing with these concerns as well as addressing issues of bullying and sexual harassment in the workplace. Since that time, the NSWPF, in conjunction with the NSW Ombudsman's Office, drafted new Section 169A Guidelines (relating to the nondisclosure of the identity of complainants) in 2010 that effectively remove the identity of complainants from complaint investigation reports. The evidence of the complainant is now presented in the investigation in the same way as any other witness. A separate annexure setting out the complainant's details, including complainant satisfaction, is maintained as a document that cannot be released. This allows the investigation report to be released without editing and indirectly identifying the complainant by reference to their evidence. The move away from reviewable action also has meant that only those complaints that may result in dismissal are the subject of evidence-based investigation. This was described by the NSWPF as reducing the pressure on internal witnesses and complainants.

Early Intervention

The NSWPF has a major project underway scoping and developing an Early Intervention System (EIS), including a working group, steering committee, and consultation. It was commented that a formal EIS was necessary as some commands were already adopting an approach of targeting "at risk" officers, but that there was inconsistency across the organisation as well as a reliance on intuition, or varying criteria regarding complaint histories, rather than a formal "scientific" approach. PSC has organised a number of consultation exercises in order to propose indicators for an EIS: "It's not easy because you've got to quantify what an indicator means in terms of an officer's conduct or behaviour." Indicators have been proposed that also encompass a health and safety perspective in order to identify if an intervention or some sort of assistance is necessary for an officer, rather than relying solely on numbers of complaints. PSC stated that "we're now thinking in a much more sophisticated way ... we know that lots of things happen in people's lives that may affect their work, so it's more focused on a person's health and well-being rather than a punitive sort of approach."

Along with early intervention regarding the rectification of officers' behaviour and assisting officers before problems become more serious, PSC also noted the concept of early intervention in terms of officers' careers. For example, it was noted that the first 2 years (while the member is at the academy and then a probationary constable) provided greater opportunities for modelling behaviour as well as easier dismissal of those identified to be problematic: "Getting them when they're on probation. There are great opportunities there to improve us overall down the track." It was acknowledged that, sometimes, recruits are accepted that are unsuitable for a career as a police officer and, for these, it was better to terminate that career early (for inadequate performance during the probationary period). PSC explained that "a probationary constable is on probation. They have certain things to do and, as an organisation, we've got certain obligations to them and that might be to say to them, 'You might have made the wrong choice in relation to your career, we don't actually think you're suited'."

Indeed, it was pointed out that many officers who engage in misconduct as sworn officers have a history of performance issues during probation and training.

Risk Management

The NSWPF operates a corruption resistance framework that requires corruption-resistance planning by local commands. This also links into a wider Command Management Framework (CMF) introduced in 2005, which functions to identify and manage local risks. Both operate to a self-assessment process based on Australian and New Zealand Risk Management Standards and encourage commands to identify their local risks and develop locally relevant process controls. A PSC review of the corruption-resistance planning process (noted in the 2007–2008 NSW Police Annual Report, NSWPF 2008) highlighted some overlap with the CMF, as well as deficiencies in the corruption-resistance planning process regarding the extent to which it addressed local command issues, and insufficient monitoring and recordkeeping. In response, corruption-resistance planning processes have been upgraded.

In order to manage many identified risks in the organisation, policies are in place to standardise practices, for example, with the execution of search warrants, pursuits, and policing public order. The NSWPF also has conflict of interest and improper associations policies, a receipt of gifts and benefits policy and guidelines, and a secondary employment policy and guidelines. With regard to the latter, secondary employment requires approval and, if that employment is considered to be in a high risk industry, the application is reviewed at a higher level and subject to a probity and risk conflict analysis by PSC. There are also policies governing the use and management of informants, and an electronic informant management system.

PSC noted that the majority of these policies have been put in place in the past 20 years, based on inquiries and particularly post-Royal Commission. PSC has a role in developing, or contributing to, reference materials, standard operating procedures, policies, and training to support best practice.

Procedural Controls

In addition to policies and guidelines, video technology is employed in the NSWPF. In-car video has been placed in highway patrol cars, and PSC stated that there had been "a significant decrease in complaints against highway patrol officers" although this effect had not been formally assessed. It was noted that recording of interactions between highway patrol officers and the public supported officer safety as well as protecting against false complaints as "highway patrol people are normally one-on-one." Further, the positive effect on officers' behaviour was noted in terms of reducing customer service complaints with "a massive reduction in rudeness-type complaints when tickets are being handed out. They know they've got to be ultra kind, they've got to be ultra polite, it's all going to be recorded."

The NSW Ombudsman commented on the use of in-car video (ICV) in his 2008–2009 Annual Report (New South Wales Ombudsman, 2009), noting that ICV had exonerated officers in complaint investigations by showing that they acted appropriately, but had also, in other cases, shown officers acting inappropriately. It was also reported:

> In other cases, the usefulness of ICV has been undermined through nonactivation, incomplete recording, or the lack of audio recording. The value of ICV also depends on commanders and supervisors ensuring that relevant footage is properly reviewed (p. 73).

At the time of interview, video capabilities were being considered for all police vehicles and were already installed in police helicopters. Tasers on issue to NSW police also have video and audio that begins recording when the Taser is activated. This was added to protect the officers, but caused storage space problems from a technical perspective. With regard to access to computer systems and information, the NSWPF conducts computer access audits. Areas considered high risk, such as "special squads" are subjected to a 100% audit of computer access.

Drug and Alcohol Testing

The NSWPF's Drug and Alcohol Policy was revised in 2007 and applies to all employees, both sworn and unsworn, such that all employees are expected to be free of impairment by alcohol or any other form of drug while on duty and abstain from using illicit drugs. In January 2011, the responsibility of the management of the Drug and Alcohol Testing Unit transferred from the Safety Command to PSC, which is currently reviewing drug testing procedures.

Sworn officers are subject to random, targeted, and mandatory drug and alcohol testing. Most unsworn members are not subject to testing, although drug and alcohol testing is conducted on unsworn pilots attached to the Aviation Support Branch, which is conducted under the Civil Aviation Safety Authority (CASA) legislation. In October 2006, the NSWPF also introduced drug testing for students at the Police College. While students at the academy are not employed by the NSWPF, drug testing serves to reinforce NSWPF expectations of its sworn officers should the students be employed by the NSWPF in the future. "Mandatory" or critical incident drug tests are undertaken following involvement in a critical incident, such as a death in custody or a shooting.

Officers can be required to undergo a breath test or submit to a breath analysis for the purpose of testing for alcohol consumption, and to provide a sample of urine (and/or hair* for mandatory testing incidents) to test for the presence of illegal (or nonprescribed) drugs. Random drug and alcohol testing is determined through the use of a random number-generating computer program. However, the policy states that "high risk work types and officers who are subject to repeat testing, having previously recorded a positive test, are subject to a degree of prearrangement for the purpose of random testing" (New South Wales Police Force†, 2007, p. 9). High risk work types are also subjected to more frequent testing for alcohol and/or drugs. High risk areas are determined by the NSWPF, but examples considered as high risk are provided where the work type or location is at a greater risk for substance use. These could include such areas as working on a drug squad or where the consequences of substance use would be more serious than for other officers, such as pursuit driving. The new Drug and Alcohol Policy also covers steroid use, where not prescribed by a qualified medical practitioner. Officers can be tested for steroid use on a targeted basis only.

The PIC explained that there are different purposes for conducting random and targeted drug tests. The aim of random drug testing of officers is

* While permitted in the legislation, the NSWPF has not used hair samples for drug tests.

† Available at http://www.police.nsw.gov.au/__data/assets/file/0010/4321/Drug_and_Alcohol_Policy.pdf

to deter inappropriate behaviour before it occurs. The PIC stated that what is important here is for officers to be aware that, if they were to use drugs, they could be drug tested and caught. The PIC stated that the effectiveness of random drug tests, therefore, cannot be measured by the number of drug tests that detect the use of prohibited drugs; it is the number, visibility, and unpredictability of the drug tests that are conducted that is relevant.

In 2002, the Committee on the Office of the Ombudsman and the Police Integrity Commission (The Committee, 2002) noted the difference between the New York Police Department drug testing program and that of the NSWPF, suggesting that the NSWPF increase the number of random drug tests (from around 4 to 20%). Similarly, the PIC in its 2005 Operation Abelia report (Police Integrity Commission, 2005) suggested that at least 15% of officers should be randomly tested each year to increase the perceived risk of being caught. Table 3.1 shows that NSW police random drug testing has since increased from around 5 to 8% (up to 2005–2006) to around 15% in the past four reporting periods. Table 3.2 shows that random alcohol tests have also increased substantially from around 50 to 60% of sworn officers tested in reporting periods from 2001–2002 to 2005–2006, rising to between 70 and 99% of sworn officers randomly tested in the past three reporting periods (in 2009–2010, 99.8% of sworn officers were subjected to a random alcohol test). Since the transfer of responsibility for drug and alcohol testing to PSC, PSC is reviewing the drug testing procedures in place with a view to conducting more random drug tests in the future.

Table 3.1 NSWPF Annual Drug Testing Statistics

		Random Drug Tests			Targeted Drug Tests		Student Testing[a]	
Year	Sworn Members	Number	% of Sworn Officers	Number Positive	Number	Number Positive	Random Drug Tests	Positive
09/10	15,633	2,309	14.8%	0	11	0	140	0
08/09	15,720	2,284	14.5%	3	20	1	153	0
07/08	15,342	2,381	15.5%	1	17	3	151	0
06/07	15,333	2,267	14.8%	1	18	0	180	0
05/06	14,634	598	7.9%	1	22	3	–	–
04/05	14,634	513	3.5%	1	22	2	–	–
03/04	15,009	582	3.9%	0	15	2	–	–
02/03	14,739	499	3.4%	0	9	1	–	–
01/02	13,716	416	4.8%	0	24	5	–	–

Source: New South Wales Police.
Note: Stats do not include steroid testing results.
[a] Student testing commenced October 2006.

Table 3.2 NSWPF Annual Alcohol Testing Statistics

		Random Alcohol Tests			Targeted Alcohol Tests		Student Testing[a]	
Year	Sworn Members	Number	% of Sworn Officers Tested	Positive	Number	Positive	Random Alcohol Tests	Positive
09/10	15,633	15,598	99.8%	5	2	2	3,383	3
08/09	15,720	13,330	84.8%	3	11	4	1,825	6
07/08	15,342	15,063	98.2%	7	19	7	2,196	27
06/07	15,333	10,996	71.7%	16	23	3	1,820	1
05/06	14,634	7,599	51.9%	4	39	10	–	–
04/05	14,634	9,057	61.9%	9	11	9	–	–
03/04	15,009	8,671	57.8%	2	27	7	–	–
02/03	14,739	7,706	52.3%	11	14	3	–	–
01/02	13,716	8,560	62.4%	4	20	8	–	–

Source: New South Wales Police.

[a] Student testing commenced October 2006.

In contrast to random drug tests, targeted drug tests seek to detect illegal drug use after the drug has been consumed. An officer is subjected to a targeted drug test only where there is reason to believe that that officer may have used illegal drugs. The PIC's Operation Abelia (2005) identified a problem of recreational drug use among police officers who saw their working life and nonworking life as quite distinct. The police, however, have a zero tolerance approach, and drug use was noted by the Ombudsman's office to be "a continual challenge" that supported the need for legislation for drug testing.

In February 2007, on recommendation from the PIC's Operation Abelia Report (2005), NSWPF authorised recall-to-duty for targeted drug testing. Prior to this, targeted drug tests could only be performed on officers who were on duty in accordance with a roster. Given the limited periods following use within which some substances can be detected, the PIC explained that there are restrictions on how effective targeted drug tests are in detecting illegal drug use. The PIC said that "depending on the drug used, it can be very difficult to detect if officers take drugs early in their off-duty time, as it will have left their system by the time that they return to work for their next rostered shift and can be tested." Recall-to-duty for drug testing commenced implementation in 2010, once associated policy and procedures had been completed. While the Act does not require it, as a matter of policy and practice to ensure fairness and integrity, the Ombudsman is notified within 3 days of any decision to recall an officer to duty for such testing.

The recall-to-duty targeted drug tests and the targeted drug tests for steroids, therefore, have become options following legislative changes that occurred as the results of the PIC's Operation Abelia report. Targeted drug tests are a tool, albeit an imperfect tool, for detecting illegal drug use. The PIC noted that, at the time the PIC conducted Operation Abelia, approximately the same number of (or slightly more) officers had come forward under an "amnesty" program and self-disclosed their illegal drug use, as had been detected through targeted or random testing.

Each year, less than 20 tests yield positive results for alcohol (including random, targeted, and mandatory) and less than 5 each year yield positive results for drugs (including random, targeted, and mandatory). Since drug and alcohol testing of students at the police college was introduced in 2006, there have been no positive results for drugs and less than 2% of tests positive for alcohol.

All positive drug and alcohol test results must be referred to an individual's Local Area Commander or Branch Manager and also the Professional Standards Command. Commanders must record any targeted drug tests and their related decision-making processes on the c@ts.i system irrespective of the results. PSC reported that, for some years, the NSWPF has provided professional and confidential counselling services for officers experiencing alcohol problems, and their drug and alcohol policy states that the NSWPF can provide financial assistance for costs of treatment and rehabilitation. However, officers who test positive for illicit drugs are likely to be subject to formal disciplinary proceedings that could result in dismissal.

Staff Screening

NSWPF applicants are subjected to a range of integrity and probity checks, and suitability checks. For example, preemployment background checks on all NSWPF applicants include criminal, traffic, employment, medical, financial solvency, evidence of inappropriate associations, personal references, and a telephone interview with the applicant. Psychological testing is also used to screen applicants, particularly to high risk and specialist areas (e.g., forensics, child protection, and the crash investigation unit). Workers in these areas are also monitored for ongoing psychological well-being. Some units also have mandatory annual health assessments. New Police College staff, both NSWPF and Charles Sturt University, are probity checked as well by the Professional Standards Manager, Corporate Services, including a check of complaint history, before they commence work at the college.

Integrity issues are assessed during the promotions process. The NSWPF has a merit-based promotions system, with merit including an appropriate standard of integrity and conduct. Promotion applicants are all checked for current and previous integrity issues, with enquiries made to PSC. The internal Integrity Review Committee assesses and makes recommendation on any integrity issues identified during this process.

Ethics Education/Training

The NSWPF offers applicants five different training and education options through partnerships with Charles Sturt University and the University of Western Sydney. All options include ethics components throughout the training. The ethics training at the NSW Police College is predominantly conducted by the college staff, although PSC provides guest speakers to talk to recruits about different perspectives, for example, PSC investigators or witness protection staff. A component of the ethics curriculum requires students to identify the background of the Wood Royal Commission and the reasons for its implementation. The NSWPF also has a Standards of Professional Conduct that is included in notebook and diary cards that are easily accessible, and recruits read and sign the code, which is then marked on their HR file and recorded.

The Ombudsman noted that the current NSWPF Standards of Professional Conduct is a clear message about what behaviour is expected and what is unacceptable and that making police more aware of general ethical standards and policies and a general framework was a more successful approach than having a large number of individual rules to follow. However, the Ombudsman's office commented that there was "constant tension … we try to go down that way, but there's always this tendency to make another policy and another procedure."

Former Police Commissioner John Avery was credited with contributing to an increase in the level of training and education of the NSWPF in and since the 1980s."The Police Recruit Education Program (PREP) actually became a benchmark in terms of the length of the time, the quality of the police recruitment, and education program." PSC noted that there had been "huge movement in terms of education and training of police officers" and that assessing the skills of recruits and concentrating on the education offered was necessary to provide a professional service.

PSC noted that, in the late 1980s, recruit class sizes became very large and this may have created problems with the standards of those officers. Recently the PIC conducted a project (People, 2009) assessing the effect of intake size on the likelihood of receiving complaints in the first 2 years of service, for intakes between 2001 and 2007. The report concluded that, for their sample, large class sizes were not related to the likelihood of those officers receiving complaints. However, it was pointed out that the 2-year period may not be long enough for problem behaviour to emerge.

Aside from specific ethics training, the NSWPF can contact PSC for advice, with PSC offering consultancy and review for investigations, critical incidents, complaint management, and employee management.

NSW Ombudsman

The NSW Ombudsman offers independent oversight of the NSWPF (and other public sector agencies) to ensure they fulfil their functions and also help them improve their public service delivery in line with best practice in administration. To this end, complaints are viewed as a source of feedback on agencies' performance, and so the Ombudsman's role encompasses a general power to keep the police complaints system under scrutiny. This involves the oversight of individual complaints, investigation of complaints, audit and inspection of complaint handling processes, and providing recommendations regarding improvements. The Ombudsman also has an own motion investigation power meaning that it can conduct investigations into matters of public interest that are not necessarily the subject of a complaint.

Complaint Handling

Much of the NSW Ombudsman's work stems from complaints. The office can accept complaints both from the general public as well as employees of the agencies that it oversees, such as the police. Complaints must usually be made in writing, although in exceptional circumstances the Ombudsman can choose to accept a complaint that is not in writing. Anonymous complaints are also accepted, but, as the Web site makes clear, the Ombudsman "will not normally investigate an anonymous complaint unless it raises a serious matter and there is enough information in the complaint to make out a prima facie case or carry out an investigation."

Complaints received by the Ombudsman must be registered on the electronic complaints handling system shared with the NSWPF and the Police Integrity Commission (unless the matter is not going to be referred to the Police Commissioner). The Ombudsman has unrestricted access to this complaints handling system.

Complaint Investigation

Most complaints about police are handled by the NSWPF. Through a class and kind agreement with the PIC, the Ombudsman determines the complaints that have to be notified to the Ombudsman's Office and those that can be handled by the police without notification. Thus, the office oversights the more serious allegations of misconduct laid against the police on a case-by-case basis, while less serious complaints, such as customer service and incivility, are generally handled directly by the police without direct oversight. The Ombudsman can override a decision by the police not to investigate a matter, but cannot direct a complaint to be investigated if that conduct is not associated with being a police officer.

Even where complaints are made to the Ombudsman's Office, they will typically be referred to the NSWPF to handle, at least in the first instance, although there may be circumstances where a complaint is investigated directly by the Ombudsman's Office. Where complaints are referred to the police to investigate, the Ombudsman can monitor the investigation. Such monitoring can include ensuring that the investigation is conducted in a timely manner, but can also involve Ombudsman officers attending interviews with complainants, witnesses, and/or police as independent observers. If the Ombudsman is not satisfied with the way an investigation is being conducted, the Ombudsman can request further investigation, suggest a course of action, or take over an investigation, at which point the police must cease their investigation. However, the Ombudsman's Office noted that in the majority of cases the police are left to do the investigation and just provide a report at its conclusion.

Once a complaint has been dealt with by the NSWPF, the Ombudsman receives the full report. The Ombudsman reviews the report and can make recommendations to improve police practices and can also request that the police consider, or reconsider, a particular outcome or action as a result of the complaint. If the police choose not to accept the recommendations, a written explanation for that decision must be provided to the Ombudsman, who if not satisfied with the explanation can ask for that decision to be reviewed, can report to Parliament, and can make a public report identifying any deficiencies. The Ombudsman also has the power of reinvestigation after the police have completed an investigation.

The Ombudsman's Office highlighted that the police complaints system had evolved significantly over the past 30 years. When the Ombudsman was first involved in police complaints in the late 1970s and early 1980s, their role was only to assess a report of the internal police investigation and make a finding as to whether the complaint was sustained. There were no direct powers to check the information provided. This was deemed inadequate and progressed to legislation supporting the Ombudsman's power to obtain further information and reinvestigate complaints where a conclusion could not be decided. However, reinvestigations could only be conducted using seconded police from the (then) Internal Affairs Branch. Subsequently, the Ombudsman was granted the power to use civilian investigators, which resulted in an increased number of reinvestigations. The Ombudsman Office said, "We started doing a lot of police investigations or reinvestigations using our Royal Commission powers because the quality of police investigations back in those days was pretty bad."

Changes over time have now resulted in a decrease of this activity. The NSW Ombudsman Annual Report (2009) reports that only 13% of complaint investigations were viewed as deficient (either in the investigation or the proposed action), but that, after advice from the Ombudsman, over 70% of the proposed deficiencies were remedied. This was reflected on positively. "I think that's a very good outcome given that there will always be cases where you can't remedy things just because of the passage of time, etc." The Ombudsman also monitors customer satisfaction with outcomes. If a complainant is not satisfied with the action of the police in response to his/her complaint, the Ombudsman can conduct a review and can also report the matter to the Police Minister and/or Parliament.

Mediation

The Ombudsman's Office noted that they have occasionally been requested to help conciliate difficult complaints.

> Sometimes we have done that with complaints by officers against other officers, where there have been ongoing or intractable problems in their working relationships and we have been able to achieve resolution by acting as the independent honest broker in a mediation of their differences.

The Office's Aboriginal Unit has also assisted a number of commanders in establishing better links with members of aboriginal communities or mediating particular conflicts. "We have also helped prevent foreseeable conflicts by being present as observers in interviews conducted in contentious investigations involving aboriginal people."

Investigative Powers

Aside from conducting an investigation on the basis of a complaint, the Ombudsman can also conduct an investigation where no complaint has been made. Section 159(1) of the Police Act 1990 states that if "any conduct of a police officer could be, but is not, the subject of a complaint, the Ombudsman may make the conduct the subject of an investigation." This own motion investigation power applies where matters arise that are considered to be in the public interest and can include conduct both on and off duty that is likely to be misconduct or bring discredit on the police force.

When conducting investigations, the Ombudsman's Office has the powers of a Royal Commission, including the power to require answers to questions in writing and produce documents, entry to inspect premises and/or items (such as documents), as well as the power to summons people and require them to give evidence under oath. It is an offence to refuse or impede the powers or investigation of the Ombudsman. There are no powers to conduct controlled operations or use covert methods. Indeed the Ombudsman's

Act has provisions that it must give notice of its investigation to the parties concerned. However, covert methods, such as surveillance and telecommunications interception were not deemed necessary for the work that the Ombudsman's Office faces:

> I don't think we think they are necessary for the sorts of investigations that we do. We have the luxury here in New South Wales of having the Police Integrity Commission, which looks at that sort of high-end corruption where those sorts of tools are useful and almost necessary. We deal with probably 99% of all police complaints, where those other powers are certainly adequate for the task.

The Ombudsman's Office does have access to the results of covert operations that are run in the course of a police internal investigation. This information is made available as part of the report on an investigation for oversight purposes. Further, the Ombudsman must audit the use of telephone interception powers, controlled operations, and surveillance devices by all the law enforcement agencies in New South Wales.

Outcomes

When the Ombudsman reviews a matter raised in a complaint, thought is given to the wider issues of which it might be indicative. "When we review any complaint in this office, we're not only looking at the merits of that particular grievance on that individual, we're always looking to see whether this particular complaint is hinting at some underlying procedure problem; is there any systemic aspect."

Similarly, when the Ombudsman's Office assesses a police investigation and considers the appropriate management action, they do not just consider the outcome for the individual officers concerned. It was explained that the Ombudsman's Office also looks at potential general deficiencies in the policies and procedures of a particular local area command, police station, or squad, etc., and will make appropriate recommendations (and track their implementation). It was also noted that, increasingly, it was found to be important to focus on particular types of complaints to see whether they are being dealt with in an appropriate manner. For example, a 2006 special report (New South Wales Ombudsman, 2006) assessed the NSWPF's dealing with domestic violence cases and made 44 recommendations, over half of which were reported to have been implemented in the 2008–2009 Ombudsman Annual Report, with further assistance planned to enable the implementation of the remaining recommendations. Indeed, the 2008–2009 Ombudsman Annual Report (New South Wales Ombudsman, 2009) states that all formal reports made by the Ombudsman about police complaints made recommendations relating to law, policy, or procedures, and half of these recommendations were supported or implemented by the NSWPF. This figure is below the target of 80% acceptance and is explained by the rejection of recommendations made in one specific report on the use of Tasers, including the recommendation to freeze further issue of Tasers to the NSWPF for 2 years. Previous years, however, have seen much higher acceptance of Ombudsman recommendations, with 89% recorded as implemented in 2006–2007, and 80% in 2007–2008 (New South Wales Ombudsman, 2007; 2008).

Witness Support

The Ombudsman's Office noted that witness support is an "important, central part of an effective complaint management approach for New South Wales police." The Ombudsman, therefore, has regular contact with the Commander of the NSWPF Internal Witness Support Unit, including meetings and collaboration on developing policy documents and procedures. The Ombudsman's Office also has experience in dealing with whistleblowers under the Protected Disclosures Act 1994 and is responsible for hearing appeals about the exercise of powers and handling complaints from people in the witness protection program. The program was established under the Witness Protection Act 1995 to protect the safety and welfare of Crown witnesses and others who have given information to police about criminal activities.

Risk Management/Complaints Profiling

The Ombudsman's Office uses a risk assessment approach to its complaint case management. The risk hierarchy is based on the nature of the allegations and determines the approach taken in handling that complaint. For example, those complaints identified as high risk go through a much more elaborate process, are allocated to more experienced staff, and are more rigorously reviewed by a number of people in the office.

Whilst the Ombudsman's Office does not directly have an early intervention system for police officers, the office uses complaint data to explore patterns and trends that may be indicative of individual or organisational risk, allowing for early identification and intervention of problems. The Ombudsman's Office has "a small intelligence unit" that develops profiles of particular officers or areas of concern:

> Individual case officers, if they're dealing with any case where they think there is some particularly valuable information that might have implications for the future, they will submit an intelligence report to our intelligence officers and that will get assessed in a fairly traditional intelligence way.

Information may be used to start a profile or be added to an existing profile. Case officers identify candidates for which profiles should be started and this profile information is used to contextualise new complaints that are received. The Ombudsman's Office noted, "We have profiles on, say, 800 officers and they're again assessed as high, medium, even low risk, and they're continually updated with new information as it becomes available."

Intelligence is required to be submitted about an officer who is being considered for reviewable action or loss of Commissioner's confidence dismissal, is subject to a serious adverse finding, or is considered for criminal charge. Factors that are considered for placing an officer on the "officer of concern master list" include:

- a high number of complaints;
- previous similar complaints;
- evidence from an investigation that suggests risk of misconduct (e.g., evidence that falls short of the standard);
- personal issues;
- conflicts of interest or lifestyle;
- previous significant management action;
- number of recent complaints;
- previous performance or conduct management plan or adverse risk assessment; and
- rank.

Also noted are investigators or Commanders of concern where there is a pattern of delays in notifying or completing investigations, deficiency in the quality of investigations, or inadequacy of management action. The Ombudsman's Office also develops profiles on individual Local Area Commands and police regions, predominantly with regard to how they are processing complaints, for example, timeliness, the degree to which they will decline complaints, and the number of internal police officers who are making complaints. That information is available to case officers when they are reviewing investigations, particularly how investigators are dealing with matters, using a risk hierarchy, and identifying what the risks might be.

Ethics Education/Training

The Ombudsman's Office is involved in officer training at the NSW Police College with respect to informing students about the complaints system and the Ombudsman's role within that system. The Ombudsman's Office also addresses investigators' courses that are run by NSWPF Professional Standards Command and is presented to a range of senior managers and police officers. The Ombudsman's Office interviewee stated, "I spend a lot of my time going out and talking to Commanders and police officers. I think every week over the last month or so I've gone out to address meetings of Professional Standards duty officers and executive officers in Local Area Commands and regions whose job descriptions involve them in some way in the complaints process or professional standards."

Although not directly involved in ethics training of police, the Ombudsman's Office does educate recruits about the role of the Ombudsman in the police complaints handling system.

Audit

The Ombudsman has a general audit function to oversee the working of the police complaints system as a whole and is required to inspect police complaints handling records at least once every 12 months (but may inspect records at any time). Inspections include audits in relation to timeliness standards (of reporting or determining management action) as well as compliance with the class and kind agreement (including both desktop and site visits). This includes checking whether complaints are being correctly classified and dealt with, which has been identified as a potential risk associated with the introduction of the new police complaints handling system with triaging of complaints and devolution of minor complaint handling to the local level.

Police Integrity Commission

The Police Integrity Commission was established under the Police Integrity Commission Act 1996 on the recommendation of the Royal Commission into the NSW Police Service (Wood, 1996). While the PIC's principal functions, as specified by the PIC Act are to prevent, detect, and investigate police misconduct, it is encouraged to primarily focus on serious misconduct in the case of police officers and serious corrupt conduct of administrative officers (unsworn members) of the NSWPF and also the NSW Crime Commission.

The PIC is independent of the NSWPF and cannot have serving or former members of the Force on its staff; its investigators are drawn from other Australian and overseas police services. Aside from its own investigative function, the PIC is also tasked with overseeing the NSWPF in its detection and investigation of police misconduct.

The PIC is primarily focused toward the more serious forms of misconduct and corruption. However, it has the discretionary power to decide which cases to investigate. The PIC can receive and investigate complaints about misconduct as well as conduct its own investigations into matters that it thinks are appropriate and in the public interest to investigate. The PIC can investigate matters that concern either on- or off-duty behaviour by police officers.

Complaints Handling

Complaints can be made anonymously to the PIC, but must be in writing (although the PIC can choose to accept a complaint that is not in writing under exceptional circumstances). Complaints can be made online, through an electronic complaint form or a complaint form that is downloaded from the PIC Web site and submitted to the PIC. The complaint form outlines the information sought (but not necessary), including the identity of the officer or officers involved, their command location, details of the incident and conduct as well as whether there are witnesses or other evidence.

Complaints received by the PIC may be investigated or referred to the NSWPF or to the Ombudsman. Complaints that are to be referred to the NSW Police Commissioner must be registered on the electronic complaints information system (c@ts.i). Access to that system is shared between the PIC, Ombudsman, and NSW police, where the PIC and Ombudsman have unrestricted access to this system to monitor and analyse the held information.

Complaints Investigation

The manner in which matters are dealt with by the PIC reflects its focus on the more serious matters, that is, matters under the PIC's jurisdiction would be too serious for resolution through mediation to be appropriate. Rather, investigation of matters would be the primary response. The remainder of complaints will be turned down with advice to contact either the Ombudsman or the NSW police or referred to those agencies by the PIC.

Thus, the PIC chooses which matters it will investigate. While many issues may be brought to the PIC's attention by complainants directly, the PIC also regularly searches the electronic complaints system (c@ts.i) for matters that have not been sent directly to the PIC by complainants, but which the PIC considers to be of sufficient interest or seriousness to warrant an investigation. Thus, the PIC can investigate matters that it becomes aware of through any means (not just a direct complaint) and can also investigate matters on its own initiative. This includes matters where no particular officer or person involved has been identified or implicated and where there is no actual complaint of misconduct or corrupt conduct.

The PIC can refer matters to the NSWPF for investigation or action. When referring a matter to NSWPF, the PIC can recommend a course of action it believes the police should take, and, if the PIC has already conducted their own investigation, they can share obtained information with the NSWPF. Where matters are referred to the NSWPF, the PIC can either require the police to furnish them with a report at the conclusion of the matter, formally oversight the handling of the complaint, or leave oversight arrangements to be determined by the Ombudsman.

If the PIC is not satisfied with a police action or investigation, it can take over an investigation, refer the matter to the Ombudsman to deal with, or inform the NSWPF directly of its dissatisfaction, and then consider the response (if unsatisfied with the response, the PIC can report the matter to Parliament).

The PIC can choose to investigate a matter itself at any time, regardless of whether the police are conducting, or have completed, their own investigation. If the PIC decides to investigate a matter that is already the subject of a police investigation, the police must cease their investigation. The PIC Annual Report 2008–2009 states that, during this period, the PIC "assessed 1,206 complaints against NSWPF officers, only 4 of which went on to become full investigations" while they "worked on 108 investigations: 68 preliminary investigations and 40 full investigations" (Police Integrity Commission, 2009a, p. 10).

Powers

The PIC has a number of direct powers as laid out in the PIC Act 1996. These include the ability to apply for search warrants for premises (including the search of people on premises) and the power to remove or take copies of documents. The PIC can also apply for an injunction to restrain conduct that is likely to impede an investigation or prevent irreparable harm because of misconduct or serious corrupt conduct. PIC investigators who are seconded police officers or approved former police officers and may exercise all the powers of a NSW police constable, including carrying firearms, handcuffs, and body armour. It is also an offence to delay or obstruct a PIC investigation.

Sections 32 and 33 of the PIC Act 1996 provide that, for the purposes of an investigation, the PIC may hold public or private hearings. The choice to hold a hearing in public depends on a number of factors, including public interest and risk to witnesses and others involved.

The PIC can summon people to attend hearings and give evidence or produce a document object. People can also be directed to answer questions under oath. However, any self-incriminatory evidence obtained through the use of PIC coercive powers cannot be used for civil or criminal proceedings against the person, but can be used for the purposes of the investigation and for disciplinary proceedings. Hearings allow the PIC to collect evidence in relation to specific acts of corrupt conduct. The PIC stated that, from a prevention perspective, it is important to also understand how the event happened and why it happened.

Matters that are the subject of public hearings must be the subject of a report to Parliament and include an opinion in respect of each "affected person" and recommendations regarding what action should be considered as a result of the investigation. Furthermore, the PIC may present a special report to Parliament at any time on any administrative or general policy matter.

Covert Operations

The PIC has the power to conduct controlled operations as part of its investigations: "We will use controlled operations when that's appropriate." Also, misconduct investigations may involve the use of undercover agents and informants, both internal police informants and external informants. Telephone interceptions and other covert techniques were considered by the PIC to be successful and necessary tools for misconduct and corruption investigations, given the expertise of those under investigation.

Outcomes

When a matter is finalised, or an investigation complete, the PIC can make recommendations to the police, or, in the case of criminal matters, can pass evidence to the Director of Public Prosecutions to determine if charges will be brought. With regard to recommendations to the NSWPF, the PIC can recommend specific action in relation to officers, which can include disciplinary actions, unless the subject officer has already resigned or been dismissed. Recommendations can be made as well in regard to changes to policy and practice.

While the PIC does not have any legislative authority to enforce the implementation of recommendations, the NSWPF is obliged to provide a response to the PIC recommendations and findings. Thus, the process of change through recommendations is a consultative process that relies on communication between agencies. The specific form that the consultation process takes depends upon the subject matter, the nature of the recommendations, and the stakeholders it affects. It may, for example, include roundtable discussions, workshops, or circulation of briefing papers or draft reports. However, the PIC highlighted the difference between acceptance and implementation of recommendations. The PIC stated that once it has made a recommendation and it has been accepted by the NSWPF, it will engage with the NSWPF as to the actions it is taking to implement it, and continue to do so until it is demonstrated that the recommendation has been implemented.

Witness Support

The PIC has a provision to protect witnesses and others who aid in investigations. The Police Integrity Commission Act 1996 empowers the PIC to make arrangements as necessary to protect the safety, including against intimidation and harassment, of anyone who is assisting the PIC.

Risk Management

With regard to risk assessment and management within the NSWPF, the PIC has conducted two major projects: Project Manta (Police Integrity Commission, 2009b) and Project Odin (Police Integrity Commission, 2009c). Project Manta has examined the identification, communication, and management of misconduct risks at the command level. The command level is viewed as the most critical level, first, because there are variations in the types of risks that are experienced by different commands, particularly between local area commands and specialist commands, and, second, because the command levels are responsible for identifying and determining how these risks are managed.

Project Manta used an Occupational Health and Safety perspective to explore workplace integrity risks rather than looking at the individuals employed within the workplace. Risks were identified through close examination of 25 commands, using documentation regarding complaints and risk assessments, and also verbal reports from commanders, to identify what the commands recognised as risks. The aim of the report was to highlight both generic and specific risks so they can be mitigated: "It's preparing people for the risks in the sorts of work that they will be doing … I mean some risks are generic to all police, but some are specific to the particular work or the particular location."

Project Odin focused on identification and management of risk at the individual officer level. Particularly, the project examined issues of the processes used to identify high risk officers, for example, those who had engaged in corrupt conduct, and how those people are managed. The project highlighted the importance of consistency in the use of the term *high risk* as well as identifying what the risk represented (e.g., high risk of engaging in a particular behaviour) and how to manage that. The project aimed to encourage and support consistency across the NSWPF in its use of terminology and identification and management of risk at the officer level.

Procedural Controls

The PIC also provides advice to the NSWPF on policy-related issues, for example, by commenting on new or amended policies, or providing advice at the drafting stage when a new policy is being considered. For example, the PIC has provided input into the drug and alcohol policy, secondary employment, and source management policies, among others. Further, Project Dresden, auditing the quality of the NSWPF internal investigations (Police Integrity Commission, 2000), led to the 2007 introduction of a process of Complaint Allocation Risk Assessment (CARA) to address issues of conflict of interest in complaints investigations. CARA works on the basis that officers assigned to complaint investigations must be assessed for conflicts of interest in relation to that investigation. For example, where possible, the investigating officer should not be from the same unit or, in some cases, the same command as the subject officer, particularly where the matter is more serious or it concerns an unidentified officer. The latter could lead to officers investigating themselves. A review of the CARA process led to five new recommendations in 2008 and 2009. The PIC reported (Police Integrity Commission, 2009a) that the acceptance and implementation of these were under discussion with the NSW Police Force.

Drug and Alcohol Testing

The PIC conducted a large project, Project Abelia (Police Integrity Commission, 2005), on illegal drug use by the NSWPF, which highlighted a number of issues and led to 64 recommendations in 2005. At the time of this study, 54 of these had been accepted (53 implemented or partially implemented), including increasing the number of random drug tests conducted. Further, it was found that some officers who used drugs off-duty admitted that they used drugs before joining the police force, but that they had not been specifically asked about their drug use during recruitment. This led to recommendations regarding making the police zero tolerance policy for illegal drug use more visible in recruitment forms, including making it clear that drug use is unacceptable and that recruits are likely to be drug tested during their training at the police college and during their career.

The PIC explained that "the whole emphasis there is to try to deter inappropriate people from applying to become NSWPF officers. It's hard to know who's going to become a drug user, but by giving clear messages at the time of recruitment that illegal drug use is not acceptable for police officers whether on or off duty, then perhaps those who consider illegal drug use to be an acceptable way of socialising may be deterred from applying."

The PIC also endorsed a former amnesty program for self-disclosure of drug use explaining that self-disclosure was an effective method of detection of illegal drug use. However, the PIC stated that this was not viewed by the NSWPF to be consistent with the NSWPF's zero-tolerance policy. Indeed, it was recognised that self-disclosure would only be effective if officers were encouraged to disclose and to receive support rather than being punished (e.g., through dismissal by loss of Commissioner's confidence). A trial of the use of drug testing based on hair samples was also recommended in order to provide longer histories of drug use. However, this recommendation was not accepted by the NSWPF. The current NSWPF drug and alcohol policy (New South Wales Police Force, 2007) incorporates the possibility of hair testing for mandatory testing incidents only.

Staff Screening

Aside from making recommendations regarding NSWPF staff screening and recruitment processes (e.g., the recruitment information regarding the drug and alcohol policy mentioned above), the PIC also conducts integrity checks for police and other agencies. For example, integrity reports are provided by the PIC to the NSWPF on candidates for promotion; the 2008–2009 PIC Annual Report (Police Integrity Commission, 2009a) states that 406 such reports were provided to the NSWPF in that reporting period. Further, reports may be provided to other agencies that are considering employing current or former NSWPF officers; the 2008–2009 Annual Report (Police Integrity Commission 2009a) reports 42 such reports were provided that year. Integrity reports will contain information on matters that have been investigated and led to some adverse finding for the officer.

Ethics Education and Training

The PIC Act 1996 outlines an education and advisory function for the PIC, including:

> … making recommendations concerning police corruption education programs, police corruption prevention programs, and similar programs, conducted within the NSWPF or by the Ombudsman or the Independent Commission Against Corruption for the NSWPF (PIC Act sec.14).

The PIC staff provide presentations at the police college, but these are not consistent components to specific courses. However, it was seen as an important role: "We see value in it, we're interested in ethics education." The PIC 2008–2009 Annual Report (Police Integrity Commission, 2009a) states that presentations were made to three NSWPF professional standards forums as well as a Detective Inspectors' development course. Further, the PIC has encouraged police staff to attend a program on corruption and anticorruption run by the ICAC and the Australian National University (ANU). The PIC also has a general role in providing advice on how police misconduct might be eliminated, which it addresses through provision of advice in response to specific requests as well as through its research and prevention publications.

Audit

The PIC can conduct audits or make enquiries into aspects of police activities in order to identify police misconduct, or the potential for misconduct. The PIC can also oversight selected investigations conducted by the NSWPF as well as monitor and audit the quality of NSWPF investigations. For example, Project Dresden, mentioned previously, audited the quality of internal investigations in order to assess improvements since the Wood Royal Commission. Further, the PIC Annual Report 2008–2009 (Police Integrity Commission, 2009a) states that 90 NSWPF internal investigations were reviewed by the PIC that year and 44 police complaints investigations were oversighted. Oversight typically involves reviewing the final police investigation report, but progress reports can also be requested and investigation activity tracked on the electronic complaints management system.

New South Wales Emerging Issues

The majority of complaints made *about* the NSWPF are handled *by* the NSWPF with notification to, and oversight by, the Ombudsman and/or the PIC. The Ombudsman's Office noted that the standards of police investigations have vastly improved, as shown by the decreasing number of reinvestigations, and direct investigations that the Ombudsman's Office undertakes, as well as the amount of police internal investigations that are sustained and lead to management action against the subject officer or officers.

The NSWPF has commenced a new process of complaint handling in order to streamline the handling of complaints. Local commands are given the responsibility of resolving the majority of minor complaint matters. The records of these minor complaints are subject to random audits by the Ombudsman as part of their overall scrutiny of the police complaints system. Indeed, much of the power of how the complaints system must run rests with the Ombudsman and the PIC, which have direct access to the electronic police complaints system to register and view complaints information. These agencies decide on what information should be entered on the electronic complaints handling system, which matters are notifiable to them, and also which matters are investigated.

Innovative Strategies

The NSWPF has introduced two new interrelated aspects to their police complaints and professionalism focus: the customer service program and streamlining of complaints handling and investigation. Both the Customer Service Program and the Complaints Streamlining Project recognise that the bulk of complaints received by the NSWPF concern minor matters related to customer service issues, such as lack of follow-up communication. While the customer service program aims to improve the level of service offered to citizens (e.g., victims and witnesses), in order to reduce these complaints, the streamlining project aims to improve the handling of these complaints.

The Customer Service Program was prompted not only by recognition of the high number of minor complaints, but also the New South Wales State Plan, which promotes customer satisfaction as one of its initiatives. In response, the NSWPF set up a working party and developed a Customer Service Charter that clearly defines who "customers" are and the level of service that the organisation must provide. This was followed by staff training and innovative survey methods, such as the "mystery shopper" methodology to assess the impact. This involves anonymous "mystery shoppers" visiting or phoning police stations at random and requesting assistance or information. The sole purpose of the contact is to assess the level of customer service provided. Further, as the Ombudsman's Office stated:

> If they actually do increase their customer service skills, potentially, there will be fewer complaints, they see that as one of the drivers for the customer service project. They're aware that complaints cost time and money and take people away from frontline policing duties.

The Complaints Streamlining Project is aimed at simplifying complaint assessment and investigation, particularly in improving the handling of these minor complaints through a triage process. This allows for preliminary enquiries in the assessment of a complaint rather than starting a full evidenced-based investigation. As the Ombudsman's Office explained:

> The police, because they are experienced doing criminal investigations, for a long time approached most complaints with that framework in mind, so, for any complaint, they conducted an evidence-based investigation, which means they over-investigated a whole range of less serious complaints.

The evidence-based approach also meant that the outcome focus was to prove or disprove the complaint rather than resolve the issue. The Ombudsman's Office explained further that changes to the legislation now enable police more flexibility over their assessment of complaints without formal investigation, for example, by allowing access to existing information holdings:

> Someone might say [that] they were assaulted in the police cells, you may have CCTV already, and you can look at that and tell was that true or not true. So, it allows you, in those circumstances, to decline more complaints easily without investigation.

These initial enquiries also allow police to assess the nature of the complaint in order to decide the best course of action, as the Ombudsman's Office stated:

> It gives them (police) more flexibility to say that this complaint is not really about misconduct, but it's about unprofessional behaviour or incompetence and really what is the complainant really wanting at the end of this, and that may be really clear. They may just want an apology, they want the officer not to do the same thing again, and that doesn't need a criminal-based investigation.

The Ombudsman's Annual Report 2008–2009 (New South Wales Ombudsman, 2009) states that, since the introduction of the Streamlining Project, the timeliness of NSWPF complaint handling has improved and the number of complaints informally resolved has increased. While this is positive, a number of "potential risks" were also highlighted:

> ... police making inappropriate decisions about whether to conduct a formal or informal investigation for complaints alleging misconduct, not taking nonreviewable management action when it is warranted for matters dealt with informally, and not properly managing the expectations of complainants (p. 67).

Further innovative practices emerging from the NSWPF was identified as rewarding officer integrity. The Ombudsman's Office noted that "police are increasingly good at identifying good practice and rewarding officers, and also publicising good work; every copy of *Police Weekly* has stories of individual police commended for good work either by the hierarchy or public." Further, the NSWPF Professional Standards Command detailed that they have an internal integrity award, "which has become a bit of a 'best and fairest' for Professional Standards Command," but which was to be broadened to outside the PSC, for example, to "reward someone that's participated in an above average act of integrity. ... Someone who's avoided the pressure to do the wrong thing." The process was explained as likely being based on nominations from the regions and judged by the PSC. "There are some reluctant heroes. We want to make it a positive experience."

With regard to the oversight agencies, the recent work by the PIC in identifying organisational corruption risks from an Occupational Health and Safety perspective shows an important shift in concentration from the officer to the environment. It also allows individualised consideration of the differences between particular areas within the police organisation that may warrant a tailored approach. As the PIC explained, "Corruption needs to be broken down into different types of corrupt conduct and specific strategies tailored to address each type." Also acknowledged by the PIC was the importance of considering the effects the particular strategies are actually trying to achieve, for example, whether a strategy is designed to detect, deter, or merely remove the opportunity for misconduct. This perspective then also allows evaluation methods to be designed in light of the expected impact.

Successful Strategies

This section details the areas that agency representatives highlighted in terms of successful practices.

Officer Education

Both the police and the Ombudsman's Office highlighted improvements in the educational levels of police as well as improvements in internal police training. The fact that it is now common for police to have tertiary qualifications, and the encouragement given by the police to members to obtain both undergraduate and postgraduate qualifications, was cited as contributing to the increased professionalism of the NSWPF.

Police Standards

The Ombudsman's Office highlighted that the strength of, and commitment to, internal standards setting of the police was a major component of improving the integrity of the NSWPF as an organisation as well as contributing to the effectiveness of the complaints system:

> I think the complaints system works effectively partly because, independently, the police are pushing integrity, professional standards, have value in themselves; they are reference points for dealing with misconduct. If that wasn't so strong then maybe the complaints system would be more at risk.

Integrity being part of the promotions system was also attributed by the Ombudsman's Office with strengthening the ethical leadership of the police: "I'm very impressed with the demonstrable seriousness with which the senior police I've come in contact with take issues to do with integrity and professional standards."

Multiagency Model

The Ombudsman's Office also commented that the policing environment presents risks for corruption and misconduct that likely make it impossible to completely eradicate such behaviour. However, a whole range of complementary strategies exist to minimise corruption and misconduct, as well as a number of different institutions that contribute to the system: "We now have a very mature and sophisticated complaints system which I think is a world leader. I think it works because of all these different checks and balances rather than any particular strategy."

Agency Consultation

Given the NSW multiagency oversight system, consultation between agencies was seen as contributing to the success of the system. The PIC commented that a process of providing briefing papers and draft recommendations and holding roundtable discussions was important to check for errors of fact and feasibility as well as receiving feedback comments or suggestions for improving recommendations. Reporting publicly and to parliament, as well as highlighting the police response to recommendations in the PIC Annual Report (which they are legislated to do), was regarded as beneficial for following up on the implementation of recommendations. As the PIC stated, "The consultation is really important to make sure you get the right sorts of recommendations and that you have the argument to sustain them. Similarly, the follow-up is important because even with the best intentions other things come up on people's agendas. ... but, also, if things go wrong or they turn out not to be practical or direction changes, we can at least know why that's happening and that might inform future recommendations."

Consultation was said to be useful as well in terms of discussing how recommendations can actually be implemented so that, while the ownership is with the police, the oversight agencies are there to help and advise on the implementation. The Ombudsman's Office also commented that steering committees can aid this process and that often someone from the Office may attend those committee meetings to monitor or check on the progress.

Research

Research that engages and benefits from the experiences of police was highlighted as a successful mechanism for both improving understanding of the issues faced by the organisation and also in building relationships between the oversight agency and the police. The PIC highlighted that such research allows an understanding of the differences across the organisation in terms of the issues faced, and was seen as an important basis for the work of the oversight agency. The police also expressed the importance of recognising local issues, particularly for the implementation of recommendations. Further, while there was an appreciation for learning from the international literature on practices and experiences, PSC noted the need to consider the specifics of the NSW context.

Investigations for Prevention

While investigations were acknowledged to be for the purpose of collecting evidence regarding the facts of particular circumstances and individuals involved, it was noted that investigations could be used to aid prevention. The PIC suggested that using investigations to elicit information on the "how and why" and not just "what and who" could provide important insights that can be used in understanding how to prevent similar cases in the future.

Legislation Reviews

All three agencies collectively highlighted the fact that new legislation typically includes a stated review period, a prescribed time after which the use of the legislation must be reviewed in order to assess both the implementation and current relevance. The Ombudsman's Office has conducted a number of such reviews of legislation regarding police powers, which are reported to Parliament. This was viewed positively in terms of oversight of the use of the legislation, particularly where it involves potentially controversial powers that can impact human rights, such as the antiterrorism powers. It was also noted that this can be difficult, though, if the legislation has not actually been used in the review period because it is hard to identify the risks associated with its operational use. The reviews were said to potentially create a sense of "use it or lose it," which may be problematic. However, the NSWPF stated that "it forces us to have better operational practices to actually try the legislation."

Emerging Ethical Issues

Both recurring and emerging ethical issues were highlighted in the interviews as needing attention. The Ombudsman's Office noted that some issues are related to risks that are inherent in police work and emerge in cycles: "You've got policies to make things a bit better, and then people get a bit more sophisticated and get around them and it pops up again." Similarly, the PIC noted that "our resources are fully devoted to coming to terms with the current issues, the current state of the environment, rather than exploring new and emerging ones." The specific issues discussed by the agencies are below.

Internet and E-mail Use

Inappropriate use of the Internet and e-mail was highlighted in a number of ways. Police use of social networking Web sites was indicated as potentially problematic, for example, with members identifying themselves on such sites, including photographs of themselves in uniform, and posting inappropriate content or comments. NSWPF commented:

> What we've accepted is that there's a generation of policing that that sort of stuff is normal social interaction, but where it crosses the line ... the approach we've taken to date is to set the boundaries of conduct up front and let people go away and comply with the standard and if they fail then we just don't let them back in.

Inappropriate e-mails, such as offensive material, were also highlighted by the NSWPF and the PIC as an issue. The NSWPF also noted that access to restricted Web sites was a concern, particularly regarding accessing pornography, including child pornography:

> They are restricted sites, but it doesn't stop some people, and there will be people who have to do that in the course of their jobs, like those who deal with child protection, they're a special category ... we have suggested guidelines so people don't get into trouble for doing their job.

Unauthorised Release of Information

The NSWPF identified concerns over unauthorised release of information, particularly in relation to relationships with journalists. It was noted that the policy over release of information could be confusing and that there were plans to look into clarifying this.

Drug and Alcohol Use

Following the PIC's Operation Abelia report, illegal drug use was recognised as a continuing area of concern, particularly in regard to recreational drug use and also attitudes toward that drug use: "The first few people who were held to account in that inquiry resigned their jobs so they could keep using drugs, so what it shows is less commitment to being a police officer." The Ombudsman's Office also highlighted the different attitudes of the new generation of police officers. Off-duty alcohol use, and its association with assaults at social events and in pubs, was also noted as an important issue.

Northern Territory

4

The police integrity model in the Northern Territory includes the NT Police Ethical and Professional Standards Command with oversight from the NT Ombudsman. The Ombudsman has been responsible for overseeing complaints against police since 1978, and the territory has seen a very low level of debate about public sector integrity systems. There have, nonetheless, been police conduct issues, described by the Ombudsman as "systemic and procedural," including mistreatment of indigenous people, drunken behaviour by police, and assaults (in *ABC News*, 2005; see also Prenzler, 2011). An unreleased review led to a new Ombudsman Act 2009, which gave the Ombudsman an own motion power to investigate matters raised outside the formal complaints process and receive complaints from police. However, the Ombudsman has stated that she lacks powers and resources to properly investigate police conduct matters (Hind, 2010).

Northern Territory Police

The Ethical and Professional Standards Command (EPSC) within the NT police is responsible for the administration, coordination, and investigation of all complaints against police as well as investigations of breaches of discipline where the conduct does not constitute a complaint against police. EPSC is also responsible for management of the disciplinary process, particularly where criminality is alleged, and provides significant input into other relevant Human Resources (HR) issues. EPSC also oversees investigations into "deaths in custody" as well as the operation of regional complaint-handling teams.

EPSC answers directly to the Deputy Commissioner and is headed by a Commander. At the time of this study, three Superintendents fulfilled roles based on task and/or geography: Alice Springs (comprehensive role), Inspectorate (internal investigations and auditing), and Complaints. The Inspectorate also included a Senior Sergeant and three investigators, and the Complaints division had two Senior Sergeants and three investigative Sergeants.

Complaint Handling

Complaints can be received and registered by the police as a result of written or verbal reports to police, referral by the Ombudsman, legal action taken against a member, or public comment (e.g., in the media). Police officers who receive a complaint against police are required to record and report that complaint; all complaints against police are required to be recorded electronically on their internal system, PROMIS (Police Real-Time Online Management Information System), regardless of how they are received. However, there was an acknowledgement that many operational police do not record minor matters because to do so would be very time consuming:

> For instance, someone walks in and says he saw the police doing this or that and you explain the legislation to him and he hadn't realised that he could do that and he walks out. Was that a complaint? Well, yes, it was. Did you conciliate it? Yes, you did. Should you record it? Yes, you should. Will you? Probably not, because it would take longer to record it than it did to deal with it.

The Ombudsman's Office also noted this same problem, although it acknowledged that only a minority of complaints were not being handled pursuant to the provisions of the Ombudsman Act. It was also noted that there is sometimes an inconsistency in how complaints are dealt with in some regional areas, since procedures rely on the officer in charge of that station or area. The Ombudsman's Office noted that, in many instances, telephone complaints are addressed by the senior officer on duty and recorded only in the Community Care Information System rather than in PROMIS. This means that the information is not referred to the Ombudsman, which is a breach of the legislation.

EPSC recognised that the recording of minor customer service matters needed to be improved to be able to adequately measure performance. NT police were reviewing their IT capabilities and planned to raise this as an issue to address for any new system.

All complaints are notifiable to the Ombudsman's office, with the exception of complaints regarding information handling (e.g., inappropriate access to or release of information), which are the jurisdiction of the Information Commissioner. It was suggested that there is sometimes a debate over whether matters are notifiable or not to the Ombudsman in relation to off-duty behaviour. EPSC stated that its test for whether the behaviour constitutes that of a police officer is whether the member is using a police power. EPSC noted that the Ombudsman's Office can take a different viewpoint, which is whether the member has identified him/herself as a police officer. The Ombudsman Office stated at interview that "if the off duty police officer identifies himself/herself as a police officer or "flashes" a badge, then our view point is he/she is acting as a police officer, otherwise he/she would not identify him/herself as one."

Complaints Against Police are categorised as either minor or serious. The Ombudsman determines the category that will be assigned to a complaint after assessing the issues of complaint. Minor complaints are those that can be dealt with through a Complaint Resolution Process (CRP) involving direct conciliation between the police force and the complainant (subject to agreement of all parties). Matters that can be informally resolved are listed in the NT Police Performance Management and Internal Investigations General Order (Northern Territory Police, 2007a) and include failure to act, incivility, misunderstandings of powers or practices, partiality, and those that appear to be without substance and likely due to mental health issues of a complainant.

The complaints resolution process infrequently involves formal face-to-face mediation between the complainant and subject member and it was commented by EPSC that little mediation training is provided. The General Order does state that "it may be of assistance to arrange a meeting between the complainant and the member(s) concerned" (Northern Territory Police, 2007a, s109) and the new Ombudsman Act also has provision for formal mediation. Where such a process had been used, its success was seen to be very dependent on the personalities of those involved. Further, it was noted by EPSC that, in practice, resolution can be achieved through simpler processes:

> Sometimes all that's required is that the police officer involved goes and sees the person and makes the apology there, which is contrary to the way the general order works ... but sometimes with the remote stations it's the most practical way of doing it.

More serious complaints are further categorised into category 1 breaches (behaviour that, if proved, would likely result in criminal or disciplinary charges) and category 2 breaches (outside CRP-agreed matters, but unlikely, even if proved, to result in criminal or disciplinary charges).

The vast majority of police complaints are dealt with through the complaints resolution process. For example, the 2008–2009 Annual Report (Northern Territory Police, 2009) states that 60% of complaints were categorised as being appropriate for conciliation while only 22% were Joint Review Committee (JRC) or non-JRC complaints (the remaining 18% were categorised as preliminary inquiries or information complaints). EPSC noted that conciliation-appropriate complaints had increased (Annual Reports show a relatively steady increase in minor complaints over the past 10 years), but this was taken as positive as the composition of the complaints (whether minor or serious), rather than the numbers overall, was a more important indicator of performance. Indeed, statistics from NT Police Annual reports show that complaints have reduced by almost one quarter (24%) since 2004–2005.

Complaints Investigations

A new policy for the management of complaints and discipline in 2007 resulted in responsibility for the management of most complaints and discipline matters to be decentralised and devolved to each division. Specifically, line managers were made more accountable for dealing with less serious matters with appropriate remedial measures. Each division has a Complaint and Discipline Management Team (CDMT) that oversees and coordinates investigations of the majority of Complaints Against Police at the divisional level.

Particularly, minor matters appropriate for conciliation and category 2 breaches are typically investigated at the divisional level, under the responsibility of the divisional Superintendent. The division will then draft a report on the findings as well as a letter to the complainant, which are both sent to EPSC for sign off. Particularly with regard to category 2 breaches, EPSC noted that a matter will not be finalised while an allegation still stands, even if a complainant decides not to proceed further: "We're quite strict in not letting an unanswered allegation stand out there … we're going to investigate it a little further and then go and discuss it with the Ombudsman and see what they want out of it." Once approved, the letter will be sent to the complainant, who has the right to seek review from the Ombudsman if unhappy with the outcome. That appeal must be sought within 21 days, although extenuating circumstances can be considered.

Complaints categorised as serious complaints were formerly oversighted by a JRC. The JRC is comprised of the Commander of the EPSC and the Deputy Ombudsman. However, this process ceased on 1 July 2009 with the introduction of the Ombudsman Act 2009. The Ombudsman's Office can now refer the investigation to EPSC to conduct, or can conduct their own investigation (the latter will be discussed in more detail below in the section on the NT Ombudsman). Typically, serious matters are initially investigated by the EPSC, which produces a report for review by the Ombudsman. If the Ombudsman's Office is not satisfied with the investigation, it can be sent back for further work. EPSC staff noted that, while there may be queries from the Ombudsman on investigations, it is very rare for a file to be sent back. This was attributed to the high level of scrutiny given to investigation files before they are sent for review; within EPSC, all files will be reviewed by the Senior Sergeant, followed by the Superintendent, and then the Commander. To reinforce timeliness standards in the process, the Ombudsman's Office contacts EPSC on a fortnightly (2-week) basis to receive updates on ongoing investigations.

When the Ombudsman's Office is satisfied that an investigation is complete, they write an assessment of the EPSC report and can provide recommendations. Under the Ombudsman Act, NT police must consider the recommendations and provide a written response. EPSC explained that, while there is typically acceptance of recommendations, there may sometimes be problems in acting on the Ombudsman's recommendations as they may be impractical to implement, cost-prohibitive, or simply "a policy issue for the Commissioner; the Commissioner has the power to ignore. He can be subject to criticism, but it's his police force."

All complaint investigations (for complaints taken externally) are oversighted by the Ombudsman's Office. Where matters are investigated internally within Northern Territory Police, only suitably qualified, impartial, and senior members are authorised to conduct investigations or conciliations. Where a disciplinary offence is highlighted by either an investigation or preliminary enquiry, the Inspectorate (internal investigations) area of EPSC is involved.

Investigative Powers/Techniques

Members of NT police have a responsibility to assist in investigations. The new Ombudsman Act states that EPSC has, in the course of an investigation, the power to direct a police officer to provide relevant information, produce a document or object, and answer questions. With regard to the latter, in directed interviews, members may be subject to disciplinary action if they refuse to answer, even if the answers may be self-incriminatory. The information obtained in directed interviews cannot be used in evidence for criminal charges against the member concerned and will not be released voluntarily to outside organisations. As EPSC stated, "We do resist other agencies having access to our directed interviews simply because it does become a trust issue."

If criminal charges are involved, for example, an assault charge, members will have the same rights as any member of the public at interview. However, it was noted that in such cases members will often refuse to talk, exercising their right to silence.

Other investigative tools are available, such as telephone intercepts. This is particularly the case where criminal matters are alleged, with the investigative tools available as they would be for any criminal investigation. However, the capacity to use such tools is not held within EPSC. Thus, operational policing areas are relied upon to provide such functions. This was seen to pose problems in internal investigations regarding maintaining the covert nature of operations, particularly if that operational area was the target. The Ombudsman's Office suggested that these difficulties could be overcome by utilising either the Australian Federal Police (AFP) or another state police force to conduct, for example, intercepts.

EPSC did not view covert methods as particularly useful, however, for complaints investigations as most would occur "after the fact." It was also noted that integrity testing would "at best … be considered for a particular investigation, but there's no broad policy. … We'd love to have the capacity." Capacity, in terms of the size of EPSC, was highlighted as a constraint for a number of more advanced integrity strategies, although it was noted that EPSC is "looking at having an intelligence capacity within the unit."

Discipline

Where a finding is made that an officer has shown unsatisfactory work performance or behaviour, but not constituting a category 1 or 2 breach, either formal or informal processes can result. The informal process would comprise the supervisor speaking to the member to identify possible causes and solutions and reaching agreement over a resolution. Notes are taken of the process, but it is not regarded as a disciplinary process. The formal process involves full exploration of possible reasons for the behaviour, and results in supervised corrective action that is monitored and reported to the CDMT. Such action may involve a Performance Improvement Plan (PIP), including a clear goal and identifying a supervisor and mentor. CDMTs are responsible for ensuring that the requirements of the PIP have been met. If an officer has not fulfilled the requirements of the PIP, disciplinary action could result, although the program could be reviewed for its appropriateness and an alternative course of action recommended.

Disciplinary offences are categorised in terms of category 1 and 2 breaches. Category 2 breaches can be dealt with at the CDMT level and result in managerial or remedial action that is nonreviewable, for example, counselling, training, warnings, or cautions. Category 1 breaches are more serious and result in reviewable action and could involve a fine, reduction in pay and/or rank, suspension, dismissal, transfer, demotion, or good behaviour bond. All actions taken for breaches of discipline are recorded centrally on the PROMIS system and maintained by EPSC. However, the general order states that "the object of disciplinary proceedings is not to punish … the object of disciplinary proceedings is to protect the public, maintain proper standards of conduct by members of the police and to protect the reputation of that body" (Northern Territory Police, 2007a, s9.6).

Witness Support

While NT police have Employee Support Services staff available around the clock, there is no formal policy or arrangements for supporting those who come forward and report the misconduct of colleagues. NT Police explained that:

> Certainly, the expectation is that no member should suffer for having come forward with something, but there is no formal arrangement. I think we would consider the needs of the victim or a witness if they suggested that there were issues for which they needed support such as informal arrangements within their workplace or with a mentor.

Further, the size of the jurisdiction was cited as a problem for maintaining confidentiality of those who report misconduct. However, it is an offence under the Ombudsman Act 2009 to commit an act of reprisal against a person for making a complaint or cooperating in a complaint investigation. This is mentioned in more detail in the NT Ombudsman section under witness support.

Early Intervention/Warning (Complaint Profiling)

In terms of early warning or intervention systems, NT police do not have a specific system that allows sophisticated tracking and flagging of officers. However, their PROMIS system can be used to review an officer's complaint history and alerts can be placed on particular individuals. Changes were planned, though, for their IT system as a whole. Further, the introduction of CDMTs has allowed easier identification at the local level where officers have received multiple complaints. However, this is not always consistent and relies on the successful operation of the CDMT concerned.

The ethos of early intervention is also addressed in the General Order (Performance Management and Internal Investigations), which identifies the need for "correcting behaviour at the earliest opportunity, with individual members accepting responsibility for their actions" (Northern Territory Police, 2007a, s4.4). The Performance Improvement Plans outlined above are designed for this purpose and are the likely action when a member attracts multiple complaints. Although there had been some initial problems with the rollout of the CDMT and PIP systems, this was seen as a step in the right direction:

> Certainly it's making us more accountable as an organisation for the management of our people because we have had problems where we don't need this person in the organisation, but we've not had the grounds on which to do anything about it because everything's minor. But, there's so much of it. So, from that perspective it makes us deal with or at least attempt to deal with that.

Further, while the complaint profiling approach has not been particularly consistent or technological in the past, EPSC reported that this had been largely because they were protected from the need for such systems by the small size of the force. However, a recent review had recommended improvements in the linking facilities of the police databases, and new IT options, including a specific early intervention system, were being considered.

Risk Management

NT police have an Audit and Risk Assessment Committee (ARAC), chaired by the Deputy Commissioner that meets on a quarterly basis to monitor corporate risk and the adequacy of internal control arrangements. For example, there is an urgent duty driving policy governing emergency driving and pursuits. This was viewed as fairly strictly adhered to, although there were problems enforcing it in the remote areas. However, it was suggested that a cultural change was occurring and that there was strong organisational support for calling off pursuits where the risk was high.

The NT police Code of Conduct regulates the terms on which members may accept gifts or benefits. There is also a process of monthly use-of-force reports that go to divisional officers, who are required to sign off on every use-of-force form generated within their division.

NT police have policies in relation to searches. For example, all search warrant applications are risk assessed by a commissioned officer before going to a magistrate or Justice of the Peace (JP) for approval. There is also video recording of conducted searches, although not necessarily in every case, but subject to the discretion of officers involved. In a related matter, officers were reported to often carry audio recorders with them by choice and, anecdotally, audio recorders have been used as a strategy to reduce complaints against individual officers where an officer was reported to have been instructed to record his interactions after having attracted a number of complaints. This was a strategy for the officer to be able to review his interactions as a training exercise, but resulted in no further complaints against the officer, presumably because the act of consciously recording himself led to more careful behaviour.

Staff Screening

For every recruit squad, including re-enlisters, the internal Police Integrity Committee and Challenge Panel will review every application and explore any integrity issues. All recruits are assessed on personal attributes, including integrity and psychological suitability. Further, those applying for the Transitional Entry Program are subject to extensive character, criminal, and background checks. The applicant's current jurisdiction is also contacted to conduct checks on integrity and internal discipline matters. With regard to integrity matters uncovered, it was noted that "the greatest offence is trying to cover up the past."

With regard to selecting and recruiting to positions within the NT police, the 2007 NT Police Annual Report states:

> A Selections Unit was formally established within Human Resource Management Branch and a new merit-based selection policy was introduced during the reporting period. It is anticipated that selections to positions within the police force will become more efficient, transparent, and consistent (Northern Territory Police, 2007b, p. 8).

EPSC provides discipline history checks of transfer, award (medal), and promotion applicants and/or candidates to selection panels. However, the Performance Management and Internal Investigations General Order (Northern Territory Police, 2007a, s258) states that "EPSC can only reveal details of a finalised category 2 disciplinary matter to a selection panel in the case of a transfer within 12 months of finalisation, or in the case of a promotion within 24 months of finalisation." Provision of these checks was said to have placed a huge workload on EPSC, particularly because of transitions through different data systems.

Education/Training

EPSC stated that it tried to have input on every relevant course run at the police college and that training is tailored to particular courses or groups. Given the large indigenous population of the Northern Territory, all recruits and lateral entry members receive cross-cultural training. Recruits are given an overview of the role of EPSC and the legislative frameworks that they operate under, including obligations with the Ombudsman's Office. Recruits are also given a lecture on the Code of Conduct so they know what their parameters are and how they are expected to behave: "It's all out there, but we also have an obligation to tell them and make sure they understand."

Senior Constables are trained in how to deal with complaints, while Sergeants and Senior Sergeants are given a half-day session on facilitating and completing minor complaint conciliations, with Senior Sergeants also given a longer session on the Complaints Resolution Process. Training is also tailored for groups of auxiliary members, depending on their function. For example, those who will work in the watchhouse will be trained more in use-of-force issues while those in the front counter or communications positions will be trained instead in communication and customer service matters. The Commissioner has also endorsed EPSC travelling to the operational areas to train members on complaint trends in terms of what attracts complaints and how they can sometimes be avoided.

In general, police training adheres to National Competencies, and ethics was identified by EPSC as "incorporating a large part of training." Indeed, it was noted that complaint numbers had been declining and improved training was credited with that effect. However, it was acknowledged that continuing training of officers was an area that could be improved, particularly in terms of members transferring between regions with very different policing issues: "If they work in Darwin, then they work primarily with indigenous people, but that is a totally different kettle of fish to working remote."

Tertiary qualifications were noted as being more frequent among employees than in the past and that this was especially useful in the EPSC area for dealing with the Director of Public Prosecutions or the Ombudsman's Office:

"We're coming from a greater level of understanding." NT police have also developed strategies for attracting and recruiting Indigenous people into the NT Police Force in a variety of roles including Aboriginal Community Police Officers and Constables. NT police has an Indigenous Policing Development Division that runs the Yidiyu Initiative, which is responsible for support, training, and recruitment of indigenous employees. There are also initiatives for attracting either former members to return to service or serving members of other jurisdictions to NT police. The Transitional Entry Program (TEP) offers experienced officers from other policing jurisdictions a modified entry process and accelerated transition and deployment. Those who do not qualify for the TEP can alternatively be fast tracked through recruitment.

Northern Territory Ombudsman

The Ombudsman (Northern Territory) Act was repealed on 1 July 2009 and replaced with the Ombudsman Act 2009. The new Act confers important new powers, particularly in relation to complaints against the police. Until 1 July 2009, the Act did not have a provision that allowed a police officer to make a complaint against another police officer. Further, the Ombudsman's Office did not have an own motion investigation power. Under the new Act, the Ombudsman's functions in relation to police are "to investigate, and deal with complaints about, conduct of police officers; to consider and prepare reports on investigations of the conduct of police officers and to make recommendations about action that should be taken in relation to them" (Ombudsman Act 2009, s.10). The Ombudsman can consider as well the administrative practices and procedures of the authorities under investigation (or subject to complaint) and make recommendations for improvement. The Ombudsman also has an audit function to inspect the records of Northern Territory police in relation to compliance with the use of surveillance devices under the Surveillance Devices Act 2007 and compliance with both the Telecommunications (Interception) Northern Territory Act 2001 and the Commonwealth Telecommunications (Interception and Access) Act 1979.

Complaints Handling

The Ombudsman can receive complaints orally or in writing, with the majority of complaints received over the telephone. Complainants need not identify the officer who is subject to a complaint. As mentioned above, importantly, the Ombudsman can now receive complaints *from* police officers about other serving members.

The Ombudsman can investigate complaints independently of police. However, this rarely occurs due to a lack of resources and staff, or the choice by the Ombudsman for the police to investigate the complaint. Where a complaint is referred to police for investigation, the process is subject to oversight by the Ombudsman. The 2008–2009 Ombudsman's Annual Report states that "of the 289 complaints finalised, 86% were referred to police to investigate" while "13% of complaints were finalised without the need to be referred to police to investigate or respond to. ... They were either found to have no substance, were discontinued, or were resolved expeditiously" (Northern Territory Ombudsman, 2009, p. 37).

Mediation/Resolution

The Ombudsman can decide to conciliate or mediate a complaint, although participation by the parties involved is voluntary. Further, the conciliator or mediator must be considered appropriately qualified and anything said during, or any document prepared for, the process cannot be used in any later investigation, nor can it be used in any proceeding, for example, for a breach of discipline. The Ombudsman's case management system documents the outcome that a complainant is seeking and it was noted that, often, complainants are seeking an explanation:

> If it's an official complaint, a senior officer discusses the matter with the complainant and once that person understands that there is legislation that supports the actions of the officer then they are happy because they have received that information.

The Ombudsman can also decide that the complaint is to be dealt with through the NT Police Complaint Resolution Process.

Complaints Investigation

The Ombudsman can determine that more serious complaints are investigated by NT Police Ethical and Professional Standards Command (this process is outlined above in the Northern Territory Police section). These investigations are reviewed by the Ombudsman and issues reported on, with relevant recommendations made. The Ombudsman's Office stated that, when reviewing the issues, they "expand the complaint to encompass all the issues that we see, regardless of the fact that the only investigation that you're required to do is the complaint itself; once you start getting footage and documents and everything else, other issues are raised so the reports include all issues that we identify during an investigation."

This was described as an area of disagreement with the police: "The view put forward by [the] police is that if the complainant doesn't raise it as an issue, then our Office shouldn't either." However, the Ombudsman's Office is of the view that complainants do not always know their rights or that actions in certain circumstances are wrong. Further, the new Ombudsman Act states that a function of the Office is to consider the administrative practices and procedures of public authorities generally, as well as specifically, of those authorities whose actions are being investigated. This suggests the opportunity to explore issues that are not directly related to an allegation.

With the introduction of the new Ombudsman Act, the Ombudsman can now determine that a complaint is dealt with by an Ombudsman investigation. Thus, there is the potential for decreasing the number of matters referred to the police for investigation. However, in reality the Ombudsman's Office highlighted a number of obstacles to their work under that function:

> Even if we did have a complaint and wanted to investigate it ourselves, we would still be reliant on the police to investigate, and then provide us with a report because of a lack of staff, other resources, and an inability to use the information in criminal matters.

The Ombudsman's Office explained that the legislation did not adequately resource them in terms of powers. The Ombudsman Act 2009 gives the Ombudsman's Office coercive powers in terms of entering and inspecting premises and compelling a person to produce documents or to answer questions. However, the Ombudsman's Office explained that information obtained through these powers cannot be used in a court of law, that is, it cannot result in police being subject to criminal proceedings. This is similar to the directed interviews conducted by police themselves, but the police have the option of conducting a criminal interview. Since the Ombudsman is not a Law Enforcement Office, it cannot conduct criminal interviews and is not legislated to use telecommunications intercepts or surveillance devices. Thus, the Ombudsman's Office concluded that "we did not have and we still do not have the ability to look into corruption issues of police officers and that is because we do not have the resources."

Outcomes

The Ombudsman's review of investigations conducted by the police, and the issues involved, can lead to recommendations made by the Ombudsman to improve processes. While there is no direct power to enforce the recommendations, the Ombudsman can request a report from the police on the actions they intend to take (or reasons for no action) to implement the recommendations.

The Ombudsman can also recommend disciplinary action or a criminal charge. While previously the Ombudsman's Office would not be informed as to what the disciplinary action taken against an officer had been, the new legislation allows retrieval of this information from the Inspectorate Division of EPSC. The Ombudsman's Office explained that there is a 6-month statute time frame in which to take disciplinary action, which can be problematic given timeliness issues of complaint investigations. The Ombudsman's Office does attempt to monitor the timeliness of particular investigations that are thought will result in disciplinary action by sending notification to the police of the disciplinary deadline date 1 month or more in advance.

Further, a file will not be closed until the recommendations have been implemented and "that might mean that the file may stay open for 2 years and our stats would not meet our set benchmarks." Where recommendations are not implemented, the Ombudsman can report to the Minister. However, while the Ombudsman's Office reported that there have been occasional police challenges to recommendations, or challenges by the Ombudsman regarding the police investigation process, agreement between the agencies was estimated at 98% of cases. It was noted that there had been rare occasions where the Ombudsman's Office had released its own report on an investigation without endorsement of the EPSC, due to police refusal to accept the views or findings. With the new Ombudsman's Act, the Ombudsman now has the power to conduct its own investigation and release its own report, independent of the police (and the now defunct JRC process).

Witness Support

Under the Ombudsman Act 2009, it is an offence to commit an act of reprisal or to harm or threaten to harm someone who has made, or intends to make, a complaint, or who has cooperated or intends to cooperate with a complaint investigation. This section protects against actions to discourage people from making complaints and actions in retribution for making complaints.

Early Intervention/Complaints Profiling

The Ombudsman is required, under the Act, to keep a register of complaints that includes details of the decision of how the complaint should be dealt with, details of that process (for both conciliations and investigations), and any finding (and outcome) that the complaint was inadequately dealt with by the police. The complaint register includes the name of the subject officer, where known, regardless of whether a matter was conciliated or investigated. The register is used to keep track of the process of individual complaints, but also to assess complaint histories of subject officers when new complaints are registered: "If an officer's name is provided or subsequently identified, it will go into our database and we'll look at their previous complaint history with our office." However, it was pointed out that any allegations involving corruption would not be in the Ombudsman's system because that was the responsibility of the Inspectorate branch of EPSC and the Ombudsman has not had access to that information.

Where officers are identified as having a number of complaints, and where those complaints have been found to be justified, the Ombudsman's Office will bring the information to the attention of the EPSC along with recommendations for addressing the issue. Recommendations could include that the officer attends remedial training or is given a mentor to minimise the repetitiveness of a complaint against that officer: "We've made recommendations that they are put with a more senior officer who oversights and supervises, micromanages really, and I think that's a very good idea because the officer might not think that he/she is doing anything particularly wrong."

Ethics Training/Education

The Ombudsman contributes to police recruit training with regard to explaining the role of the Ombudsman in police complaints and what recruits can expect if they receive a complaint about their on-duty behaviour. While not involved in ethics training per se, the Ombudsman's Office does provide information on case examples that are taken from their annual reports, which allow an understanding of the types of complaints that are received about police.

Audit

Legislation in place for use of telecommunications interception and surveillance devices provides the Ombudsman with the power to audit the compliance of Northern Territory police with their obligations under those Acts. However, the Ombudsman's Office pointed out that there is no controlled operations legislation for the Northern Territory, meaning that police functions, such as undercover operations and the use of informants, were unable to be audited in similar ways.

The Ombudsman's audit and review functions can lead to recommendations. For example, new police powers may require new policies: "When the new legislation, for example, the Surveillance Devices Act, came into effect, our first suggestion was that they (NT police) wrote a General Order, which is a policy, a guidance for staff."

Northern Territory Emerging Issues

Innovative Strategies

The introduction of the new Ombudsman Act 2009 has shown improved powers of oversight in the Northern Territory, and the Ombudsman's Office viewed the new powers positively. However, a lack of associated resources in terms of staffing and further legislation for use of coercive powers for the purpose of gathering evidence for criminal proceedings were seen as major impediments to this function. The representative of the Ombudsman's Office expressed the opinion that every state or territory should have an independent anticorruption agency for the purposes of accountability, openness, and transparency: "Complaints against police being handled by their colleagues can be perceived as biased or a conflict of interest."

While the above comment relates to a general perception of conflict of interest in police investigating themselves, the size of the NT police was raised as potentially increasing the likelihood of such conflicts of interest, for example, where the EPSC investigating officer may socialise or have worked for many years with the officer that is the subject of investigation. While NT police are obliged to consider such conflicts of interest and reassign the investigation to another staff member, the representative of the Ombudsman's Office suggested that the issue should be formally addressed on record at interview and, should a conflict be declared, it (and the subsequent action to address the issue) should be documented, so that this process is made transparent.

The Ombudsman's Office was not dismissive of police conducting internal investigations. Indeed, the Ombudsman's representative acknowledged the expertise and powers of the NT police in this area and, in light of the new Ombudsman powers, suggested a potential change in practice to share the workload, in that the Ombudsman's Office takes responsibility for interviewing civilian witnesses and the complainant in order to free up resources at EPSC to devote to gathering evidence from police. It was suggested that this would likely reduce the time taken to investigate and finalise complaints. However, implementation would depend upon the agencies, their budgets, and resources.

Successful Strategies

In terms of current complaint-handling processes, both the EPSC and Ombudsman's Office commented on the good practice of prompt action. EPSC highlighted the importance of prompt action for both increasing the satisfaction of complainants as well as preventing issues from becoming more serious: "The message we've been sending is, as soon as someone rings up, it might not even be a formal complaint, the supervisor should be on the phone back to them as soon as possible, and quite often it is resolved at the first instance."

The Ombudsman's Office was keen to highlight that NT police are very good at handling complaints and handling them quickly. The fact that EPSC involves a dedicated and consistent group of staff who are experienced was noted as aiding the quick resolution of complaints. EPSC also voiced optimism for the divisional CDMTs, but that it required a cultural shift: "There are some areas where it is done extremely well and other areas where it's sort of lip service only."

In support of the delegation of complaint handling to the local level, EPSC commented that education and training regarding minor complaint handling had improved. Particularly, EPSC noted that, in the last 18 months to 2 years, they had concentrated on training supervisory applicants: "I think we've had a good result out of it. The upper echelon level complaints have reduced, which means that we are dealing with them (the issues) at a lower level, where they should be."

On a more general level, the Ombudsman's Office noted that learning from other jurisdictions was important as well. Particularly, the merit of conference attendance was highlighted, as was identifying and contacting certain agencies that have conducted worthwhile investigations and discussing the methods used and lessons learned.

Emerging Ethical Issues

The Ombudsman's Office noted that they consider that "the Northern Territory police are a very professional organisation and couldn't say that there was anything seriously concerning about the Northern Territory police." When specifically asked to identify potentially emerging ethical issues for Northern Territory police, the EPSC and Ombudsman's Office mentioned the issues detailed below.

Protective Custody

Section 128 of the Police Administration Act states:

> Where a member has reasonable grounds for believing that a person is intoxicated with alcohol or a drug and that that person is in a public place or trespassing on private property the member may, without warrant, apprehend and take that person into custody.

The Act defines "intoxicated" in this section as "seriously affected apparently by alcohol or a drug." It was reported that NT police are making 30,000 to 40,000 protective apprehensions under this section every year. Given that the population of the Northern Territory stands at approximately 220,000, this number of apprehensions was considered extremely high. Determination as to whether a person is "seriously affected" is discretionary and both the EPSC and the Ombudsman's Office commented that these decisions were very hard to review or challenge. The Ombudsman's Office noted that apprehensions under Section 128 had been problematic for a number of years and they had received complaints by people who stated that they were not "seriously affected." Clearly, such a term can be subjectively determined by both those who are under the influence of alcohol or drugs as well as those observing them.

Communication

Both the Ombudsman's Office and EPSC noted that the majority of complaints are minor and concern issues or incivility, inaction, or questioning the legality of police actions. The Ombudsman's Office noted that many minor complaints could be minimised if police provided information to citizens during encounters, particularly in relation to informing as to the legislation that supports their actions:

> Officers carry little police cards around with them and merely explaining in writing on the back of the card the legislation for which the person is being accused and under what section, would be a sufficient explanation. ... That might minimise these minor complaints. Giving a member of the public this explanation should be enough to satisfy them that they haven't been harassed or mistreated or unfairly dealt with.

EPSC also raised a communication issue by operational police. It was suggested that communication abilities were decreasing as the range of options for dealing with situations (particularly in relation to additional 'use of force' accoutrements, such as Tasers, OC spray, etc.) has increased. "I think we also recognise that we don't talk as well as we used to; the on-the-street police ... because we're giving them more options, they'll tend to go to those options earlier."

Tasers

In relation to use of force options, Tasers were reported to have been issued to NT police officers for approximately 18 months at the time of interview. While it was reported by EPSC that it had not received a large number of complaints regarding the use of Tasers, Tasers were recognised as an area of concern that had recently been reviewed. The review had particularly recommended against "dry tasering" (where the Taser is held against the target without firing the projectiles). A number of other problems had also been identified, including not following procedures for booking out Tasers to individuals, but passing them to colleagues ("hot handover"). In response, new accountability processes have been introduced. Further, the Inspectorate division of EPSC audits use-of-force forms and the use of Tasers. However, resources were an issue: "It's about the size of the units because there's only so many audits you can have." It was noted that the audits are not subject to oversight from the Ombudsman's Office.

Policing Indigenous Communities

It was highlighted that policing an indigenous population was core business for the Northern Territory police. Approximately one-third of the Northern Territory population is indigenous, with a significant number of those being rural and many traditional. EPSC have received a number of complaints from indigenous people and noted that there is often a tension between police action and cultural issues. An example of efforts to minimise this tension was given through the promotion of police activity to protect communities, giving the following message: “What we’re about is respecting the people in this community, so we will do these searches and we will target these people who are bringing in substances that are ruining your lifestyle.” The fact that the police action is specifically explained as protecting the community was described as “being really well received.”

Supervisory Staff

Issues were raised by EPSC in relation to staffing at the supervisory level. One issue identified was that members were more motivated to attend training courses and seek promotion for the pay increase rather than the actual supervisory role. This meant that staff who reached such roles were not necessarily motivated to supervise others. Further, it was raised that, often, supervisors are acting in the role short-term. This creates difficulty in building and maintaining any level of objective authority.

Domestic Violence

An emerging area of interest for EPSC is also domestic violence committed by members of the Northern Territory police, including the Aboriginal Community Liaison Officers. EPSC oversees investigations of allegations against members of NT police for domestic violence. At the time of this interview, the extent of such incidents had not been quantified, but it had been highlighted as a potential area of concern that needed analysing.

Queensland

5

The integrity system in Queensland includes the Queensland Police Service (QPS) Ethical Standards Command and the Crime and Misconduct Commission (CMC). Queensland was the site of numerous allegations and suspicions of police corruption over many decades. In 1989, the landmark Fitzgerald Inquiry documented significant corruption, especially in protection rackets. The recommendations led to the establishment of the Criminal Justice Commission (CJC), which was responsible for investigating misconduct across the entire public sector, including the police. In 2002, the CJC merged with the Queensland Crime Commission to form a new agency, the Crime and Misconduct Commission (CMC). The CJC and CMC have enjoyed considerable public support, but have been in conflict with police management over disciplinary decisions, and there has been consistent criticism of the commissions for the practice of "devolution," in which the large majority of complaints continue to be investigated by police with minimal oversight (Queensland Council for Civil Liberties, 2010). The CMC investigates less than 2% of the thousands of complaints it receives each year, despite a staff complement of approximately 350 and despite public opinion showing 91.5% support for the proposition that "complaints against the police should be investigated by an independent body not the police" (Crime and Misconduct Commission, 2008, pp. 25–26, 67, 76; 2009a, p. 54). The Commission's investigations have exposed diverse forms of misconduct, with disciplinary outcomes, but it has had limited impact in problematic areas, such as police abuse of Tasers, assaults by police, indigenous deaths in police custody, and deadly vehicle pursuits (Prenzler, 2011). The Queensland police complaints, discipline, and misconduct system is currently under review, following the publication in December 2010 of the CMC Report *Setting the Standard: A review of current processes for the management of police discipline and misconduct matters* (Crime and Misconduct Commission, 2010a).

Queensland Police

QPS launched a Corruption Prevention Plan in 2007, and currently endorses the Corruption Prevention Plan 2009–2013 (Queensland Police Service, 2007). The plan places the onus for corruption prevention on the individual with the clear message that "integrity is everyone's business," encouraging self-monitoring, but also monitoring the "behaviour and professional conduct" of work colleagues.

While the Commissioner of Queensland Police has overall responsibility for issues of professional standards and integrity throughout the organisation, in practice that responsibility is delegated to the Assistant Commissioner, head of Ethical Standards Command (ESC). The QPS Web site explains the role of ESC in the following way:

> The goal of the Ethical Standards Command (ESC) is to ensure the community has full confidence in and respect for the Queensland Police Service. The Command manages the internal discipline process whilst being responsible for promoting ethical behaviour, discipline, and professional practice*.

ESC comprises five work areas: Ethical Practice Branch, Inspectorate and Evaluation Branch, Internal Audit, Legal and Policy Unit, and Internal Investigations Branch. The Ethical Practice Branch takes responsibility for education and training throughout the organisation as well as capacity building in terms of encouraging people to report unethical practice and supporting internal witnesses. The Inspectorate and Evaluation Branch, along with Internal Audit, is responsible for conducting inspections, evaluations, reviews, and operational audits as well as coordinating research. The Legal and Policy Unit provides advice to members on the disciplinary process and policy. The Internal Investigations Branch largely responds to, and investigates, complaints against the QPS as well as deaths as a result of police-related incidents or police custody, and other critical incidents.

Complaint Handling

The QPS Web site includes details on the procedures for making complaints against members of the Service, including options of complaining both directly to the QPS and to the CMC. Complaints can be made in writing and by e-mail and anonymous complaints are accepted. However, the QPS is clear that its preference is for complaints to be made in person (at any police station) in order to ensure provision of the details necessary to adequately deal with the complaint. When making a complaint, it is also encouraged to provide information on the outcome that is sought or expected (e.g., an apology, disciplinary action, etc.). ESC explained that "there are times where, in every complaint, what's important to us is to find out what the informant or

* Online at: http://www.police.qld.gov.au/aboutUs/the_service/structure/esc/ (accessed 29 June 2010).

complainant, what do they hope to achieve as a result of this. The organisation has an expectation, but the expectation of the person that was aggrieved is also important in this."

When complaints are received, they are assessed by a commissioned officer according to whether they constitute lower-level customer service issues or breaches of discipline (e.g., rudeness, delayed response), or more serious matters, such as police misconduct or official misconduct. Lower-level complaints and breaches of discipline are dealt with exclusively by the QPS. Misconduct matters are passed on for further assessment by the State Coordinator. Under the Crime and Misconduct Act 2001, the QPS must notify the CMC of complaints of misconduct. Notification of such complaints are dealt with through a formal direction issued by the CMC, following consultation with the QPS, which separates misconduct in category A and category B matters. The CMC must be notified immediately of category A matters for assessment and such action as the CMC considers appropriate. Application of the devolution principle under the Crime and Misconduct Act 2001 means that the CMC refers the majority of these matters to the QPS to deal with where possible. Category A matters include complaints involving possible official misconduct (where the complaint, if proved, could lead to a criminal charge or a disciplinary breach where dismissal is a reasonably possible outcome). Category A also includes complaints involving an indigenous complainant or alleged victim concerning assaults in custody or failure to provide medical treatment while in custody, inappropriate associations with a criminal or outlaw motorcycle gang, and matters likely to be the subject of significant media attention. Category B misconduct matters, which also include possible official misconduct, have in effect been preassessed by the CMC and concern less serious matters that are more suitable for the QPS to deal with. The QPS notifies the CMC of all category B matters by way of schedule on a weekly basis. Typically, these are reviewed at weekly meetings between the QPS and the CMC.

The CMC has access to category A and category B matters on the QPS complaints database. The CMC can monitor how the QPS deals with these matters in a range of ways, which may involve the CMC reviewing the full investigation file and proposing a further course of action before a matter being finalised, to auditing a sample of less serious matters for which information about the outcome has already been provided. ESC explained that, in practice, the majority of matters are referred back to the QPS to deal with: "Almost all of these matters come back to the organisation to be investigated, to have preliminary investigations, or to be managerially resolved."

In order to increase consistency in the assessment and categorising of complaints across Queensland, each geographical region and command has an assigned Professional Practices Manager (PPM) to ensure complaints have been assessed at the correct level and who passes complaints to the relevant District Officer or Branch Manager. While the PPM was described as an "emissary" for ESC, he/she is not actually under the command of ESC, but belongs to the region. He/she does provide a consistent point of contact for ESC staff and allows a point of responsibility for addressing concerns with complaint handling at that local level.

The CMC also has real-time, unrestricted access to the QPS complaints database and so can check on the appropriateness of how the QPS is handling the complaints. ESC supported this: "That's a good thing, it needs to occur. That's the degree of transparency and accountability that we have."

Local Resolution of Complaints

Recent years have shown increasing QPS responsibility for dealing with complaints, misconduct, and, particularly, minor or lower-level issues. A joint project between the QPS and the CMC, Project Verity, has taken this devolution a step farther and tested local-level (outside ESC) complaint handling responsibility in two regions. Project Verity aims to devolve responsibility for complaint handling and decision making to the lowest level possible, which would be the Officer in Charge or Unit Manager. This encourages supervisors to take a more responsibility for the conduct of their staff and encourages minor matters to be handled less formally through management processes, such as managerial action, where the emphasis is on learning and improvement rather than placing blame.

While alternative resolution is an available outcome in non-Verity areas, Project Verity is aimed particularly at both improving complaint handling (especially timeliness) and early correction of behaviour. Managerial action is described as a process for the supervisor or manager to discuss the issues with both the complainant and officer in question, while mediation offers an opportunity for the complainant and subject officer to discuss the issues face-to-face, facilitated by an independent trained mediator. While the majority of minor matters were described as being resolved informally, mediation was said to rarely occur:

> It's all subject to the officer (and complainant) wanting to participate; you can't compel an officer to participate in mediation, but having said that, there are certain times when an officer might not want to participate, but a senior person on that officer's behalf, representing the organisation or the work unit, would be prepared to do that.

Mediation also was described by ESC as being an important option for particular indigenous communities "where they don't want a report, they want to sit down with people and talk about these issues face-to-face."

Complaints Investigation

Investigations of complaints have also followed the path of increased devolution to police, with the majority of matters received by the CMC actually referred back to the QPS to deal with. ESC coordinates and directs the complaint process within the QPS and acts as a central point of contact for the CMC. The ESC Internal Investigations Branch (IIB) is primarily responsible for complaint management and investigating allegations of misconduct. IIB is Brisbane-based, and investigators are dispatched to regions to conduct investigations, thus, all investigations into more serious matters are conducted by central staff.

While the importance of devolution was recognised, difficulties were highlighted regarding the growing size of the organisation and the resulting volume of complaints. It was highlighted that the increased number of matters that are referred to QPS to investigate presents an issue over the ability to maintain standards of investigations. Decentralisation of responsibility for minor issues to the local level was recognised as potentially alleviating some of this workload from ESC, but it was highlighted that the rollout to the regions was likely to be slow. Further, while the work of ESC may be decreased by this project, clearly, the workload of local level officers in charge will increase with this additional responsibility.

There is an option for conducting joint investigations with CMC, which is likely where more independence or security of information is wanted or the CMC's powers are needed. For example, the QPS does not have the means to conduct directed hearings, but can utilise the powers of the CMC through a cooperative investigation arrangement, where "we (QPS) will give them (CMC) a list of people that we want subject to such a process and they will pursue that on our behalf. So, when we do that, we do it as a joint investigation with the CMC."

The QPS can conduct directed interviews with members. While a criminal interview offers the member the same rights as any citizen, such as the right to provide no comment, in the directed interview, members are compelled to answer questions. Information gained through directed interviews cannot, however, be used against the member in any criminal proceedings as information gained under duress is inadmissible in court. As ESC explained, the utility of the directed interview is a "trade off … it's about the administration of justice, it's about internal justice, we need to know what's occurred and it goes to their fitness as a police officer." However, the information gained can be used in criminal proceedings against others, or for a charge of knowingly or recklessly making a false or misleading statement.

Covert Operations/Integrity Testing

With regard to the use of controlled operations for misconduct investigations, ESC explained that they can access these resources within the organisation, but generally prefer to engage the CMC to provide these services:

> When we need extra support or resources, we can go to the CMC. … we much prefer to leave that (controlled operations) external to the organisation and use our capacity with the CMC, and the reason for that is to keep the information really tight, to prevent leaks.

Informants are used as well, but it was explained that this does not constitute a large proportion of the work of ESC: "… given that a lot of the work that we do comes very much from people making complaints … or alternatively they're from internal police officers and staff members who actually make a complaint."

Integrity testing was also discussed as an available option for uncovering misconduct, but is not currently used, partly because the CMC undertakes this task. Integrity testing was also viewed by ESC as an investigative tool and a last resort, only to be used where there is some evidence base. Thus, integrity testing was seen by ESC to have value only if used in a targeted way, rather than on a random basis, because the targeted form would have the goal of adding evidence to a case, while random testing was seen not to advance the organisation's learning while it also provided a moral question regarding trust of members. As ESC stated, "I'd like to think that we start with a philosophical problem at the front end … and I just don't know that I'd feel very comfortable on a personal level in seeing who's going to succumb to temptation."

Outcomes/Discipline

While sworn and unsworn employees of QPS are governed by separate legislation (the Police Service Administration Act 1990 and the Public Service Act (Qld) 2008, respectively), the Internal Investigation Branch (IIB) of ESC manages the QPS internal discipline process for all employees. However, breaches of discipline are the responsibility of regions or commands and directorates and are dealt with at that local level. Sanctions include reprimand, reduction of salary, forfeiture or deferment of salary increment, and deduction of a fine from the salary for breaches of discipline, as well as dismissal or termination and demotion for misconduct. The QPS also has the power to stand down officers and suspend members from duty.

ESC is currently conducting a review of the internal discipline system. ESC highlighted that the current system was problematic in terms of the time taken to impose sanctions: "… from the action of the individual to the intervention being imposed is sometimes 12 or 18 months. … The educative effect of that is completely lost." This was true even for minor sanctions where the effect of the delay in deciding on the sanction was seen as particularly destructive to the individual's relationship with the organisation. Further, it has long been recognised that police behaviour, which may be the subject of a complaint, is not always serious enough to warrant a sanction, but, rather, managerial, corrective action is more appropriate than discipline (Criminal Justice Commission, 1997a).

The joint CMC–QPS Project Verity was raised as aiming to improve the speed and efficiency of the disciplinary process and devolving the responsibility, particularly for these minor matters back to the appropriate local level, for management action. However, more serious matters are still dealt with through the discipline system.

One particular focus of the Project Verity trial has been the introduction of an improved process for dealing with disciplinary matters that are not contested by the officer who is the subject of the complaint. Rather than requiring a full investigation and hearing, the new Administrative Consensual Discipline Process (ACDP) is an administrative (paper) process that allows faster resolution where the subject officer is willing to admit to the alleged conduct and accept the nominated disciplinary action. Advantages of the expedited process are put forward as reducing the resources needed for lengthy investigation, but more importantly decreasing the stress caused by the uncertainty and length of time between the allegation and an outcome. This, in turn, increases the impact of the discipline by being timely and enabling the subject to take responsibility for his/her conduct.

The CMC said that "it just makes a great deal of sense" to have a process to deal with a matter in a timely way when a subject officer has made admissions, rather than unnecessarily prolonging the process and causing stress and strain. However, the CMC also pointed out the danger of using it to "plea bargain," explaining that while a manager can take into consideration the fact that the officer is willing to admit to the behaviour and can reduce the proposed sanction according to mitigating circumstances, the process should not be seen as saying "if you do this (admit to the behaviour), then I'll only give you this (disciplinary action)." The process, therefore, involves checking comparative sanctions as a guideline in order to keep sanctions consistent across similar cases.

Witness Support

Section 7.2 of the Police Service Administration Act 1990 provides an obligation for members of the QPS to report misconduct or breaches of discipline. In support of this, the Act also provides for the offence of victimisation: It is an offence to intimidate, harass, or do (or threaten to do) any action likely to be detrimental to, or prejudice the safety or career of a person because that person complied with the mandatory reporting requirement. QPS is also obliged, under the Whistleblower Protection Act 1994, to protect those who make disclosures in the public interest against reprisals. This Act is soon to be replaced by the Public Interest Disclosure Act, which also provides for oversight of compliance through monitoring by the Public Services Committee.

Due to the mandatory reporting requirement there is no option for anonymous reporting of misconduct by members of the QPS. However, there are a variety of ways that the information can be reported, including completing a complaint form on the internal electronic complaints system, reporting to a supervisor who can complete a complaint form on their behalf, reporting directly to ESC (via the telephone), or reporting outside to the CMC.

Further, in January 1998, an Internal Witness Support Program was established in the ESC "to provide guidance and support to members who report misconduct by another member of the Service" (Criminal Justice Commission, 2001). The Ethical Practice Branch (EPB) is responsible for the program to advise, assist, and support QPS employees and proactively promote reporting suspected inappropriate behaviour of peers. ESC explained that, also, where officers come forward about their own behaviour, or behaviour of others that they too were involved in, their reporting is looked on favourably and they are offered support.

Employees receive practical support both centrally and locally:

> … we encourage them to get that level of support at the local level as well to make sure that people are looking after their needs, that they aren't being targeted, that they aren't being treated like a pariah for coming forward and doing what they needed to do.

The QPS reports that, during the 2008–2009 reporting period, 116 members were provided with advice and assistance in relation to internal witness issues, with 152 contacts in 2009–2010 (Queensland Police Service, 2009; 2010). This shows a marked and steady increase since the program's early years.

Early Intervention

Over 10 years ago, it was recommended that the QPS adopt procedures for identifying and managing officers who receive multiple complaints (Criminal Justice Commission, 1997b). Such an "early warning system" was recommended to take into account multiple sources of information including:

- personnel records;
- sick leave;
- use of force reports;

- number of times an officer is assaulted or resisted while making an arrest;
- number of injuries sustained by an officer or civilians as a result of conflict;
- number of critical incidents in which the officer is involved;
- supervisory evaluations, letters, and other reports of the "image" of the officer.

It was also recommended that officers identified by the system could be dealt with by interventions, such as counselling, retraining, transfer to other duties, and psychological evaluations.

An update on the QPS reform published by the CJC in 2001 (Criminal Justice Commission, 2001) identified that the QPS had, indeed, through the Ethical Practice Branch, adopted processes for profiling officers who account for disproportionate numbers of complaints. This information was said to be provided to those officers' supervisors with an encouragement to use remedial action.

Currently, the QPS profiles individuals, units, and stations in terms of complaint or behavioural trends with the goal of reducing complaints and improving service delivery. ESC highlighted that it was recognised that profiling only on the basis of numbers of complaints attracted by officers was one-dimensional and that opportunities for incorporating a broader range of information into the process were being explored. Previous work history was highlighted as an important source of information, as was the type and timeline of complaints. However, there was recognition that, while this information may highlight that a problem exists, a range of information was necessary to identify the nature of the problem and an appropriate intervention.

Information on "at risk" officers is sent to the region for action. It was acknowledged that, if systems are working well, the officer should already be known to the region and that the central identification should only be a "fail safe." ESC also highlighted that complaints themselves should be early warnings to the organisation and opportunities for intervention. This was framed in terms of the organisation learning from complaints "as opposed to a lost opportunity—there was a complaint and there was a finding—we can look at that forever and a day, or we can say to ourselves 'well, what is the institutional learning here?'"

Risk Management

The QPS has a Risk Management Committee that maintains the QPS's risk management policy and practice. The committee is a high-level executive committee, including the Commissioner, Deputy Commissioners (regional and specialist), and a Risk Management Coordinator, among others. The committee ensures accountability for risk management, determines risk priorities, particularly high-level risks, and generally oversees the risk management of the entire organisation.

The Ethical Practice Branch of ESC is responsible for risk analysis related to professional practice and performance management and provides corruption prevention support and risk assessments for the QPS. However, corruption risks are also managed at the local level, with the QPS Corruption Prevention Plan for 2009–2013, developed by ESC, stating, "Regions, commands, and divisions are responsible for monitoring and reviewing progress of corruption prevention plans at district, station, or work unit level" (Queensland Police Service, 2007, p. 3). These risk management plans are monitored through the Operational Performance Review, but also through ESC inspections. ESC also provides a central point of coordination regarding the organisational expectations with respect to risk management and, through its inspections, can check that work units also have controls in place for managing the risks identified.

ESC inspection priorities are reestablished every year, particularly in line with what is learned through the main ESC branches, including investigations. ESC explained that this meant "risk management is fluid, more organic than linear, ticking off things to see if we have risk management plans." However, there are some identified risks that all business units are obliged to include. For example, since the CMC Dangerous Liaisons Report (Crime and Misconduct Commission, 2009b), all business units are obliged to include Corruption Prevention and Professional Standards as a risk in their risk management plans.

Procedural Controls

External independent oversight also provides identification of organisational risks and recommendations for managing them. For example, the QPS implemented a use of force policy and a Police Operational Skills Training Course in response to specific recommendations of the CJC in 1997 (Criminal Justice Commission, 1997b). Furthermore, there have been several calls for the use of audio and video recording of police–civilian interactions in a variety of settings. The QPS are testing Taser cameras in some Queensland districts and recently announced that they are testing the use of body-worn video and audio recorders for use by Taser-qualified officers. The trial is in response to a recommendation of a recent joint QPS–CMC Review of Taser Policy, Training, and Monitoring and Review Practices (QPS–CMC, 2009). The Taser cameras become operational automatically when the Taser's trigger is engaged, while the body-worn video can be activated manually at any time and is aimed to record the deployment of a variety of use of force options as well as the interaction that leads up to that deployment. The cameras are aimed at improving accountability and identifying opportunities for learning and improvement in use of force as well as protecting officers against false allegations.

Drug and Alcohol Testing

All Queensland police officers and recruits are obliged to comply with the QPS Alcohol and Drug Policy. The Police Service Administration Act 1990 states that members must not have consumed alcohol over the limit of 0.02g (in 100 ml of blood or in 210 L of breath) when reporting for duty, on duty, or on call for duty. Members must also not have the presence of a dangerous drug in their system, or any targeted unlawful substance that may impair mental or physical capacity. All police officers and recruits can be subjected to drug (urine) and alcohol (breath) testing, as well as staff members who perform duties in critical areas (e.g., communications, driver training, police armoury, watchhouse, facility for storing dangerous drugs). The Alcohol and Drug Awareness Unit is responsible for the coordination of testing as well as managing internal alcohol and drug programs, including education and clinical support.

Alcohol testing can be conducted on a random basis, targeted due to reasonable suspicion that a member is over the prescribed alcohol limit, on applicants undergoing a medical test, or on members involved in a critical incident. Mandatory critical incident testing relates to incidents that involve discharging a firearm in circumstances that caused or could have caused injury, a death in custody, or death or serious injury following a vehicle pursuit or workplace incident.

Drug testing (or targeted substance testing) is also conducted in the case of critical incident involvement. Critical incident drug and alcohol testing involves investigators from ESC attending the site and facilitating the testing program (both a breath and urine analysis). Members can also be drug tested in cases of reasonable suspicion (targeted testing). Further, any member engaged in a controlled operation can be subject to a test, as can recruits before commencing training and applicants in the course of a medical test to decide suitability.

For all drug testing, the major substances of interest are benzodiazepines, amphetamine/methamphetamine, cannabis, and opioids. There is a capability to test members for other drugs; however, it was highlighted that an evidence base would be necessary for such a test. The main issues regarding the substances tested related to the legality of the substance and also the impairment of performance: "If we test for those four main drugs plus alcohol, that's going to catch 99.9% of the substances that we'd be interested in, certainly the ones that impair performance."

The 2008–2009 QPS Annual Report states that, during the reporting period, 1,249 members (8.5% of all employees) had undergone a random alcohol test, with one positive result (Queensland Police Service, 2009). Further, in relation to mandatory testing incidents, 33 urine drug tests and 31 breath alcohol tests were conducted following critical incidents, all with negative results.

If an alcohol or drug test is positive, the Police Service Administration Act 1990 provides for a range of actions including: suspend from duty until no longer under the influence, guidance, counselling and rehabilitation, undergo medical examination for fitness to perform duties, transfer to performing other duties, disciplinary action, and also requiring the member to submit to further testing from time to time until satisfied that it is no longer necessary.

Staff Screening

Recruitment applications require applicants to self-disclose any integrity-relevant information, and the QPS further undertakes integrity checking of all applicants. Community background enquiries are also conducted, including standard referee reports, checks with current and former employers, and also residence checks: "We do detailed background checks that include talking to family, friends, and neighbours … for example, we'll knock on the doors of neighbours and have a chat about the person. It's a very effective strategy." Any integrity issues raised through the checks are evaluated by an Integrity Committee within the QPS, consisting of representatives from ESC, the Academy, and Recruitment. Psychometric (psychological) assessment of applicants is also conducted as well as with staff entering and leaving particular specialist units, such as child protection, forensic computing, the special emergency response team, and other critical areas of the organisation.

ESC is responsible for conducting probity checks in relation to promotions and awards. Decisions in relation to successful nominations for appointments or awards are subject to that vetting, but the ESC Assistant Commissioner can overturn a vetting decision:

> If a person is subject to investigation, I would look at the matter, you know if it was a senior appointment or a specialist award, I would look at it and I'd need to satisfy myself that the allegation was incredibly light or it was unlikely to be proven or it was a relatively minor matter.

Ethics Education and Training

The EPB is responsible for providing statewide support, advice, and training in all aspects of ethical awareness, corruption prevention, discipline, and risk management processes. Indeed, training was described by ESC as the principal work of the Ethical Practice Branch, both in terms of central training provided at the police academy, talking to every recruit group, and also training at various work units with respect to specific issues: "They conduct hundreds of hours of training a year to scores of people all over to the furthest corners of Queensland." For example, the 2008–2009 QPS Annual Report states that 117 courses and sessions were delivered to 2,177 participants on the QPS Complaints Management System, ethics, and ethical behaviour during that reporting period (Queensland Police Service, 2009).

ESC commented that ethics training should be about identifying issues and that presentations were given specifically to people in districts, regions, and commands about the risks that are identified from internal investigations and inspections. Further, while discrete ethics and integrity training occurs in the form of specific units or programs, ethical considerations are also incorporated into more operational training courses:

> So, the ethical issues are clearly identified, but they're weaved into the training. It's not just "okay, we're going to teach you how to arrest these people, and now we're going to bolt on a chapter on ethics," it's not like that; it's weaved into the training.

A recent initiative has seen the introduction of an interactive training resource related to police pursuits by the First Year Constable Program, which focuses on ethical decision-making processes during a "staged" pursuit. QPS also is investing heavily in a new academy, which will provide a significantly improved environment for training delivery.

Audit

Both ESC and the CMC audit and review how complaints are dealt with. Further, all matters of misconduct must be overviewed by ESC before any action is taken. This overview is the responsibility of the IIB, as is overviewing and auditing regional and command disciplinary actions.

The Internal Audit branch of ESC provides an appraisal function to examine and evaluate service activities. Together with Internal Audit, the Inspectorate and Evaluation Branch (IEB) is responsible for conducting inspections, systems analysis, operational audits, reviews, and evaluations. ESC highlighted that inspection and audit functions are closely related to Internal Investigations with respect to development of areas of focus and organisational learning. ESC said that problems highlighted by individual internal investigations form part of the inspection process, in which IEB will review procedures and policies at the local level:

> So, there is this learning that occurs in each of those branches that is then communicated to each of the others. … That's a pretty good model. If you don't subscribe to a model, then ultimately Internal Investigations is just about punishment and an individual's aberrant behaviour being dealt with in a very cloistered confined environment; where's the institutional learning from that? The only one that learns anything from that is the investigators and the subject member.

Crime and Misconduct Commission

The Queensland Crime and Misconduct Commission (CMC) was a result of a merger in 2002 of the former Criminal Justice Commission and the Queensland Crime Commission. The CMC was created under the Crime and Misconduct Act 2001 to fight crime and promote public sector integrity and reduce misconduct. Thus, the CMC has a wide remit, part of which is to enhance integrity in the Queensland Police Service (which is the focus of this chapter). The CMC offers a range of functions in this arena, including investigations, monitoring, capacity building, prevention, conducting research, intelligence gathering, and protecting witnesses.

Complaint Handling

The CMC deals with complaints of official misconduct and police misconduct. Official misconduct involves wrongdoing in carrying out official duties or exercising powers. The allegation in question must be capable of constituting, if proved, either a criminal offence or a disciplinary breach for which dismissal is a reasonably possible outcome. The conduct "must also involve one of the following: dishonesty or lack of impartiality; a breach of the trust put in a person by virtue of their position; or a misuse of officially obtained information."* In contrast to official misconduct, police misconduct can apply to off-duty behaviour and includes any (other) conduct "that is disgraceful, improper, or unbecoming a police officer, or shows unfitness to be or continue as a police officer, or does not meet the standard the community reasonably expects of a police officer."† QPS must notify the CMC of all complaints that it receives pertaining to suspected official misconduct and police misconduct.

Complaints can be made to the CMC in person, in writing, by e-mail, fax, by phone, or using the complaint form provided by the CMC on their Web

* Source: CMC Web site: http://www.cmc.qld.gov.au/asp/index.asp?pgid=10760 (accessed 26 July 2010).

† Ibid.

site. The CMC Web site also offers advice concerning useful information to include when making a complaint. Anonymous complaints are accepted, but it is made clear that these can be difficult to investigate. The CMC encourages complainants to provide contact details in order to be able to provide follow-up information for investigation.

The CMC is looking at improving accessibility to the complaints system, particularly for remote and indigenous communities, and developing more culturally appropriate, effective ways to deal with indigenous complaints against police. However, while the CMC seeks to be accessible for complainants, it is also made clear that the organisation's preference is for complainants to approach the agency in question initially, where possible, and that they do not deal with low-level cases of rudeness or other misdemeanours.

Where complaints do fall within the CMC's area, the CMC can choose to investigate the allegations or refer the complaint to the agency concerned, subject to the CMC's monitoring role. Indeed, the legislation (CMC Act 2001) calls for the CMC to refer as many matters as possible to the relevant agency for handling. As such, the vast majority of complaints *against* the QPS are dealt with *by* the QPS. The CMC monitors how agencies deal with complaints by conducting reviews and audits as well as providing advice. For example, the CMC assists agencies in building their own capacity to investigate matters that do not require the resources or special powers of the CMC and provides guidelines for investigating and providing scenarios as example situations. There is also the capacity for the CMC to conduct cooperative investigations with the QPS.

The CMC commented that the percentage of complaints that it actually investigates has decreased over recent years. This was explained as partly due to the impact of the "devolution" principle (referring a complaint to the relevant agency) in the CMC Act and the resultant increased focus on monitoring and the low threshold for notification to the CMC that is set by the CMC Act. With regard to the latter, the CMC explained that quite often an individual can perceive or suspect that the conduct that has given rise to their complaint is serious, but, when examined, the complaint does not actually involve such conduct. Approximately 80% of matters are referred to the QPS to deal with, with the CMC conducting investigations in about 2% of matters; the rest are the subject of preliminary inquiries usually resulting in a decision of "no further action warranted." The comparatively small number of CMC investigations (to number of complaints) was noted and the resulting practice of police investigating themselves was commented on. The CMC acknowledged that there are members of the public who will never be comfortable with police investigating police; however, a recent CMC report states:

> The CMC is strongly of the view that one of the most effective ways in which the QPS can engender public confidence, protect its reputation, and maintain high standards, and the self-esteem of its members is to be seen to take certain, timely, responsive, and decisive action when there is a failure to meet these standards (Crime and Misconduct Commission, 2010b).

The CMC does, however, continue to monitor *all misconduct* matters that are handled by the QPS, typically by "desktop" review. In practice, the CMC reviews, on an individual case basis, just under 10% of complaints that are handled by the QPS as well as auditing samples of complaints. For example, the 2008–2009 CMC Annual Report (Crime and Misconduct Commission, 2009b) states that, during the reporting period, 130 such reviews were conducted, constituting 9% of the complaints that were dealt with by the QPS. CMC satisfaction with these cases is generally high; of those 130 reviews in 2008–2009, 83% were satisfactory, and two further reviews of specific classes of complaints raised no significant issues.

If complainants are concerned or unhappy about their matter being referred to the QPS for resolution, the CMC does offer the option for complainants to bring the matter back to the CMC if they are not satisfied with the QPS investigation (or outcome). The CMC will, where appropriate, examine the matter and make recommendations to the QPS to respond to a complainant's legitimate concerns. In serious cases, the CMC may assume responsibility for the matter.

The CMC can also monitor the QPS in its investigations of referred matters. This can include receiving regular reports on activities in the investigation, requesting or requiring a certain course of action, and requiring a provision of an investigation report before an outcome decision is made. The CMC can, if the matter involves suspected official misconduct, also direct the QPS to make further inquiries and, in the case of major concerns, the CMC can assume responsibility for the investigation. The CMC is of the view that it is unsustainable and, in the long term, inappropriate and ineffective for the CMC to provide close scrutiny for every complainant, let alone investigate every complaint. The CMC also stated that it is important that the QPS takes responsibility for ensuring high standards of conduct and maintaining public confidence.

In 2006, the Parliamentary Crime and Misconduct Committee noted that timeliness of misconduct assessments and investigations both by the CMC and by units of public administration was a concern and recommended that timeliness be carefully addressed and closely monitored (Parliamentary Crime and Misconduct Committee, 2006). In response, the CMC has implemented processes that allow devolved decision making and complaint assessment based on defined levels of complaints and seriousness. This includes a process described as "preassessing a whole range of types of conduct complained about" to identify those that are suitable for the QPS to deal with straight away. This is allowed through Section 40 of the CMC Act 2001, which provides the CMC with the power to modify the obligation to notify it of complaints, and give directions as to the way in which complaints must be referred by the QPS. These directions allow the QPS to notify the CMC of less serious complaints in the form of a schedule, once a week, rather than notify each individual complaint immediately and have to wait for it to be assessed by the CMC and referred back before the QPS can take any action. The process was described by CMC as "working reasonably well" and the 2009 Parliamentary Committee review of the CMC stated that, while submissions were still received in relation to timeliness, "in the main, timeliness does not seem to be the problem it once was" (Parliamentary Crime and Misconduct Committee, 2009, p. 33).

Complaint Resolution

Also aimed at reducing timeliness of complaint handling is the CMC–QPS joint Project Verity, focused on local management of complaints within the QPS (discussed in more detail in the first section, Queensland Police). Verity particularly focuses on resolving complainants' concerns, and mediation, in the broader sense, was mentioned: "... mediation that covers a broad range of bringing together the parties and working through the issues." This was highlighted as particularly relevant for indigenous complaints where it was noted that often complaints are an indicator of underlying broader concerns where, as the CMC explained, if you deal strictly with the complaint, you do not necessarily deal with the issues that have led to it, which may cause continuing concerns.

Complaint Investigation

While a very small proportion of complaints received by the CMC result in CMC investigations, it was noted that "some very important investigations have come by way of complaints" and that complaints were responsible for approximately half of the investigations conducted. The remaining investigations were said to have stemmed from a variety of intelligence-gathering sources, including the CMC's own crime-related functions, human sources, and covert operatives. The CMC also has a Strategic Intelligence Unit that identifies targets for investigation as well as recommending methods for proactive investigation of official misconduct.

While the CMC does employ its own civilian investigators, it also has police officers from the QPS "seconded" to the CMC due to the particular skills and experience of police officers in investigations. QPS officers can spend time attached to the CMC working in both crime and misconduct areas investigations, and can be seconded from the QPS to work on specific operations. The 2008–2009 QPS Annual Report (Queensland Police Service,

2009) states that, during that reporting period, 73 QPS officers were on secondment (temporary assignment) to the CMC.

Powers

The CMC has a range of powers to aid its misconduct investigation function. Powers under the CMC Act 2001 include requiring a person to produce records or other items relevant to an investigation, including financial documents, and the power to compel people to attend hearings, both public and private. Witnesses can be required as well to answer questions even where the answers could incriminate them. However, self-incriminating evidence gained through this coercive questioning cannot be used against the person in either civil or criminal proceedings (unless witnesses give false answers, which would constitute perjury). The power to conduct hearings is viewed as "a potent investigative tool because it greatly enhances our ability to break through the 'wall of silence' that frequently characterises major crime and misconduct" (Crime and Misconduct Commission, 2009c, p. 11).

The CMC can enter agencies to inspect, remove, or take copies of documents or items relevant to an investigation and can apply for a warrant to enter and search any "relevant" premises and persons on those premises. The CMC can also search without a warrant if there is reasonable suspicion that evidence will be destroyed, concealed, or diminished if not immediately searched and seized.

The CMC also has powers to use covert techniques to investigate corruption and misconduct. The CMC can use controlled operations, including allowing covert operatives to use assumed identities and to engage in unlawful activities for the purposes of the investigation to gather evidence. Physical and electronic surveillance is possible through applications for warrants, for example, applications can be made to the Supreme Court for a surveillance device to intercept conversations, and this has been broadened to allow warrants to be obtained for a "relevant place" even where a named person cannot be identified as a suspect.

Through the Telecommunications Interception Act 2009 (Qld) and an amendment to the Telecommunications (Interception and Access) Act 1979 (Cth), the CMC was granted the power to use telephone interception devices through application for warrants. The Parliamentary Crime and Misconduct Committee (2009) recommended that "the Crime and Misconduct Commission be funded to operate its own telecommunications interception (TI) facility, separate from any to be utilised by the Queensland Police Service" (PCMC, 2009, p. ix). However, in practice, the CMC's utilisation of the TI function is not totally independent of the QPS.

Integrity Testing

The CMC engages in integrity testing of Queensland police officers, but on a targeted rather than random basis. Random integrity testing was not seen as a productive use of resources, while targeted was viewed as an investigative tool. However, criteria have been developed in order to assess the seriousness of the response against the seriousness of the case, for example, only in cases where a criminal offence that might warrant dismissal is suggested. The CMC explained that "it's really about having a good framework, making appropriate inspections, integrity testing with some good criteria, and some good operating procedures." The CMC stated that it communicated with other agencies in trying to develop best practice and to make the most of resources. The CMC also explained that tests could be used as a tool to inform an operation or to gather evidence, and that investigative tools complement one another depending on the aim. Most importantly, it was stated that it is necessary to plan for a pass as much as a fail of an integrity test: "In the old days the thought of [an] integrity test was really trying to make someone do the wrong thing. It almost steered them toward that path, and now it's purely a true test, and you need to manage for the pass as much as manage for the failure."

Outcomes

CMC investigations were described as not only focused on the conduct of the individual and whether there's evidence to support (or refute) specific allegations, but also "public hearings have shown what the systemic issues are here, what lessons can be learned across the sector." Indeed, the importance of investigations was highlighted to be beyond individual conduct, but about changes to the organisation as a result of investigations and recommendations. Thus, implementation and impact, in terms of the effectiveness of implementation, of changes needed to be monitored. In light of this observation, the CMC noted that it encouraged prompt incident reviews within the QPS in order to gather information, learn how to respond to the issues, and train and educate members of the service.

In terms of more direct outcomes for the subjects of investigation, the CMC does not have the power to make findings (of guilt or otherwise) from an investigation or to discipline people directly. However, it can refer the evidence gathered on a matter to the Director of Public Prosecutions to decide whether to pursue criminal prosecution, or to the appropriate agency to consider disciplinary action against those involved. The CMC can also bring disciplinary proceedings for official misconduct to the newly established Queensland Civil and Administrative tribunal; previously, these proceedings were conducted before the Misconduct Tribunal.

Witness Support

The CMC has an important witness protection function offering Queensland's only witness protection service for witnesses assisting law enforcement in general crime matters as well as corruption or misconduct. Witness protection can be provided where a person's safety is at risk or he/she may be subject to intimidation or harassment because of assisting the CMC. The CMC can apply to the Supreme Court for an injunction to restrain conduct or proposed conduct that would constitute victimisation. The CMC offers an Advanced Diploma in Witness Protection course to the QPS for police officers who work in relevant areas; it is offered as well nationally to other agencies. The course is registered through the Department of Education and Training.

The importance of whistleblowers was highlighted as a source of information, and particularly useful in investigations. Indeed whistleblowers were described by the CMC as "a very important stakeholder in many of our strategies." This importance is recognised through ensuring an appropriate framework to manage whistleblowers and giving whistleblowers confidence in the process. The CMC, therefore, had conducted an audit of complaints that involve whistleblowers and to ensure that they are dealt with appropriately and it was stated that "we're certainly seeing evidence that in recent times police services do deal with those well."

Early Intervention/Complaint Profiling

The CMC uses data on "associations" between recorded matters in its complaints management system to pick up those that are linked. This enhances the profiling of, for example, individuals, districts, stations, and allegation types as part of a quarterly monitoring process in order to highlight issues of concern that may require attention. Responses to such issues could include an investigation or close monitoring by the CMC or a discussion with the QPS in terms of action it could take. The analysis could also form the basis for a more formal audit. Patterns may arise as well in complaints that, individually, might not be serious enough to warrant CMC attention, but in number may indicate a more serious underlying issue that the CMC will explore. It was noted by the CMC that this was the case where similar complaints are received both from the public and internally from police themselves.

Risk Management

The quarterly reports described above are used to identify potential risks and emerging complaint trends and issues at a strategic level. The CMC also conducts misconduct prevention system reviews and risk management system reviews to identify activities and practices that pose a risk of misconduct, and designs strategies to minimise those risks. The CMC also provides advice on how agencies can formulate their own anticorruption plans, providing checklists for assessing the plans in terms of coverage and assisting in developing corruption risk assessments and misconduct prevention strategies.

Risks in targeted areas are identified through specific reviews and evaluations, either conducted by the CMC or with CMC involvement with the QPS committee that conducts the reviews. For example, the CMC has reviewed the QPS dog squad, use of OC (pepper) spray, and, more recently, together with the QPS, conducted a review on the QPS Taser policy including their training and monitoring practices.

In terms of managing risks from a longer term perspective, Project Verity was highlighted as being designed to influence risks within the QPS through embedding a strong culture of integrity within the service and providing the opportunity for managers at the appropriate local level to take responsibility and be accountable for the culture, conduct, and behaviour of their officers. The CMC noted that "to maximise the opportunity to reduce misconduct, you've got to get that happening from within, rather than imposed upon from an external source."

Ethics Training and Education

CMC staff from the Research and Prevention area and also Integrity Services deliver lectures to the Queensland police recruits at the academy on ethics as well as the role of the CMC. The CMC also conducts ethics surveys of recruits and first-year constables annually or biannually. The process of these surveys has recently been updated in order to provide more timely feedback to the academy: "We're now giving virtually instant feedback to the academy on the findings so that they can actually make it more useful." Improvements to the survey itself were described in terms of updating the scenarios presented and improving the integration of these items with theory. However, while this has improved monitoring and feedback, some concern was expressed regarding a "slippage" in ethical standards of new officers. This was also noted to reflect the results of public attitude surveys, also conducted by the CMC yearly from 1995: "The public attitude surveys suggest perhaps the ethical attitudes of the recruits and certainly the first-year constables is not as high as it was a few years ago. That the standards are dropping."

The CMC also provides a range of written guidance resources, including advisory papers, training materials, toolkits, checklists, and guidelines. The Building Capacity series offers written guides designed to build an agency's own capacity for dealing with particular problems. The series focused on specific issues, such as conflicts of interest, outside employment, and development and revision of codes of conduct to highlight potential risks and provide advice for managing, preventing, and dealing with those risks.

Misconduct prevention advice is provided during complaints assessments and misconduct investigations and the results of audits and reviews are used to help agencies build their capacity to prevent and deal with misconduct. Outreach activities are also conducted including making regional visits to deliver advice through presentations and seminars, and conducting meetings with agencies about concerns in relation to any individual complaints. Thus, regional visits can be focused around particular issues that have been highlighted through complaints or audits, or can be used to provide an opportunity for regions to highlight their own areas of concern and seek advice. This work, however, was described as resource intensive and it was noted that it is important to ensure that such work is carried out in a way that is most productive. The CMC also keeps in contact with agencies and stakeholders through distribution of an electronic newsletter, for example, to agency liaison officers.

Queensland Emerging Issues

Innovative Strategies

The Queensland police oversight model is seeing increasing devolution of responsibility for investigating police complaints, with more matters being referred to the QPS to deal with and only the most serious matters investigated independently by the CMC. A recent report by the CMC stated its position as strongly supporting devolution of responsibility for action in relation to QPS standards, stating:

> The CMC is strongly of the view that one of the most effective ways in which the QPS can engender public confidence, protect its reputation, and maintain high standards and the self-esteem of its members is to be seen to take certain, timely, responsive, and decisive action when there is a failure to meet these standards and obligations (Crime and Misconduct Commission, 2010b, p. xxviii).

Indeed, the CMC has a wider task than dealing with complaints against the QPS. The CMC provides independent oversight to all public sector agencies in Queensland and also performs witness protection and serious crime investigation. With regard to the latter, the CMC is, therefore, both a law enforcement agency and an oversight body of law enforcement. Indeed, Queensland police officers are regularly seconded to the CMC to aid investigations, both in the crime and the corruption and misconduct fields, while the QPS is able to utilise the benefits of the CMC's powers, if necessary, through joint investigations. Some have highlighted the perceived difficulty in "walking a fine line" between maintaining a hard edge to ensure independence and that police are held accountable, and the softer edge of cooperative working, particularly in relation to specific investigations; the level of independence and reputation that may aid a deterrent effect may then hamper relationships when conducting an investigation.

The CMC noted that, in the longer term, it is better that more of its resources are utilised for activities, such as monitoring and investigating more serious matters, rather than receiving, recording, assessing, and dispatching complaints to the appropriate agency. The CMC explained that this does not mean that they are "taking a step back totally from complaints," the focus remains on making sure that they are dealt with appropriately. Thus, the CMC has been developing strategies around preassessment as well as engaging in greater communication with the QPS Ethical Standards Command to aid devolution of responsibility to the QPS for matters that do not meet a prescribed threshold. However, monitoring is still seen as important, particularly making sure that the minor issues are dealt with appropriately so as not to allow an environment that could lead to more serious issues.

Within this model is also a trial of devolution within two areas of the QPS. This is a movement away from centralised complaint handling to share the workload and responsibility for staff conduct among local managers. Project Verity aims to build the capacity of regional and local managers to deal with the issues that arise within their communities and involve their staff, and provides the opportunity for managers to offer a nondisciplinary response designed to correct behaviour, where appropriate, and communicate with complainants to resolve issues. Project Verity, therefore, removes a number of stages in the decision-making process regarding complaint handling with the aim of improving timeliness as well as providing additional outcomes to aid improvements for both individuals and the organisation.

This increase in responsibility and shift to nondisciplinary options for correcting behaviour has involved a shift in the disciplinary system for those areas subject to the Project Verity trial. The disciplinary system of the QPS has been highlighted as problematic in a number of ways, including the length of time for disciplinary action to be taken as well as the likelihood of the misconduct tribunal not supporting the decisions that are taken, particularly overturning dismissal decisions. While the Administrative Consensual Discipline Process has also been introduced to improve timeliness of complaint handling and the discipline process in appropriate cases, the entire discipline system is being reviewed and redrafted.

The CMC has recently published its report: *Setting the Standard: A review of current processes for the management of police discipline and misconduct matters* (Crime Misconduct Commission, 2010a), and its recommendations are under consideration by the Queensland government. The CMC stated that implementation of the response to these recommendations may well have a significant impact on the police oversight model.

Successful Strategies

This section outlines the strategies that the agencies identified as being particularly successful.

Early Intervention

The QPS identified early intervention systems as "a very worthwhile initiative." Identifying at-risk individuals and work units, and utilising information from multiple sources to assess a problem and get an appropriate response was seen as the way forward. Particularly, though, the opportunity to enact an intervention in "real time" and consistent with a Human Resources, nondisciplinary approach was seen as key: "… where you encourage people to be honest and forthright. … If you bring them in and talk about their complaint history and they tough it out and say 'there's nothing wrong I'm alright,' well, where has that taken you, what have you learnt from it? I don't think that's particularly helpful."

Good Leadership and Management

Related to the point above, the QPS identified good leadership and management at the appropriate levels of the organisation: "The greatest opportunity we have to reduce complaints is by having leaders lead and managers manage." The problem of utilisation of the disciplinary system as a surrogate for good management techniques was mentioned, as was the danger that a centralised complaint system allows managers to defer responsibility for their staff. The CMC noted that Project Verity was positive in terms of its aim at shifting responsibility for minor matters back to the local management level. However, the CMC also noted the importance of good leadership for the QPS and that attention needed to be paid to supervisors and managers in terms of their skill level and support.

Monitoring and Audit

While the QPS Ethical Standards Command noted the value of its inspection and evaluation process, including audits of work units, it was highlighted that there may be room for improvement to maximise the impact of this function. Particularly, the notion of using the internal investigation area (generally reactive to complaints or other matters brought to its attention to investigate) to generate information that can be used proactively for subsequent audits of more systemic issues was highlighted as offering a good opportunity. This targeted approach was also noted for its potential deterrent effect: “There’s nothing that sends a shockwave through the organisation more than knowing that a certain practice is the subject of an internal investigation.” The CMC also said that its own audits and reviews are increasingly used in a more targeted approach: “... our monitoring activities, we’re getting more sophisticated in terms of the types of audits we do and our reviews, how we target those and the use we make of the information—that’s been very good.”

Prevention Advice

The CMC noted that it had increased its focus on prevention and particularly the ability to offer advice on evidenced-based strategies. Increased research as well as the increase in the availability of more practitioner-oriented research was credited with aiding this function. The CMC has produced prevention brochures and publications and, in an interview, spoke about targeting the integrity framework of agencies, looking at identifying areas of risk and working in an advisory capacity regarding best practice of risk management strategies.

Powers and Flexibility of Investigation Tools

The CMC noted that, in its investigation function, the suite of tools and powers available to it was particularly important. The options were said to allow flexibility to address matters on a case-by-case basis, think laterally, and choose the best course of action to suit the problem. The public hearing power was also noted very positively by the CMC as a particularly effective tool, including the publications and case studies that can be used subsequently for advice and training.

Emerging Ethical Issues

When asked to identify any emerging (or current) ethical or integrity issues facing the QPS, the agencies noted the issues outlined below:

Inappropriate Associations

The QPS mentioned that inappropriate associations are always going to be a challenge for police. Associations with criminal and outlaw motorcycle gangs were mentioned as well as associations with informants. Also mentioned as problematic were associations that were not necessarily problematic for criminal reasons, but for legal behaviour that was considered improper for police officers. An example of the latter was having a financial interest in a legal brothel. Such an interest may be considered misconduct under the Act definition if it is deemed “improper or unbecoming an officer” or may “not meet the standard of conduct the community reasonably expects of a police officer” (Police Service Administration Act 1990, p. 13).

Culturally and Linguistically Diverse Communities

The QPS mentioned the challenge of meeting the needs of culturally and linguistically diverse communities, and disadvantaged groups, particularly those moving to Australia from overseas who may have negative experiences with police in their home country. The expectations of communities in terms of police performance and standards of behaviour were seen as a critical issue. The QPS raised that it is important to know "what the level of service is that they want in terms of us meeting our obligations of the law, but also protecting the public."

Standards Slippage

Both the QPS and the CMC noted that a slippage in standards is an issue that needs to be monitored and risk managed. As mentioned previously, the CMC regularly surveys QPS recruits and first-year constables with regard to ethical awareness and attitudes. These surveys have highlighted a potential decrease in ethical standards over recent years. This was an area noted as needing closer inspection and monitoring.

The CMC noted that, while a great number of initiatives and policy changes have been implemented since Fitzgerald, there may be a tendency to be complacent over time. "It's been a long time since Fitzgerald and sometimes you need something like that to actually remind everybody." Further, with the introduction of accountability measures in terms of recordkeeping and decision making, the CMC noted that there was a danger that the increased workload this may generate could lead to corner cutting or avoidance of action in order to avoid the associated administrative load. The CMC stated that this was an area that needed to be monitored more closely to see what the risks are: "We need to take a look and see if that really is so or whether it's just an excuse." It was stated that there may be a balance required whereby more trust is given to the QPS and the CMC can be more focused in terms of the accountability requirements that they set.

The fact that the agencies are results-driven was seen as being potentially problematic when faced with diminishing resources, as that may produce a "breeding ground" for ethical issues. Cutting corners to avoid spending the resources that are needed to follow correct procedure was viewed as, potentially, the start of the "slippery slope" that could lead to more serious or widespread "slippage" of standards.

QPS also mentioned the effect of lack of resources affecting slippage, but in the context of recruitment in a tight labour market. While this was not considered a problem at present, it was an area of risk for the future, where police-to-population ratios need to be maintained. If the QPS finds it difficult to recruit the numbers needed, it was mentioned that changing its standards for recruitment might be an option for increasing the pool of potential recruits. ESC stated that "that's going to have great consequences. … I would never advocate that. I'd rather have numbers really lean than have the slippage."

Off-Duty Behaviour

The QPS noted that off-duty behaviour was an issue of concern, whereby officers engage in behaviour considered unacceptable for a police officer while off duty. Such behaviour could be engaged in during their off-duty hours locally or while on vacation overseas. In regard to the latter, ESC stated that "while they escape the jurisdiction of Australia, the reality is a police officer is a police officer is a police officer, no matter where they are, irrespective of whether they're on duty or off duty." Such behaviour is primarily that which would be considered improper or unbecoming, or fall below the standards expected of a police officer: "It'd be about bringing the organisation into disrepute." Despite being off-duty, police officers do not escape the disciplinary provisions and are expected to behave appropriately.

Generation "Y"

Generational issues were mentioned by the QPS as a challenge with which police have always grappled. The generation gap between recruits and senior members of the organisation was mentioned in terms of a potential difference in values.

Social Networking Sites

A rise in police officers' use of social networking sites, such as Facebook and Second Life, was viewed as a concern in terms of the information that officers are sharing on sites as well as their general behaviour and attitudes that are expressed and whether that meets the organisation's expectations.

Use of Force

The CMC mentioned police use of force as an ongoing issue. The largest category of complaints received by the CMC against the QPS involve assault or excessive use of force (approximately 20%), typically in relation to police interaction and arrest and not involving a weapon. However, the majority of these are unsubstantiated and, as the CMC stated, "Nobody comes out of those complaints with any degree of satisfaction." The CMC further explained that such complaints can often be an indication of an underlying issue, such as poor policing decisions, that needs to be addressed. Thus, it was stated that investigations of these matters are unlikely to be helpful in many cases, but resolving issues through alternative means and working with the QPS Ethical Standards Command and Cultural Advisory Unit to identify trends and issues in terms of individuals, stations, districts, or communities was seen as the way forward.

The CMC mentioned that the increasing options for use of force was also likely to bring some challenges in terms of ethical decision making by police. Indeed, use of force is a current area of interest for the QPS in terms of research, and the recent QPS–CMC review of QPS Taser policy is an initial step in seeking to improve use of force practices.

South Australia

6

The police integrity framework for South Australia consists of the South Australia Police (SAPOL) Ethical and Professional Standards Branch and the Anticorruption Branch, with independent oversight provided by the Police Complaints Authority (PCA). South Australia has not seen the systemic corruption problems experienced in the larger Australian jurisdictions, but police actions have not been without controversy. Perhaps the most notable case involved the jailing in 1988 of the head of the Drug Squad for on-selling large quantities of seized drugs. Police have been subject to oversight by the PCA since 1985. Its role is largely limited to monitoring police internal investigations of complaints, but it does have discretion to investigate matters as it sees fit (Police Complaints Authority, 2010, p. 2). Despite the relative quiescence in relation to police and public sector corruption, there have been repeated calls for an anticorruption commission as a precautionary measure against hidden or future misconduct (Prenzler, 2011).

South Australia Police

The Ethical and Professional Standards Branch (EPSB) incorporates a number of sections that review the ethical performance of South Australia police. The Internal Investigations Section (IIS) investigates conduct and criminal matters in relation to SAPOL employees. The section has a staff of approximately 15 detectives with experience in conducting serious investigations. The Professional Conduct Section has six staff members and is responsible for overseeing conduct and criminal charge processes regarding employees as well as providing advice or policies on ethical issues. EPSB also incorporates the Investigations Assurance Section (for managing Commissioner enquiries, e.g., into deaths in custody), the Audit and Risk Management Section, and an Intelligence Unit.

SAPOL has an Anticorruption Branch, separate from the EPSB (although there is liaison between the two). The Anticorruption Branch investigates corruption across the entire public sector under the direction of a Government Minister. The Anticorruption Branch also works in partnership with EPSB to monitor and review performance within the organisation with the objective of minimising internal corruption.

SAPOL has a Code of Conduct under part 5 of the Police Regulations Act 1999 and expands upon this with a Code of Conduct booklet. The booklet defines the standards expected of all staff and emphasises accountability and responsibility as well as encouraging an appreciation of the consequences and impact of conduct on the community. SAPOL has also developed a Leadership Charter that outlines characteristics of effective leaders who model integrity.

Complaint Handling

The SAPOL Web site provides information for those wishing to make a complaint about services received. The information encourages complainants to contact the branch that provided the service and speak to the officer in charge. Should this be unsatisfactory, complainants are encouraged to write to the Commissioner of Police to make their complaint, or report the matter to the Anticorruption Branch (when the matter concerns a corruption issue) or PCA. However, it is suggested that complainants try to resolve their issues at the local level in the first instance before considering central or external notification of their complaint.

Public complaints can be made anonymously and do not have to name the subject officer. However, members of SAPOL have an obligation to report a breach of the Code of Conduct. Section 38(1) of the Police Act 1998 requires police to report a suspected breach of the Code of Conduct to a supervisor or manager. Complaints must then be referred to the Internal Investigations Section, which, in turn must notify the PCA in writing and provide details of the complaint. Thus, all external complaints are registered with the PCA. Complaints are assessed daily by the Internal Investigations Section and any matters concerning corruption are referred to the Anticorruption Branch. Subject to determination by the PCA, SAPOL can carry out investigations or inquiries into complaint matters centrally through the IIS or, where matters are minor, pass the matter to the appropriate local area to investigate, make inquiries, or attempt to resolve the matter by conciliation. Annual Reports for 2007–2008 and 2008–2009 (South Australian Police, 2008; 2009) show that approximately 28% of matters received were conciliated each year, while 31 to 41% were determined (by the PCA) to not warrant investigation. This latter category includes those complaints where the PCA determined that the complaint was minor and only warranted an informal inquiry. Thus, the majority of matters are reportedly not investigated fully by either PCA or SAPOL, but subject to a less formal and, presumably, faster process.

Conciliation

Conciliation is an option for resolving complaints about minor matters reported by a member of the public (such as officer incivility to a member of the public) that even if proved would not warrant a criminal or disciplinary charge. Conciliation is aimed at fast resolution of matters with the process intended to be completed within 14 days. Conciliation can only be attempted with the consent of the PCA, SA Police Commissioner, and the complainant. Typically, conciliation will be conducted at the local level (local service area or branch). While not involving face-to-face mediation, conciliation allows discussion between a conciliating officer and the complainant to resolve the matter to a satisfactory outcome. At the conclusion, a report is provided to both IIS and the PCA to check the process and the outcome. If the matter cannot be resolved, it will be referred back into the complaints handling system.

Complaints Investigations

The Police Act 1998 allows minor misconduct to be dealt with through an informal inquiry rather than an investigation. As with formal investigations, the subject member is still given the opportunity to make submissions relating to the allegation, or to admit the allegation, and a report is still produced on the results and determined action (and a copy provided to the subject member as well as the Commissioner). Where inquiries find a member to have breached the Code of Conduct, that member can apply for a review of that outcome or the action determined in response. All such inquiries must be monitored and reviewed under the Police Act 1998 to ensure consistency and proper practice.

Where the PCA determines that a matter should be formally investigated by SAPOL, IIS will typically conduct the investigation if it is of a serious nature. At the conclusion of such an investigation, IIS must provide a written report to the Commissioner (delegated to the Officer Commanding (OC), EPSB) and the PCA. IIS is the primary investigator of public complaints and breaches of the Code of Conduct, and, when appropriate, also oversees investigations of allegations relating to police misconduct or criminality. Internal complaints (by members of SAPOL against other members) are generally not registered with the PCA, but are reported to the OC EPSB. The IIS will then determine the level of investigation of the complaint, where serious complaints will be investigated by IIS and minor complaints by the Local Service Area with some oversight by the Internal Investigations Section.

Powers

In the course of an investigation, IIS can seek information or property, including documents, from a person. Under the Police (Complaints and Disciplinary Proceedings) Act 1985, it is an offence to refuse to comply with such requests without a reasonable excuse or to knowingly provide false information. However, an officer can refuse to provide information if it may be self-incriminating, but this failure can be dealt with as a breach of discipline.

IIS also has access to resources to conduct covert operations in the course of their investigations, subject to legislative requirements. However, telephone intercepts and listening devices were discussed at interview as only used for criminal matters rather than internal conduct matters due to the legislative restrictions. Targeted integrity testing is also an available tool that has been used to aid internal investigations, but more associated with the Anticorruption Branch than the Internal Investigations Section. Random integrity testing is not used and was raised at interview as having significant resource issues.

Discipline

Proven or admitted matters of minor misconduct can be acted upon at the local level where officers can be subject to a transfer (for not more than 4 months), receive recorded or unrecorded advice, counselling, education, or training for minor breaches. The process is subject to oversight by the Professional Conduct Section (PCS). Outcomes of all other matters are dealt with centrally by PCS, and, where charges of a breach of Code of Conduct are brought, but not admitted by the subject officer, the charges are heard by the Police Disciplinary Tribunal. The Tribunal is headed by a Magistrate who is selected by the Minister and so is external from SAPOL. The Tribunal can require attendance of any person and the production of any document object or material, require answering under oath, and require a person to answer relevant questions. Failure to do so is an offence, unless answering or otherwise producing information would be self-incriminating. The purpose of the Tribunal is to pass judgment in respect to the charges brought against a member. The matter is then passed to the Commissioner to appoint a sentencing officer (typically an Assistant Commissioner or Deputy Commissioner) to decide on the appropriate action.

The Officer in Charge of EPSB determines which matters go to the Tribunal and also indicates the likely appropriate sentencing level of A, B, or C (where A represents termination, suspension, or reduction in rank; B represents transfer, reduction in pay or seniority, or fine; and C represents withdrawal of rights or privileges, recorded or unrecorded reprimand, counselling, education, or training). The sentencing officer will take into account this and any assessment of the Tribunal regarding the seriousness or otherwise of the breach of discipline, when making a determination of appropriate action.

Alternatively, where investigations uncover evidence of criminal behaviour, officers will be prosecuted in the criminal court. At interview, SAPOL highlighted that prosecutions of officers for criminal matters, as well as serious misconduct charges, were generally successful. However, it was also stated that, increasingly, officers will resign when faced with serious disciplinary charges rather than face the possible penalty. One SAPOL interviewee noted that this could be seen as a positive outcome:

> ... because they are no longer a risk to the organisation. There's a significant amount of work and effort in fighting a Police Disciplinary Tribunal matter, so all those resources that go in to that. So, if the person's willing, it's a fairly fair penalty.

This was noted as an issue for outside employers, though, where such officers who resign will leave "without a black mark against their name" such that their (alleged) conduct will be unknown to future employers. While members who resign are no longer affected by the code of conduct and thus cannot be held to account for alleged breaches, criminal matters are still pursued where there is evidence.

Witness/Staff Support

South Australia Police employees are supported through the Whistleblower Protection Act 1993, which provides confidentiality to those who make public interest disclosures and makes it an offence to victimise such "informants." It is also an offence under the Police (Complaints and Disciplinary Proceedings) Act 1985 to prevent or hinder someone from making a complaint. That Act also has a secrecy provision, whereby it is an offence for officers of the PCA or IIS to divulge information that was disclosed or obtained through the Act (other than for official or welfare purposes defined in the Act).

SAPOL has a witness protection unit that can provide witness support in criminal investigations, which can be utilised in internal investigations if necessary. There is also an occupation health, safety, and welfare section of Human Resources that can be drawn upon to support members who are the subject of internal investigations and/or disciplinary proceedings, and the PCS ensures that this section is made aware of individual cases. At interview, SAPOL noted that support was more often necessary, and utilised, by subject officers than internal witnesses. However, the PCA stated that it was important that members have lines of reporting available that offer support.

Early Intervention

The EPSB has an Intelligence Unit that identifies trends and patterns in complaints and misconduct. This is linked to the use of the specialised software system that supports SAPOL's Early Intervention System. The system was purchased in June 2007 and allows increased reporting capabilities and also the use of a range of specified indicators to flag individuals that meet particular thresholds (indicating that their performance or behaviour may require some form of intervention). Thresholds can be set at different levels depending on the position or work area, for example, probationary constables have a lower alert level. Indicators mentioned at interview included numbers of complaints (and of specific types of complaints), numbers of use of force, speeding infringements, and arrest–release (release without charge). The process also takes into account the context, including identifying the number of contacts that the subject officer has had in the community; for example, the number of arrests made or infringement notices issued. At interview, SAPOL spoke about the difficulties of comparing complaint numbers across different activity areas and the potential of trying to identify a benchmark ratio of complaints to contacts for different service areas in order to provide more contextualised indicators.

Reports and analysis from the system by the Intelligence Unit are raised centrally at biweekly Tactical Coordination Group (TCG) meetings. The TCG includes all branch managers and is responsible for identifying emerging issues and making strategic decisions, including deploying resources for managing identified problems. Patterns in performance and conduct that may require intervention are identified at both the individual officer level and the work unit level.

At the time of interview, SAPOL were also testing a process of identifying issues with local commanders and deploying EPSB members to the local area to talk with both the commander and the subject officer or officers. Rather than a disciplinary process, this was seen as offering guidance to prevent further similar problems. As SAPOL stated at interview:

> (It's) not a disciplinary process, we're saying, "Are you aware this is happening, how can we help you to reduce the number of complaints?" And, so we've gone down that road to try to reduce the risk to them as an individual and to the organisation.

Indeed, the goal of the early intervention process is to change behaviour and reduce complaints against individuals. While a disciplinary process may follow later if the intervention fails to correct the behaviour, the first stage is to highlight the issue and try to address it through counselling, advice, and, potentially, training. SAPOL stated that "the whole idea is to stop those individuals and to make people aware and consider why they're getting complaints."

However, while the focus for employees is on correcting behaviour, SAPOL noted during the interview that there was a move to harsher dealings with cadets and probationary constables with the view that unacceptable behaviour or performance at these early career levels was likely to be indicative of problems later in an officer's career. SAPOL stated that termination at this early level was a simpler process than the discipline system involving permanently appointed members:

> I think that's a good early warning system, since if they are behaving in a way that shows a lack of integrity, then the conventional wisdom is get rid of them then because (a) you can, and (b) they are only going to get worse later on. So, that's the conventional wisdom and I think it's a pretty valid one.

Risk Management

SAPOL has a Corruption Prevention Strategy booklet that was made available to staff in August 2007. The strategy provides a general framework for activities, responses, and procedures designed to minimise opportunities for corruption and build upon more specific policies regarding conduct of members. This is supported by the Fraud and Corruption Control (FCC) Plan general order, which outlines the roles and responsibilities of employees at specific levels throughout the organisation with respect to implementing effective measures in the areas of prevention (including auditing and risk management), detection (including intelligence, auditing, reporting, and protection), and response (including assessment and investigation). The FCC Plan includes the development of a corporate risk register (the responsibility of the Audit and Risk Management section of EPSB) as well as assigning responsibility to local service areas or branches for assessing their own fraud and corruption risks in local risk management registers.

Within this framework, a number of operational orders and general orders govern policy in relation to particular activities, such as policing public order, conducting raids and searches, and urgent response driving (pursuits). For example, the general order for pursuits identifies how pursuits will be managed, supervised, and the considerations that each individual police officer should take into account when conducting a pursuit. Compliance with these orders is audited by the Audit and Risk Management Section that also identifies best practice (and poor practice), although audits are typically of administrative processes rather than operational issues.

Procedural Controls

SAPOL has in place a requirement for police officers to video tape all interviews with suspects (under Part 17 of the Summary Offences Act 1953) where interview means any conversation. This includes interviews in the field as well as at stations. Where it is impractical to video record, options are to audio record or take a written record that is then read back to the suspect while being video recorded, giving the suspect the opportunity to highlight any errors. In the interview, SAPOL commented that, while this requirement was initially met with some opposition in the field, it was now viewed very positively, as are videotaping of cells and charge areas. SAPOL noted that such strategies "have really decreased a lot of allegations of misbehaviour

(a) because the police know they are being taped and (b) because an allegation can be easily refuted because it's all on tape." To aid the video-recording requirement, SAPOL has tested the use of personal body-worn video for officers, which was being evaluated at the time of the research. Tasers equipped with audio- and video-recording capabilities (automatic when the Taser is armed) are being rolled out as well.

Information technology (IT) access is recorded and audited regularly, with the ability to retrieve information on keystrokes retrospectively to the 1990s. Audits are conducted both reactively, where a complaint is received, and also proactively. For example, audits can be conducted to check who has access to particular pieces of information as well as what information a particular officer has accessed. Detectives are also required to keep an electronic journal on the networked computer system of their activities chronologically, including time, place, personnel in attendance, and what was done. Entries into this system must be completed within a fixed time frame before the system closes.

SAPOL also requires mandatory disclosure of criminal associations and conflicts of interest. Conflicts of interest must be reported to a supervisor or manager. SAPOL also described having a very strong policy regarding secondary employment with a variety of restrictions on the sort of work that officers are permitted to do. This was said to impact on the general integrity level of the organisation and that weakening that policy would create a risk.

Drug and Alcohol Testing

SAPOL does not have random drug testing for all members, but does randomly drug test undercover operatives who sign a deed of understanding when they enter that role, stipulating the random drug testing process. There is also mandatory drug and alcohol testing of officers involved in pursuit-related collisions, where the driver of the police vehicle is obliged to provide a sample of blood for testing. However, drug and alcohol issues were not regarded, at interview, as a common problem among SAPOL employees. Isolated incidents of drug use have occurred, and members at the cadet and probationary constable stage were said to have been terminated at that early stage due to incidents. Alcohol was said to be slightly more of a common problem, given general societal acceptance of alcohol use.

Staff Screening

After completing (and passing) an initial entrance exam, applicants complete a personality profile questionnaire. The next stage involves a panel interview using a "behavioural interviewing" method. This method asks interviewees to draw on specific experiences to offer examples of their skills in areas such as leadership, decisiveness, problem solving, stress management, and integrity. Applicants may also be interviewed by the police psychologist for further psychological assessment. Aspects of applicants' character and background are taken into consideration, as well as fingerprint checks, and any integrity-related issues, such as criminal activity or drug use, may be debated by an Integrity Committee comprising the officers in charge of HR, the Anticorruption Branch, and EPSB. Recruitment into special squads can involve additional screening, for example, provision of financial records and disclosures in relation to conflicts of interest and associations prior to appointment.

The Professional Conduct Section of EPSB also provides probative reporting in relation to the conduct of candidates for promotion and awards and medals. This involves detailed checking of applicants' records for any conduct issues and patterns. The promotional application also specifies integrity and conduct as the first selection criteria, asking applicants to identify behavioural examples of how they dealt with integrity issues and conduct issues. Integrity was seen as the key feature of the promotions framework. SAPOL stated that "you can have varying levels of suitability, but, if you don't meet the integrity one, then you shouldn't be getting a promotion, a medal, even a transfer."

Ethics Education and Training

EPSB is involved in ethics training at all levels of the service, including cadets, sergeants, officer training, protective services officers, and call centre operators. While ethics is taught generally within the cadet courses by the trainers at the cadet academy, EPSB provides sessions to enforce particular points. Ethics is also involved in promotions courses.

EPSB also provides advice and information to the entire organisation through the release of current issues papers. These papers concentrate on specific identified issues that have been highlighted as significant, widespread, or emerging. They focus on improving readers' understanding of the problem and consequences, including clear guidelines as to what is acceptable and unacceptable behaviour, and suggestions for response or prevention. Particularly, low-level breaches have been noted in this way, to increase understanding of expected standards with specific examples of behaviour cited as being inappropriate or breaches of the code of conduct. The SAPOL 2008–2009 Annual Report (South Australian Police, 2009) states that, at the time of publication, four such current publications issues had been released on SAPOL's intranet.

Police Complaints Authority

The Police Complaints Authority (PCA) was established in South Australia in the wake of other jurisdictions introducing police oversight models rather than any established dissatisfaction with South Australian police. The PCA was established under the Police (Complaints and Disciplinary Proceedings) Act 1985 to provide external monitoring, or oversight, of SAPOL's handling and investigations of complaints, rather than providing an independent investigative agency. Thus, while the PCA does have the power to receive and investigate complaints as well as an own motion investigative power, the expectation is that SAPOL will investigate the majority of complaints.

The PCA maintains a register of complaints and assesses the merits of the complaints that it receives. It aims to resolve issues, where possible, but primarily exists to provide independent scrutiny to the complaint-handling process and reports to Parliament on SAPOL's complaint handling. To ensure its independence, none of the PCA staff are police officers. The person designated as the Police Complaints Authority is appointed by the Governor for a term of 7 years and must be "enrolled as a barrister or solicitor, or both, or legal practitioner, of the High Court or the Supreme Court of this State or another State or Territory of the Commonwealth and has been so enrolled for not less than 5 years" (Police (Complaints and Disciplinary Proceedings) Act 1985, s.5.2).

Complaint Handling

The PCA can receive complaints directly from the public or will receive complaints referred through SAPOL (all public complaints made to SAPOL must be registered with the PCA). Complaints can be made to the PCA concerning the conduct of SAPOL officers as well as policies, practices, or procedures. Where the conduct of an officer is the subject of a complaint, the conduct must be in relation to official conduct where the officer identifies him/herself as a police officer. The PCA does not accept complaints about "purely private acts done while off-duty simply because the person is a police officer."*

The PCA can receive anonymous complaints (and also complaints from people who do not wish their identity to be made known to the police), but can refuse to investigate (or have investigated) anonymous complaints, usually on the basis of lack of information and the inability to contact to request further information. In order to increase the relevant information obtained in a complaint, complainants are often required to reduce their complaints to

* Online at: http://www.pca.sa.gov.au/PCAmain.htm (accessed 2 November 2010).

writing and a standard complaint form is provided (this is available online; it can be provided to complainants who wish to make a complaint in person at the PCA office, or can be posted or faxed to complainants by request). The complaint form asks for contact details of the complainant, details of other persons involved and the police officers involved (where known), details of when and where the conduct occurred, a description of what happened, and the conduct subject to complaint.

Complaints made directly to the PCA must be notified to SAPOL. All complaints received by the PCA are assessed and a determination made. This can involve referring the matter to SAPOL for conciliation, informal inquiry, or for formal investigation, with PCA oversight or direction; determining that investigation is not warranted; or determining to investigate the complaint itself. All complaints are sighted by the head of the PCA as well as other PCA staff to ensure thoroughness.

Conciliation/Mediation

The PCA can determine that, where complaints allege minor matters, attempts can be made to resolve the issues through conciliation. Conciliation typically involves a process of local management intervention by SAPOL. While not face-to-face mediation, the process is relatively informal and attempts to discern what outcome the complainant is seeking and to address that, if possible. The Act requires the PCA to attempt to resolve complaints where possible, but such a process is usually reserved for less serious incidents where the alleged conduct would not ordinarily justify a criminal or disciplinary charge even if proved. Resolution is usually successful where an explanation or apology can be given or where the complaint is the result of a misunderstanding that can be rectified.

The PCA explained that most complainants are looking to be heard, and the conduct that has affected them to be addressed, in order to improve the quality of service for others. Many complainants were described as very reasonable in accepting explanations of conduct, while some look for an apology. In relation to the latter, the PCA pointed out at interview that civil law now allows formal expression of regret without admitting liability.

While the PCA may not act as the conciliating officer, it does determine if the complaint is suitable for conciliation attempts and may conduct initial inquiries or review matters to aid the conciliation process. The PCA also receives a copy of the report on the matter, reviews the action taken, and considers whether conciliation was successful. This can involve the PCA contacting the complainant directly to discuss his/her satisfaction with the outcome.

Complaints Investigations

While the majority of investigations are carried out by SAPOL's Internal Investigations Section (as determined by the PCA), the PCA does investigate some complaints independently. These matters include cases of complaints against police officers who are of equivalent rank or senior to the head of the SAPOL Internal Investigations Section (IIS), complaints that concern officers within the IIS as well as public servants who are employed by SAPOL, and also complaints that relate to issues of policy or procedure rather than conduct per se. Aside from these special categories of complaints, the Police (Complaints and Disciplinary Proceedings) Act 1985 also provides for the PCA to investigate any matter that it considers necessary, or indeed where there are no reasons that SAPOL IIS should investigate. Such cases are rare, however.

Where matters are referred to SAPOL's IIS for investigation, the PCA can oversight that investigation, direct the investigation, or conduct an investigation jointly with IIS. In practice, the PCA noted that they "maintain fairly close links with the investigation as it goes along." In determining a response to complaints, the PCA stated that they consider the inherent significance of the allegation and the complaint, what various methods of investigation are likely to ascertain, how serious it is, the likelihood of proving it, and the likelihood of being able to take remedial action.

The PCA can determine to conduct an investigation itself in relation to a received complaint. Further, the PCA has an own motion investigation power, whereby it can decide to investigate matters in the public domain (not subject to specific complaint) that are of public interest, and that concern possible misconduct or raise questions regarding policies and practices of police. Decisions to investigate such matters must be communicated to the Commissioner of SAPOL and can only begin with agreement of the Commissioner, or in case of disagreement, determination by the Minister.

When conducting investigations, the PCA has powers to make inquiries and obtain information, or relevant property, documents, and records. This includes the power to enter and inspect police premises (and inspect documents found there), or to apply for a warrant from a magistrate to enter residential or nonpolice business premises. The PCA may also require a person to furnish information in writing, and require the complainant or a SAPOL member to attend and answer questions. Failure to comply with such PCA requests, in the absence of a reasonable excuse, amounts to an offence (for non-SAPOL members) or a breach of discipline (for SAPOL members). SAPOL members are not excused from furnishing information that might show that they have committed a breach of discipline, but they can refuse to answer self-incriminating questions. Furthermore, the PCA can direct a person (in writing) not to communicate to any other person that an investigation is being, or has been, carried out or that he/she was requested to provide information.

At interview, the PCA explained that, in practice, because of staffing and financial constraints, PCA investigators often recruit the aid of police officers who act under the direction of the PCA: "What I would normally do is own the investigation, but negotiate with police regarding the people who I want to run it under my direction and in conjunction with my own investigator." Indeed, the PCA noted that conducting PCA investigations using police personnel was advantageous in some instances because police officers have powers that are not available to the PCA. For example, where investigations may need to use covert methods, such as telephone intercepts, surveillance, listening devices, undercover operatives, targeted integrity tests, and informants: "They are all facilities that are available to us within the statutory scheme ... they (police) can (use those strategies), under my direction and subject to a warrant, if that's what's needed." Thus, PCA investigations are often conducted closely with SAPOL's Internal Investigations Section.

Outcomes

For all complaint cases handled by SAPOL, a report is provided to the PCA and the PCA reports to Parliament on the handling of complaints about police. In the case of IIS investigations, the PCA examines the investigation report and can request further investigation if it is deemed necessary. The PCA explained at interview that, while approximately 20 to 25% of investigations might likely be sent back to IIS for further work, this was not necessarily due to inefficient investigation, but an advantage of an independent viewpoint that may highlight a different perspective that warrants attention:

> We will often send them back because we think there are issues that aren't fully addressed or we've seen issues that the investigator hasn't ... not so much because the investigation was deficient in the first place, but that a different set of eyes has seen the problem in a different way.

Indeed, the PCA noted that investigations on the whole were done well and that quality had improved greatly in more recent years: "We're sending a lot less back than we would have 10 years ago. The police are doing a lot more in terms of quality control."

When investigations are completed, the PCA can assess the outcome in relation to whether allegations have been substantiated and whether action should be recommended. As the PCA explained in an interview:

> We can either decide to do nothing else on the basis that there doesn't appear to be a problem, or we can assess it formally if there appears to be deficiencies in either conduct or practices and we make recommendations.

Thus, PCA consideration of investigation reports must include a written assessment of the conduct of the officer in question and any recommendations arising from that assessment in terms of charges, reconsideration of decisions, actions to rectify the effects of a decision, or alterations to a rule of law or policy and practice.

Any recommendations made by the PCA are communicated to the SAPOL Commissioner. Where SAPOL does not agree to follow a recommendation, the reasons must be given and, if the PCA does not accept those reasons, the matter can be taken to the Minister. In the case of agreement, or Minister's direction, the Commissioner is obliged to implement those recommendations. Recommendations can target policy or practice issues as well as disciplinary or other action for officers subject to complaint. All matters that go to the Police Disciplinary Tribunal, and their outcomes, must be relayed to the PCA, regardless of whether the action was recommended by the PCA. All outcomes are registered in the PCA complaints database so that they can be monitored and taken into account if further complaints against the same officer or for the same conduct are received.

Early Intervention

The PCA does not have a formal Early Intervention System (EIS). However, the PCA does keep a register of all complaints under the Police (Complaints and Disciplinary Proceedings) Act 1985, which allows a less formal process of complaint profiling to complement SAPOL's formal EIS. The PCA explained that, when it receives a complaint, it will check the history of the officer concerned against the new allegations: "You use your history to build an informal profile and to tailor your tactics to the situation." This allows for patterns to be identified in terms of particular officers or particular types of conduct. The PCA and SAPOL communicate regarding patterns and potential emerging issues identified, including appropriate response strategies. The PCA also highlighted a process of "environmental scanning" to pick up on emerging best practice in response to particular issues.

Ethics Education and Training

The PCA provides presentations on all recruit and promotions training courses. Presentations include information about the role of the PCA and involve discussion regarding the police complaints system, causes of complaints, and some suggestions about how to avoid complaints. For promotions courses, particularly to the rank of Inspector, trainers provide ethical scenario role play strategies. With recruits, sessions involve discussions around highlighted issues; as the PCA explained, "I get them to work things out for themselves, what they talk to me about will shape that conversation, and I'll feed in trends, recent cases." The PCA noted that this method was designed to encourage internal understanding of ethical issues and encourage recruits to take responsibility for their ethical decision making: "If motivation is not internal, you're whistling against the wind. You can put up rule books, codes of conduct, but all you're doing is creating a catch-me-if-you-can culture." The PCA 2007–2008 Annual Report also states that courses encourage participants to view complaints as opportunities "for learning and improving performance and to approach the task of resolving particular complaints in that spirit" (Police Complaints Authority, 2008, p. 3). The PCA highlighted that the sessions it provides are also successful at promoting good relationships between SAPOL members and the PCA, and breaking down misconceptions. An example of this success was highlighted through the fact that the PCA receives contact from SAPOL members seeking advice or answers to questions.

Audit

The PCA has several audit functions with respect to inspecting records of SAPOL's use of telecommunications interceptions under the Telecommunications (Interception) Act 1988, operations under the Listening and Surveillance Devices Act 1972, and also providing external review of applications to SAPOL under the Freedom of Information Act 1991. Written audit reports are provided to the Attorney General on a 6-month basis, while applications for external review of freedom of information (FOI) applications have averaged at about 12 a year in recent years.

South Australia Emerging Issues

At interview, SAPOL and the PCA were asked to outline their experiences of the integrity environment in South Australia. This included practices they regarded as successful, emerging, or innovative and also emerging ethical issues that might need addressing.

SAPOL has had external oversight since 1985 when the Police (Complaints and Disciplinary Proceedings) Act 1985 came into effect. This increased the level of scrutiny of SAPOL and aimed to ensure public confidence in police. While the Act sets the specific model of oversight, the PCA explained that strategies have been built around that framework based upon experiences and what was known to be best practice at the time. Thus, strategies are subject to continuous review against the environment.

Innovative Strategies

Internal Conciliation Process

While the Act allows for the PCA to determine that a complaint can be conciliated, only public complaints are generally dealt with under the Act. More recently, SAPOL has introduced a similar process of conciliation for internal complaints regarding minor matters. This has meant that, instead of going to a full investigation that might take many months to resolve, minor internal matters can now be dealt with much faster via a managerial support process at the Local Service Area level.

Stakeholder Communication

The PCA noted that a conscious strategy had been to communicate with the main stakeholders in police integrity—the SA Police Association as well as SAPOL. Particularly, the PCA emphasised that the common goal of each of the agencies is to support the majority of police officers who are being let down by a small minority that act inappropriately. Thus, it was seen by the PCA as particularly important to have "respectfully, properly distanced conversations with all the players so that we're trying from each of our perspectives to put pressure on the same sort of misbehaviour and deal with it in a consistent way because it's in all our respective and quite proper interests to do that."

For example, it was seen as in the interest of the majority of Police Association members that the Association considers communicating with the PCA when making decisions of financially supporting members who face charges arising from PCA/IIS investigations. Such communication was only seen to be likely if a good working relationship exists.

Successful Strategies

Leadership/Management

Leadership and management issues were raised by both SAPOL and the PCA as impacting integrity. The PCA noted that effective and accountable line management has been consistently considered as important. Strategies that challenge and empower line managers to manage all but the most serious issues regarding the performance and conduct of members were endorsed, as was providing nondisciplinary management strategies that allow behaviour to be rectified without assigning blame or criticism: "You don't have to be wrong to be advised or sent on a course to do the job properly, to get skilled up. 'I'm doing it because I'm your manager and you need to know, not because you've done anything wrong.'"

SAPOL noted that the leadership offered by the present Commissioner had impacted positively on the integrity of the organisation. The Commissioner was said to have sent a strong message that integrity matters are dealt with very seriously.

Integrity Impacting Promotions/Medals

Linked to the point above, integrity, as a promotions criterion, was highlighted as being effective because missing out on a promotion due to integrity-related matters has a financial impact that can have a very real consequence for members. Furthermore, the Good Conduct Medal for members was also viewed as an incentive for good performance with integrity. As SAPOL noted, "I think that's a good method because people know that proven misbehaviour will prevent them from getting promotions and medals." SAPOL said, though, that decisions to exclude a member from receiving a promotion or medal must be based on sound data records and proven matters of misconduct.

Targeted Integrity Testing

While targeted integrity testing is not used extensively in South Australia, both SAPOL and the PCA noted that it can be, and has been, very successful in internal investigations.

Experienced Investigators

SAPOL noted that the Internal Investigations Section was improving as it maintains a "core group" of investigators who have built up skills and experience in conducting internal investigations. Thus, both consistency of staff and also staff training was viewed as benefitting the quality of investigations. This, in turn, was thought to impact positively both on complaints and on the reputation of IIS among the Service: "If the reputation gets round that these people do quality, impartial investigations, then that can only be good for everyone." Further, beyond investigations, the "collective wisdom" of the experienced individuals in the EPSB, with respect to the broader picture, was noted to act as a successful early warning system, where members are aware of internal and external matters of consequence. As SAPOL stated, "We see all the files, are aware of what's going on around the place, interstate, and what's in the media. We pick up on the issues and discuss them ... we don't just mechanically deal with all our files."

Early Intervention System/Complaints Information Management

The PCA noted that integrating information and intelligence regarding conduct issues works well since indicators for risk behaviour or poor performance may come from a variety of sources. Particularly, the PCA noted that identification may require the use of secondary indicators, for example, the proportion of an officer's arrests that are resisted, where it is not possible to observe the primary problem. SAPOL noted that the software system had enabled better statistical identification of such patterns and was a move in the right direction, but that the system could be utilised better to take full advantage of its capabilities as a proactive strategy for identifying problems. The system was credited with improving the tracking of complaint investigations, particularly those that are conducted outside IIS. Thus, the system also offers administrative improvements in following up the timeliness of stages of investigations.

Termed Appointments for Rural Postings

The PCA noted that termed appointments have been recognised as an important strategy for high risk areas, but that an emerging area that should be subject to this is remote area postings. The PCA noted that SAPOL was actively looking at this area in relation to the risks associated with small country stations that have few officers and various potential influences from the community, coupled with a lack of supervision of activity.

Emerging Ethical Issues

Generational Differences

SAPOL noted that generational differences posed some challenges around differing values or experiences in new officers from generations X and Y as compared with earlier generations:

Drug Use was noted to be more frequent generally among people of these generations than previously. Thus, expectations of applicants to have no history of drug usage were said to be potentially naïve and unrealistic. Applicants are required to self-disclose any drug use history, which is then considered by the Integrity Committee. Essentially, honesty in disclosure was viewed as a more important indicator of integrity than having never previously used drugs.

Inappropriate associations or conflicts of interest were also raised as an issue that may be more prevalent with new generations. This was said to be due to the fact that recruits were older and, therefore, entering the organisation with a wider variety of experiences and associations that may present certain conflicts or risks to their role. However, these risks may not be understood by the member. As SAPOL mentioned, "I think that is true about people not seeing that line between the sorts of people you can liaise with, then once you have those inappropriate associations, there's either the perception or the reality that favours are being done and I think that's a real risk."

Technology and information security was highlighted as an issue that was becoming more prominent. This was stated as due to the increasing reliance on technology as well as younger generations being more habituated with its use, which may mean that potential risks or integrity issues are overlooked or not recognised. As SAPOL explained, "The younger generation is so reliant on technology, they just take it as second nature, but it [the risk] is in the use of that information, the movement of that information."

Social networking sites were similarly sited as a growing concern for the Service, predominantly regarding conduct or portrayal of members on such sites. SAPOL is working toward a policy regarding conduct on social networking sites and potential conflicts between personal conduct and responsibilities as a member of the police service. As a SAPOL interviewee said, "some members really struggle to see any nexus between what they do off duty and what their job is and how it's seen." Aside from identification as a police officer on social networking sites being problematic for potential conduct reasons, identification may also pose risks to the member in terms of creating a vulnerability to be put in an inappropriate position, for example, by an organised crime group or other criminal element.

Increased Police Powers

Legislated increases in police powers were cited as a potential cause of ethical concern. However, the issue was stated by SAPOL as a concern regarding the legislation framework regarding human rights, rather than an actual conduct concern of the officers working within this legislation. Examples were given by SAPOL of changes to legislation that have given police increased powers, such as the introduction of organised crime legislation and the weakening of search warrant legislation. The PCA agreed that such legislation poses potential problems in that it indicates a shift toward increasingly harsh measures to deal with particular forms of behaviour. The PCA stated that "the biggest ethical issue I think is that we'll go back to the era of the ways and means act … where these are desperate measures, but they're for your own good, and historically that's always put societies on a slippery slide to nowhere."

Domestic Issues

Domestic breakdown was noted as an area of concern that can affect members and their conduct. Whether relationships are between two members of SAPOL, or one member and a person external to the service, relationship problems or breakdown can create welfare issues as well as potential risks. Examples of risks were given, including members using their position as a police officer to access information without permission or official cause or for one to use his/her position to have power over the other individual (in employment situations or more generally).

7 Tasmania

Tasmania Police has an Internal Investigations Unit (IIU) responsible for the investigation and management of complaints against police. Oversight of the Tasmania Police during the period of this study (2008–2010) was exclusively provided by the Ombudsman. Tasmania is another state where serious police corruption and misconduct have not appeared to have developed in any organised or recurring form. One of the most serious corruption cases involved charges of drug trafficking against Northern Drug Bureau officers in 1999 (Prenzler, 2011). Concerns have also been expressed about conflicts of interest in police investigating police. However, corruption allegations have been focused on politicians, especially in recent years, resulting in the establishment in 2010 of a new Integrity Commission, including jurisdiction over police. The Commission has investigative powers, but its primary emphasis is on education and advisory services for public sector institutions. In relation to police, the Commission's investigative work will focus on allegations of serious misconduct by senior police officers.

Tasmania Police

Tasmania Police has an Internal Investigations Unit (IIU) staffed by six full-time members (in 2008–2009), including a commander, an inspector, an analyst, and three investigators. Internal Investigations is responsible for the investigation and management of all complaints made against police. IIU also is responsible for investigating police shootings and fatal or life-threatening injuries caused to persons in custody or during the conduct of police operations. IIU staff mentioned that the coroner regularly reports his satisfaction with Tasmania Police internal investigations of deaths in custody.

Complaint Handling

Complaints can be made in writing, by telephone, or in person (with no appointment necessary). Indeed, the Internal Investigations Unit is based at police headquarters in a central position in Hobart and members of the public can walk in with a complaint and be seen by a member of IIU staff: "We don't tell them to come back another day, we give them the face-to-face contact." Complainants do not have to identify themselves in order for their complaint to be registered and dealt with, although most are happy to provide their names and details.

Complaint Categorisation

Complaints received by, or referred to, Tasmania Police were assessed and differentiated (at the time of our research) in terms of two categories: Complaints Against Police (CAPs) and Customer Service Complaints (CSCs). A CAP generally will include a complaint involving allegations of the commission of an offence or crime or complaints by persons arrested, intercepted, or interviewed alleging assault, unjust arrest, or other mistreatment. A CSC is one where it is clear from the outset that, even if proved, the complaint would unlikely result in action more serious than advice, caution, or counselling, but does not include circumstances where a crime or offence charge could be likely.

Initial assessment and categorisation is carried out by the Commander of Internal Investigations. The differentiation between CSCs and CAPs was introduced as a mechanism to improve the timeliness of complaint handling processes with "lower end" complaints, i.e., CSC, directed to the district level. The 2008–2009 Annual Report explains the CSC process:

> The objective of the Customer Service Complaint process is to record, investigate, and, where possible, resolve minor complaints in an effective and timely manner. District Commanders are responsible for the management of Customer Service Complaints, with Internal Investigations auditing the process. (Tasmania Police, 2009, p. 68)

The district will apprise IIU as to how the matter has been dealt with and IIU will also audit the process of district complaint handling. The focus at the lower level is resolution and, in 2008–2009, 40% of CSCs were conciliated (Tasmania Police, 2009). Conciliation could involve an explanation of police behaviour, for example, with regard to powers or legislation, or could involve an apology by, or on behalf of, the officer subject to complaint.

Complaints Investigations

All CAPs (the more serious matters) are investigated by Internal Investigations rather than at the district level. This is made possible in part by the low numbers of complaints received. Internal Investigations has three investigators with the rank of sergeant who conduct the investigations into CAPs, or, if the complaint is against a senior officer, then the Inspector or Commander of Internal Investigations will take on the investigation. The investigation reports are subject to a high level of scrutiny with the Inspector and Commander reviewing and assessing all completed CAP investigation files.

Further review is then provided by the Deputy Commissioner. The Deputy Commissioner also signs off on all disciplinary action.

After an investigation has been completed, the Deputy Commissioner and the Commander will discuss an appropriate outcome and write to the affected member. Outcomes can include one or more of the following: counselling, reprimand, fine, reduction in pay, reassigning duties, transfer, probation, demotion, and termination. The member has a right of reply, after which a determination is made about the outcome by the Commissioner. That outcome is recorded against the member's complaint history held by Internal Investigations as well as in the member's district dossier and internal dossier.

During the 2009–2010 reporting year, Tasmania Police developed a new system for investigations of CAPs, called the Graduated Management Model (GMM). The GMM's aim is for complaints to be dealt with "at a level commensurate with the seriousness of the allegation and likely sanction should a complaint be sustained" (Tasmania Police, 2010, p. 32). The process is designed to improve the efficiency of resolving complaints in order to improve the experience for both subject officers and complainants. Timely outcomes are said to decrease the level of stress experienced by officers as well as increase the impact of the outcome on learning (ensuring that outcomes are associated with specific allegations).

In cases involving criminal allegations, members have the right to a standard criminal interview with the right to decline to answer questions. Alternatively, a disciplinary interview (directed interview) can be held where the member can be directed to answer questions under the provisions of the Police Services Act 2003. The advantage of the directed interview is to uncover the truth, but the directed answers cannot be used in a criminal law proceeding against the individual, only for internal disciplinary matters.

Criminal matters also involve liaison with the Director of Public Prosecutions. The office of the DPP is consulted routinely by the IIU in cases of assault or prima facie evidence of commission of a crime or significant offence. The DPP will be consulted to independently review the file and provide advice as to whether or not a prosecution is warranted. IIU staff explained that they "do not prosecute anything without the sanction of the DPP." Aside from the expertise gained from the DPP review with regard to successful prosecutions, the review also provides independent support for the IIU to explain outcomes to complainants, particularly where the decision had been made not to proceed with a prosecution.

As part of the suite of investigative tools available to Tasmania Police, the IIU has the capacity under the Police Service Act 2003 to use covert operations, integrity testing, and drug and alcohol testing as well as provide witness support. However, none of these were considered necessary at the time of the interview and, thus, were not used. With regard to integrity testing, it was seen that a targeted approach could be used based on the threat posed or the information available, but that the behaviour of officers was not serious enough to warrant that tool at present. A drug and alcohol testing policy was under discussion for potential future implementation.

Complaints Profiling/Early Intervention

While complaints are investigated as they arise, patterns in complaints are also monitored at the officer, district, and behaviour (type of complaint) levels to proactively identify broader systemic issues. Spikes in particular types of complaints are met with tailored solutions. For example, where a number of complaints involving arrest and restraint tactics were identified, information was passed to the academy Operational Skills unit, which adjusted their defensive tactics training accordingly to target the behaviour. Further, where a number of assault complaints were identified, district Commanders were provided with information to enable them to identify the problem areas and the police officers involved in allegations of assault.

Members' complaint histories are recorded and monitored on the rationale that a member with a history of attracting complaints will continue to attract complaints (past behaviour predicts future behaviour). Previously, officers have been identified on the basis of having multiple complaints, or particular types of complaints, with a view to taking proactive measures to reduce the likelihood of further complaints.

More specifically, in 2003–2004, Internal Investigations, in its annual report (Tasmania Police, 2004), stated that it provided districts with multiple complaint profiles. Officers with five or more complaints against police through analysis of complaints received between 1999–2000 and 2003–2004 or who had gathered at least two complaints (from separate incidents) during the 2003–2004 reporting period were identified. Since 2003–2004, Tasmania Police data show that no officer has received more than three complaints in any 1 year (Porter, Prenzler, & Fleming, 2011).

While the small size of the jurisdiction has allowed fairly easy identification of problems in the past, in a bid to capture more diverse "warning signs" than complaint numbers and types, Tasmania Police now has software to facilitate this process. The use of such software allows more sophisticated and standardised monitoring of a range of behavioural indicators that go beyond complaints. For example, indicators may include firearm discharges, police vehicle accidents, or excess sick leave. The software also allows various levels of access for both inputting and viewing data, which allows responsibility for misconduct issues to be less centralised. With regard to access to information, the Operational Skills and Tactics Unit at the academy has access to view data, which will allow staff there to monitor problems that they can address through training (either by addressing issues in future training, or by retraining particular members if necessary).

Indeed, the approach taken toward identified problems is considered preventative rather than punitive or disciplinary. Where unsatisfactory behaviour is identified in a member, he/she will be encouraged to review his/her own performance. They may be recommended for training or for counselling by a senior officer at their district level in the first instance, with the potential for counselling (or reprimand) by IIU staff or the Deputy Commissioner if behaviour is persistent or more serious.

Staff Screening

Staff screening in Tasmania Police force is carried out at entry level by the recruiting division and academy staff. This includes high level vetting, a demanding assessment day incorporating scenario-based individual and group activities, a job suitability test (an initiative from the Australian Institute of Forensic Psychology in Melbourne), contact with former employers, and home visits to speak with the applicant's family. In addition, a psychologist reviews all applications.

Internal Investigations also provides reports on integrity matters on members who are seeking promotion, are nominated for awards or medals, and those seeking to extend their tenure within high risk areas (e.g., the drug squad). These reports include issues relating to the member's complaint history or any other relevant issue that is apparent.

Ethics Education

As well as complaint-related functions, IIU is involved in training courses within the service. In addition to regular communication with the Operational Skills unit at the academy (mentioned above), IIU staff speak to recruits and to the professional in-service courses at the academy. Sessions may be up to a half day and include information on issues affecting integrity, topical issues from complaints trends, and advice on how to prevent attracting complaints (or further complaints).

While all training courses have an ethical component, the academy also offers specific ethics training for recruits that is independent of Internal Investigations. The Police Ethics module for the recruit training program is delivered jointly by an Inspector at the academy and the University of Tasmania, and comprises thirty 50-minute periods.

Tasmania Ombudsman

The Ombudsman's role is to investigate complaints concerning the administrative actions of government departments, councils, and public authorities, including the police. The aim of the office is to resolve individual complaints and to promote fairness, openness, and good public administration. The Ombudsman can report on findings of administrative deficiency and make recommendations to improve future action: "While the Ombudsman has no power to enforce recommendations and is dependent on persuasive arguments, it is rare for an authority not to accept the Ombudsman's recommendations" (Tasmania Ombudsman, 2004, p. 4).

In relation to the police, the Ombudsman can receive and investigate complaints from the public regarding administrative actions (e.g., failure to perform required duty or whether policy was adequately followed). Complaints about operational police behaviour are outside the remit of the office and would be referred to Tasmania Police to investigate themselves with no further involvement from the Ombudsman. Where complaints are within jurisdiction, the Ombudsman provides an oversight role including monitoring the progress of police internal investigations and providing independent review of all IIU files and outcomes.

The Ombudsman also has an own motion investigation power, although limited resources for such a function, noting that such work was becoming increasingly difficult on a financial basis. The Ombudsman stated that his office is only able to conduct one own motion investigation at any one time and expressed the desire to expand this area in the future. While he explained that there were no issues in Tasmania Police that currently warranted such an investigation, the need could certainly arise.

Complaint Handling

Complaints can be received orally or in writing (and the Ombudsman can request that an oral complaint be confirmed in writing). The Ombudsman can attempt to resolve the complaint through conciliation, but participation is voluntary. Further, anything said, written, or done during conciliation is not admissible in subsequent proceedings held or action taken, for example, in a court or tribunal (unless the person to which that evidence relates consents to its use).

Where a matter is investigated, the Ombudsman's investigation methods are inquisitorial, but the work tends to be desktop, meaning through exchange of documents with the police rather than conducted in the field. Usually matters will initially be sent to the police to conduct an internal investigation in accordance with the procedures outlined previously (see the first section, Tasmania Police). The Ombudsman oversees the progress and outcomes of these investigations. Depending on the seriousness of the matter, the Ombudsman will then receive either a summary of that investigation and outcome, or a copy of the file including statements taken. Even where matters are less serious, the Ombudsman can request the complete file if it is deemed necessary. Furthermore, Ombudsman review of the investigation may involve interviewing the parties to the complaint and, at any time, the Ombudsman can conduct a fresh investigation of the complaint.

The Ombudsman's powers include the power to obtain information, make inquiries, and enter premises occupied or used by the police, and inspect the premises and items within the premises. It is also an offence to obstruct, hinder, or resist the Ombudsman in performance of functions, or fail to comply with any lawful requirement made. The Ombudsman also has search and seizure powers to support the investigative function. However, the Ombudsman stated, "I have confidence that I can rely upon police to provide me with what I need. So I wouldn't hesitate to use those powers if I had to, but it's just not likely to happen."

The Ombudsman commented on the process of police conducting complaints investigations and his office having oversight instead of a more independent model. While initially such a process seemed to lack transparency, he saw several advantages to it, and faced several obstacles to adopting a different model. While the Ombudsman lacks resources to employ investigators with the level of skills necessary for investigating police, there are advantages in having police investigated by officers who are senior and at a distance from them. Further, given that the complaints received are largely of a low level, the current systems were viewed as adequate. In addition, police had, on occasion, sought to increase public confidence in the process by proactively requesting full oversight in certain investigations of importance.

Another option for increasing independence and transparency in investigations involving police has been to involve an outside jurisdiction. The Ombudsman recalled:

> I've been involved in Royal Commissions in this state where we've been investigating police and we deliberately seconded police from the Australian Federal Police to come and do that work because we wanted to make sure there was complete transparency in what we were doing. That really is a matter of good practice.

Aside from the power to review investigations and their outcomes, the Ombudsman can make recommendations, for example, to change policies or procedures, or recommend disciplinary action against an officer. The latter would be the responsibility for the police internal disciplinary system to consider. With regard to making recommendations to the police, if the Commissioner of Police does not respond to the recommendations (either with steps proposed to address them or reasons as to why they will not be addressed) within a reasonable time, the Ombudsman can send a copy of the report to the Premier and Police Minister and could also report to parliament.

A further option is that the Act allows the Ombudsman to release a public report on a case investigated.

Where an investigation or inquiry reveals evidence of criminal conduct, the Ombudsman can refer the case to the Director of Public Prosecutions or to the police to investigate as criminal conduct (and to pass to the DPP).

Audit

The Ombudsman has an audit function in relation to police, regarding records maintained under particular legislation. This includes twice yearly audits of the records that they maintain of telephone interceptions under the Telecommunications (Interception) Tasmania Act 1999. The legislation requires Tasmania Police to keep records of, for example, applications for warrants, the discharge of those warrants, and the exercise of powers under those warrants. Similar audits are conducted for the Police Powers (Surveillance Devices) Act 2006 and for the Police Powers (Controlled Operations) Act 2006.

The Ombudsman also carries out a number of reviews of decisions not to release information under the Freedom of Information Act 1991, with police being the agency that has the greatest number of FOI requests. In addition, the Ombudsman is charged with overseeing the witness protection arrangements that are put in place by police under the Witness Protection Act 2000. However, the Ombudsman explained that this has never been used due to the absence of serious organised crime problems in Tasmania.

Tasmania Emerging Issues

Innovative Strategies

The Ombudsman provides an independent review and investigation function for Tasmania Police. However, in practice, the office is limited in terms of resources, jurisdiction (administrative matters only), and power to effect change. While the size of the jurisdiction and its apparent lack of serious or organised crime or corruption served as arguments for the adequacy of this system of oversight, recent developments have seen the call for a new system and the introduction of an Integrity Commission to strengthen oversight in Tasmania. However, given that its focus is confined to investigating serious matters against senior officers, the Ombudsman will remain an important part of the oversight framework that will continue to require resources for its police oversight function.

Further, much as the Ombudsman has jurisdiction over all public authorities, the new body will not provide specialised oversight exclusively to police. Given that the current Ombudsman commented on the lack of resources for employing appropriately skilled people for investigating police, it is important that the new body is adequately resourced to allow it to fully execute its powers of independent investigation in the police sphere should the need arise.

Clearly oversight in Tasmania is experiencing change with regard to the introduction of a new independent Integrity Commission. While it has been recognised that an independent body is crucial to maintaining and enhancing public confidence in the police, the Ombudsman stated that he was happy with the quality of police internal investigations, but that involvement of police from other jurisdictions to independently investigate police has also been good practice, on occasion.

In the context of the Joint Select Committee on Ethical Conduct in Tasmania, the Ombudsman did suggest that an audit system was needed to demonstrate the quality of the systems to the public. The Ombudsman suggested that a random audit system to check internal investigations would help to reassure the public and demonstrate that they can have confidence in the system.

Successful Strategies

Further examples of successful or innovative practices in the area of integrity systems were cited by Tasmania Police in relation to the falling numbers of complaints seen over the past decade. Figure 7.1 shows that police complaints in Tasmania have been decreasing. Since the division of matters into Complaints Against Police (CAPs) and Customer Service Complaints (CSCs), CAP have decreased by 70% from a peak of 185 in 1999–2000 to 55 in 2009–2010, while CSCs dropped by 54% from a peak of 161 in 1998–1999 to 74 in 2008–2009, but unfortunately rose to 100 during the 2009–2010 reporting year. Complaints received by the Ombudsman have also decreased by 46% (from 81 in 2001–2002 to 44 in 2009–2010).

Tracking and targeting officers receiving repeat complaints was deemed a successful strategy for reducing complaints against officers. The recent acquisition of the Early Intervention System software was aimed at increasing this capability to allow for more standardised and consistent identification as well as broadening the range of behavioural indicators of interest.

Increasing awareness of members, particularly operational police, in relation to current integrity issues or complaints trends was seen to be particularly beneficial. Initial reductions in complaints, potentially gained through the strategy above, has allowed Internal Investigations more time to devote to travelling out to the districts to discuss current issues with members as well as contributing to the more formal education and training events:

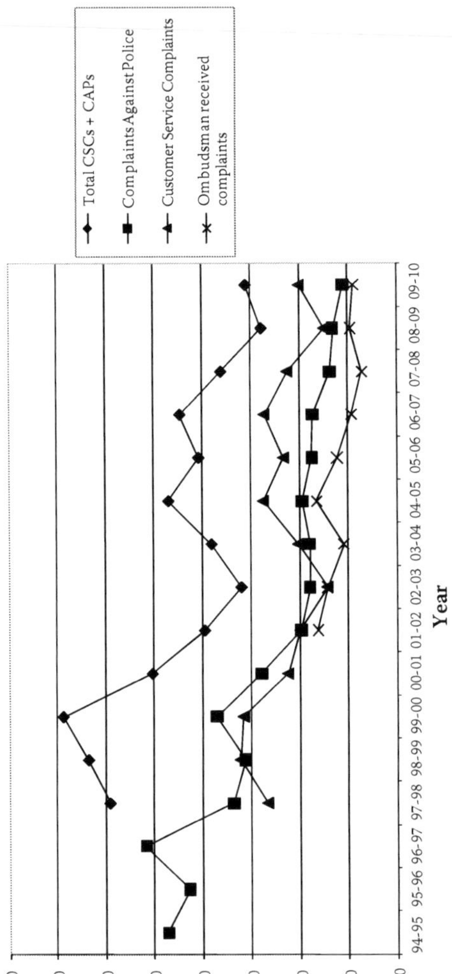

Figure 7.1 Complaints against the Tasmanian police. (From Tasmania Police Annual Reports.)

> On their training day, (we) speak to each member once a year at least. It's not a formal sit-down talk fest, it's a discussion about why complaints are where they are, strategies for the members to avoid them, we discuss their rights when they are under investigation, we discuss some very basic means by which they can protect themselves.

Proactive reviews of practices are also conducted by Internal Investigations to ensure that they are contemporary with the needs of the organisation. Particularly, current practices are reviewed to identify any potential gaps in the integrity framework that may need addressing with the introduction of a new strategy or policy.

Operational skills training at the academy has also undergone change since 2003. Training has become more scenario-based with an increased focus on deescalation and communication techniques. Increased realism in training allows for stress inoculation, while video recording performance in training allows exercises in accountability. Close links between the Operational Skills unit and Internal Investigations also allows for training issues to be identified from complaint trends and addressed.

Emerging Ethical Issues

Regarding emerging ethical issues, the Ombudsman did not highlight any specific areas of concern regarding the police. Internal Investigations identified a number of recent cases of plagiarism at the academy that are recorded as internally generated complaints. Internal Investigations is working with the academy and district training to address the problem and are testing a software package to detect plagiarism. Tasers were highlighted as an area for future concern that should be monitored for potential problems, particularly given experiences of other jurisdictions and the media attention that the topic attracts.

Victoria

8

The Victoria Police integrity framework consists of the Victoria Police Ethical Standards Department, with independent oversight from the Office of Police Integrity (OPI). In addition, oversight of Victoria Police's management of law enforcement data is provided by the Commissioner for Law Enforcement Data Security (CLEDS). Chapter 1 (Introduction: Police Misconduct and Integrity, International and Australian Perspectives) outlined some of the key corruption issues and scandals that have plagued the Victoria police. The Police Complaints Authority (PCA), established in 1986, uncovered a litany of misconduct cases. Nonetheless, there was widespread dissatisfaction with its limited powers and resources, and with police subversion of its recommendations (Prenzler, 2011). The state government came under increasing pressure to establish a commission of inquiry, especially in 2002–2003, with the escalation of the "gangland wars" on the streets of Melbourne and allegations of police complicity. In 2004, the government restructured the Ombudsman's Office to create the Office of Police Integrity (OPI), with royal commission powers reviewed by a Special Investigations Monitor.

The OPI has exposed corrupt practices in the Victoria police force, but it is limited to making disciplinary recommendations to the police commissioner or referring criminal matters to the public prosecutor. It has reported that police "accepted" 90% of approximately 330 recommendations (Office of Police Integrity, 2010a, p. 23), but it has struggled to influence genuine cultural change in a force that has long been seen as a law unto itself. A 2007 survey by the Police Ethical Standards Department found that two thirds of complainants were dissatisfied with most aspects of the way their complaints were managed, and this was related to the fact that over three quarters wanted their complaint investigated independently of police (Prenzler, Allard, Curry, & Macintyre, 2010). In 2009–2010, a number of failed prosecutions against high profile police figures and allegations of inaction and leaks put the Office under a cloud. Responding to these problems and to calls for a public sector-wide anticorruption commission, in 2010 the government announced the introduction of a new broad-based Victorian Integrity and Anticorruption Commission (Brumby, 2010).

Victoria Police

Victoria Police (VICPOL) acts within a number of legislative and policy provisions that impact upon the conduct of members, including the State of Victoria Charter of Human Rights and Responsibilities Act, 2006. The *Victoria Police Manual*, available on the police intranet, contains a section on Professional Standards and Conduct that includes all policies and information in relation to this area (rather than finding policies and codes in separate places). VICPOL has both a Code of Ethics and Code of Conduct. The code of ethics is a simple statement: "I uphold the right in my role within the Victoria Police Force by acting impartially, with integrity and by providing service excellence to everyone." The code of conduct is the SELF Test that asks whether the decision would stand up to scrutiny and is ethical, lawful, and fair. VICPOL also has a set of organisational values that underpin its activity in all areas and they relate to integrity, leadership, flexibility, respect, support, and professionalism. Responsibilities of managers and supervisors are outlined in the Professional Standards and Conduct section of the *Victoria Police Manual*, and include demonstrating and reinforcing ethical and professional behaviour, including rewarding good performance, taking action when employees are not upholding the standards, and providing supervision.

Specifically, it is the mission of VICPOL's Ethical Standards Department (ESD) to "enhance and promote a culture of high ethical standards throughout Victoria Police through effective prevention, deterrence, and investigation of unethical behaviour ensuring the continued respect and confidence of the community" (Victoria Police, 2008, p. 2). ESD reports directly to the Chief Commissioner, and the Assistant Commissioner of the ESD is a member of the Corporate Committee, which is the board of governance for the Victoria Police. ESD has approximately 165 employees, approximately one-third unsworn members, across a number of functional areas:

- Conduct and Professional Standards Division
- Risk Mitigation Division
- Targeted Operations Division
- Special Operations and Intelligence Division
- Investigations Division
- Financial Investigations Unit
- OPI and Ombudsman Liaison

Complaints Handling

The Conduct and Professional Standards Division of ESD incorporates a call centre for complaints, but can also be contacted in writing, including by fax or e-mail. VICPOL also stated during the interview that it will send a member out to take a complaint in the form of a statement if necessary. However, complaints about the actions or behaviour of VICPOL members are encouraged to be made in writing and/or using a complaints form that can be completed online or downloaded and printed. The online form contains an option to submit a complaint anonymously (the form can be one without the "contact details" fields). The complaint form asks for details of the incident, including date and time, witness details, police officers involved if known (names, numbers, rank, station), and comments (e.g., specific location, details of incident, actions of police).

VICPOL stated at interview that complaints were viewed as important forms of communication with the public and that VICPOL is trying to increase the numbers of complaints that it receives: "It's about maximising community engagement, openness, and responsiveness to people raising concerns about our service." VICPOL launched the Koori Complaint Project in 2006 to increase communication from indigenous people. The project is a joint venture between VICPOL's Ethical Standards Department and the Department of Justice's Indigenous Issues Unit.

Complaints received by VICPOL are assessed by the Complaints Classification Committee and recorded on ROCSID (Register of Complaints, Serious Incidents, and Discipline). The Complaints Classification Committee consists of a Triage and Initial Action Team that classifies files into category 1 or category 2 complaints. Category 1 includes misconduct, minor breaches of rules or procedures, workplace harassment, and performance issues. Category 2 includes criminal allegations; corruption; serious, deliberate, or intentional misconduct; recidivist behaviour; harassment of internal sources; and breaches that may result in serious disciplinary charges. Details of all complaints are forwarded to the OPI for assessment and reviewed regarding the appropriate action to be taken.

ESD provides a central service of monitoring and coordinating the handling of complaints against VICPOL. However, the majority of matters are now dealt with at the regional level, with ESD only dealing with those matters that involve serious misconduct or corruption (outside of those retained for investigation by OPI). To aid with regional responsibility for complaint handling and staff performance management, VICPOL has introduced Professional Development Committees (PDCs) for each region. The PDCs are responsible for promoting ethical standards and managing and monitoring local complaint investigations and resolutions, including timeframes.

Complaints Resolution

The Police Regulation Act 1958 allows VICPOL to try to resolve complaints through conciliation. The OPI must be notified of decisions to conciliate, as well as outcomes of conciliation. However, OPI can recommend that a complaint is appropriate for alternative dispute resolution, not requiring OPI review, which is then handled through the Management Intervention Model (MIM). Complaint matters suitable for MIM are typically lower-level, category 1 complaints. Such matters are reviewed by a coordination officer and the regional Professional Development Committee, which then assign a resolution officer at the region or department level. The resolution officer will speak to both the officer concerned and the complainant and may arrange a face-to-face mediation session between all parties, if appropriate. This might involve a police officer providing a personal apology to the complainant, or simply an opportunity to talk through the issues. While face-to-face mediation between all parties is uncommon, it is increasingly likely between the complainant and resolution officer. The ESD Annual Information Report for 2008–2009 states that, during that period, 57% of public complaints and 25% of internal matters were dealt with through MIM. This is described as a significant number that "could be partly attributed to the increased efforts by ESD to engage other departments in restorative justice discipline measures, thus moving away from the more traditional approach of punitive discipline" (Victoria Police, 2009, p. 5).

Complaints Investigation

Where a matter is assessed as concerning criminality, corruption, or serious misconduct, VICPOL must conduct a full investigation. Serious misconduct is defined as conduct that "constitutes an offence punishable by imprisonment… likely to bring the force into disrepute or diminish public confidence in it… disgraceful or improper conduct." Details of such complaints must also be provided to OPI (although in practice, OPI's access to ROCSID satisfies this requirement), as well as details of the investigation once it has commenced, and a final report with details of any action (to be) taken. VICPOL can also investigate where there is a reasonable suspicion of a breach of discipline.

The ESD has an Investigations Division containing approximately 60 detectives who have a focus on reactive investigations, primarily criminal investigations, but also longer term corruption and complex crime matters. VICPOL noted at interview that the Investigations Division of ESD uses the full range of investigative tools and also "a very close cooperative arrangement with OPI where we share capability." For example, VICPOL, when investigating a possible breach of discipline, can direct members to produce information or answer questions (although evidence obtained under direction is not admissible for criminal proceedings against the person). However, having no such power over nonpolice civilians, VICPOL stated that it can seek to leverage the coercive and inquisitorial powers of OPI in such instances: "If there are civilians involved in police corruption or criminality,

OPI's capacity to summons and secretly and coercively question them has proven incredibly useful."

During an investigation, VICPOL can transfer the subject member to other duties, suspend the member from duty, with or without pay, or order the member to take accrued leave.

Covert Operations

The Special Operations and Intelligence Division of ESD provides covert investigative support services to investigations. This includes three surveillance teams, a telecommunications monitoring unit, a police technical unit, and an intelligence unit with analysts and tactical analysts who are outposted to the investigations teams. Telecommunications and surveillance capabilities were stated to be used frequently, particularly for complex crime and corruption matters.

Undercover operatives are also utilised in investigations in both controlled operations and specific integrity testing incidents. VICPOL stated at interview that there was a strong interstate collaboration with the use of undercover operatives, where VICPOL can source operatives from other jurisdictions outside Victoria as well as providing operatives to other states.

Integrity Testing

The Targeted Operations Division of the ESD includes VICPOL's Integrity Testing Unit. VICPOL was clear at interview that random integrity testing was not seen as an effective use of resources and that only targeted, intelligence-led integrity tests are conducted. Thus, integrity tests are used as an investigative tool, typically directed toward achieving an investigative outcome for a specific operation. As VICPOL explained, Targeted testing is able to tailor specific testing incidents to particularly suspected behaviour, for example, drug or alcohol testing; "invariably we've found it much more effective to leverage a piece of work where the key protagonists have already displayed a propensity for a particular type of behaviour and then it's pretty easy to set up a scenario around that to test it. And, you also avoid potential arguments around entrapment."

Random integrity testing was discounted as a strategy because of a belief in the detrimental effect on staff morale: "It generates this sense of fear and mistrust in the workplace, which is antithetical to what you're trying to achieve."

Outcomes and Discipline

In 2007, OPI produced a report on VICPOL's disciplinary system (Office of Police Integrity, 2007b) making a number of recommendations for reform. Primarily the report recommended simplifying and streamlining processes as well as an increased focus on rehabilitation rather than punishment. In response, minor matters dealt with by VICPOL under the Management Intervention Model can result in members being issued with a Management Action Plan (MAP). MAPs were recommended by OPI to detail an agreement between the subject officer and his/her manager as to the behavioural changes expected and the action to produce those changes, such as reeducation, mentoring, increased supervision, counselling, or changes to employment such as a change of shift or duties. The MAPs are recorded on the subject officer's personnel file and the progress is monitored by the manager and fed back to the subject officer.

In more serious matters where an internal investigation has been conducted, the Conduct and Professional Standards Division provides a Discipline Advice Unit to assess briefs of evidence and make recommendations about disciplinary action or criminal prosecutions. Any criminal charges recommended must be referred to the Director of Public Prosecutions who will make the decision as to whether to prosecute, based on the evidence.

Where there is evidence of a breach of discipline, disciplinary charges can be brought against a member. Charges are inquired into through a hearing. Such inquiries are bound by rules of natural justice rather than the rules of evidence. The Police Appeals Board provides oversight of disciplinary charges with members able to appeal for a review of disciplinary decisions.

At interview, VICPOL explained that cases can involve both the criminal and disciplinary hearing process, but that criminal matters are typically pursued before any disciplinary matters: "We have to be very careful about pursuing a discipline matter if criminal matters are outstanding." VICPOL explained that this was due to a danger of obtaining evidence through a disciplinary, directed, interview that is inadmissible in court due to the view that the coercive questioning undermines the person's right to silence. Thus, disciplinary charges can be pursued after the conclusion of a criminal hearing, regardless of whether the prosecution was successful or not; where a prosecution was unsuccessful, members can still be charged with breaches of discipline and, where a member is convicted of a criminal offence, they can also be disciplined.

Where disciplinary (or criminal) charges are proved, VICPOL can make a number of determinations:

- Reprimand
- Adjourn the hearing on the condition of maximum 12 months good behaviour or other requirement
- Impose a period (maximum 2 years) of ineligibility for promotion or transfer
- Reduction in rank or seniority
- Reduction of pay
- Transfer
- Dismissal

Members can also be ordered to pay compensation, if relevant. Further, an inquiry can be made as to the person's fitness for duty.

Where a person is deemed to be unsuitable to continue as a member of the police due to either a matter of his/her integrity, or the belief that retaining the member would decrease community confidence in the organisation, the Chief Commissioner can dismiss the member. The Commissioner's Loss of Confidence provision was described by VICPOL as quite difficult to use due to the way that it is structured and that it is a nondelegable power (it has to be exercised by the Chief Commissioner). While VICPOL said that, where it has been used, it has generally had an effective outcome, VICPOL noted that the process was long and complex. Indeed, VICPOL noted that due to the length of time that it takes to dismiss a member under the current legislation, many members resign or retire before they are dismissed. Such an outcome, though, was stated to be positive for the force and encouraged. VICPOL commented that they have pursued legislative reform over a number of years to provide the Chief Commissioner with similar powers that are available to all CEOs of businesses and corporations. However, to date that process has not been successful.

VICPOL said the vast majority of issues do not merit dismissal and that there has been a shift in focus to rehabilitation rather than punishment. Indeed, OPI's report on VICPOL's disciplinary system recommended that punitive sanctions be reduced only to dismissal and that performance development instead be enhanced. VICPOL noted that many of the existing disciplinary sanctions, such as fines, do not resolve the underlying behavioural issues. Instead, VICPOL noted that the use of good behaviour bonds has been encouraged "as a way of getting binding commitments from members to change their ways. And, if they meet those requirements, then ultimately the matter is dismissed." VICPOL commented that the use of good behaviour bonds with conditions, such as attending recruit courses and writing essays, has been a positive development and a key part of the rehabilitation process for members.

Witness Support

All members of VICPOL are obliged to report any act or suspected act of corruption or serious misconduct. To support this mandatory reporting, the Police Regulation Act 1958 states that it is a criminal offence to victimise a member through taking (or inciting others to take) detrimental action due to their fulfilling this duty or otherwise cooperating with an investigation." Support for witnesses is coordinated through the Internal Witness Support Unit, which consists of one staff member who assists in access to support services throughout the organisation, such as through the ESD or local managers. VICPOL is accountable to the Victoria Ombudsman in relation to the management of whistleblowers.

Early Intervention

At the time of interview, VICPOL was in the process of exploring possible upgrades and expansion of its complaint management information technology (IT) system. The system in place at that time, ROCSID (Register of Complaints, Serious Incidents, and Discipline), was used for complaint management and tracking of outcomes as well as generating data for its Early Intervention System. It was hoped that the expansion of the system would allow inclusion of information regarding use of force deployments, secondary employment, declarable associations, as well as the integration of data around operational performance, particularly operational performance that has the potential for adverse outcomes. The new IT support is envisaged to aid cultural change in early intervention and staff development, with the intention of supplying real-time information to line managers regarding the performance of their business area and staff.

The system in use, driven by ROCSID, was described as requiring a fair amount of manual work to generate data that will run a profile or benchmarking process. The profiling process is designed to identify at risk individuals and workplaces, based largely on complaint data. Risks are identified through benchmarking complaint numbers of similar individuals, for example, by gender, rank, years in service, and duties, followed by region. The senior management responsible for each identified person or workplace then meet with ESD to discuss the issues and must develop a treatment strategy, which is reported to ESD within 3 months. ESD can also provide managers with individual profiles on request where a local manager has identified an at-risk employee who may need some form of intervention strategy. Here ESD, through its Research and Risk Unit, can undertake and prepare a risk summary for the identified individual from information held within ROCSID.

Risk Management

Risk management in VICPOL is largely addressed at the local level with central support from ESD. A corporate risk management reporting database was purchased during 2007–2008 to aid this process. Each department of VICPOL conducts a yearly strategic assessment that identifies its top strategic risks. This informs ESD's Action Plan, which generates, from the departments' assessments, the top operational priorities for the year ahead. Key priorities are also informed by a range of data sets, such as complaints data and civil litigation cases. Conflicts of interest were highlighted at interview as an example of an identified risk. For each area of risk, ESD provides suggested strategies and performance measures. This is detailed in a working template risk assessment for use by local level managers to identify and address their own risks. The VICPOL Annual Report (2009) states that, during the reporting period, information and guidance on identifying and managing risks was provided to regional and departmental risk managers in the form of a new training program.

At the corporate level, VICPOL has adopted a strategic approach to its integrity strategies, launching its first Ethical Health Strategy in 2005. This has since been replaced by two mandated items that all regions and departments have had to adopt and incorporate into their action plans: (1) conduct an ethical health risk assessment, and (2) implement a strategy to manage electronic information use (disclosure of information, accessing without good reason, etc.). The ethical health strategy has been redeveloped into an ethical health risk guide to support these activities. The guide provides practical advice on how to conduct the risk assessment and develop response strategies.

Procedural Controls

VICPOL noted that a great deal of work has been conducted to enhance procedures with regard to property management as well as interviewing and obtaining confessional evidence. Information management and IT security was stated to be an ongoing area of concern that was receiving investment.

VICPOL discussed the use of audio and video recording equipment for enhancing accountability. Initial rollout of in-car video took place in the latter half of 2007. VICPOL described that, at the time of the interview, a pilot of mandatory recording of certain specified interactions with the public was being conducted in one region. VICPOL explained that many general duties officers personally record their interactions and that this creates problems regarding controlling the use and storage of that data. Further, VICPOL discussed the debate around recording all police–citizen interactions: “One of the philosophical problems with mandating the recording of all exchanges with the public is the message that sends the community about whether or not we trust them.” However, VICPOL expressed the view that certain interactions that have the potential to lead to an adverse outcome should be recorded, such as arrests, use of force, traffic stops, and complaint situations. It was pointed out that such recordings should be conducted overtly rather than covertly, with officers disclosing that they are recording. VICPOL noted that recording of incidents had led to a reduction in complaints, including vexatious complaints: “It’s very, very rare for us to get a complaint where an engagement’s been recorded through in-car video or a team member of traffic management unit has walked up with an audio recorder. … It’s a great complaint reduction tool." Recording the interaction was noted to regulate the conduct of the officer as much as it does the members of the community.

VICPOL has worked to improve its management of informers, or human sources, in line with recommendations from OPI. Since 1992, VICPOL has required all criminal informers to be officially registered with VICPOL and has more recently worked to implement an Informer Management Unit and Dedicated Source Unit handling teams. The current Ethical Health Strategy Action Plan calls for the implementation of a "Declarable Associations instruction" for all staff, and also policies and registers for gifts and benefits as well as secondary employment. Professional Development Committees are tasked with reviewing all secondary employment approvals annually.

In relation to the Declarable Associations policy, members must register certain associations, such as with known criminals, and management plans are enacted for every association. VICPOL noted that compliance with the requirement was high as every member that was expected to have completed a declaration had done so. However, cases had come to light where internal investigations of members for criminal misconduct and corruption had uncovered associations that had not been declared (i.e., the member had completed the declaration falsely, or had not updated the declaration in light of a new association). VICPOL noted that, increasingly, workplace knowledge and communication was valuable in uncovering compliance with the policy:

> People in the workplace have a pretty good idea of who you're associating with and they also have a pretty good idea of what you've declared, and if they know you haven't declared it then they know that something isn't right and so we hear about it. So, that's actually one of the expected benefits of the policy.

Drug and Alcohol Testing

VICPOL commenced its "alcohol and other drugs" program in August 2008. The program incorporates drug and alcohol testing procedures for members, and revised policies and guidelines for drug and alcohol consumption. These services complemented and expanded existing counselling services available to members regarding alcohol and other drugs, with referrals for support being available through the Clinical Services Branch.

The VICPOL policy for alcohol and other drugs clearly states that illicit drug use is a criminal offence and never acceptable, and that consumption of alcohol off duty should be engaged in responsibly and should not affect a member's ability to meet the requirements of the policy. The Police Regulation Act 1958 allows for drug and alcohol testing of members under circumstances where it is reasonably suspected that a person's performance is impaired (targeted testing), after involvement in a critical incident (mandatory testing), and where a person ought to be tested for alcohol or a drug of dependence for the good order or discipline of the force. Critical incidents that require mandatory testing include an incident that resulted in death or serious injury or an incident that involved firearm discharge, use of force, the use of a motor vehicle, or death or serious injury to a person in custody. VICPOL does not have a random drug testing program.

Tests can be directed by ESD, but also by local managers at Inspector level. Department heads or Assistant Commissioners can also declare their workplaces to be high risk and, therefore, subject to mandatory testing. Thus, all employees in a workplace designated as high risk will be tested, typically once a year. Drug tests involve a urine analysis, typically looking for drugs, such as opiates, methamphetamines, and cannabinoids. Alcohol is tested by breath and blood test. Members cannot be prosecuted for failing a drug test. Results of a test can only be used as evidence against a member in proscribed circumstances, such as in accordance with the health and safety act, accident compensation act, and proceedings arising out of a critical incident, among others.

Staff Screening

The recruitment process for VICPOL was, at the time of the interview, undergoing review, and responsibility for recruitment had been moved from the Human Resources Department to the Education Department. Applicants to VICPOL are required to undergo a psychological screening test and provide details of any criminal charges, traffic penalty notices, cautions, and official warnings as well as history of bankruptcy and outstanding warrants. VICPOL noted that there was a move to developing a behavioural-based assessment process and moving to the introduction of an assessment centre approach as the final stage of the recruitment process.

All promotions applicants within VICPOL undergo assessment in the form of a risk summary that is considered by the selection panel. ESD also provides risk summaries for candidates for particularly high risk jobs or locations, for example, selection for high risk task forces, on an ad hoc basis. ESD also provides a number of targeted questions for panels based on the rank being sought, designed to test the applicant's thinking and response to ethical dilemmas in the workplace. Similarly, ESD provides a number of questions on the promotion eligibility exams, for example, for those seeking the position of sergeant or inspector. These exams are stringent multiple choice tests that are very difficult to pass, but which are a prerequisite for gaining a place on a promotion training course.

Ethics Education and Training

ESD has recently significantly increased its engagement with training and education in integrity-related matters. The Conduct and Professional Standards Division of ESD incorporates a Training and Communications Unit as well as regional Ethical Standards Professional Support Officers, who provide strategic advice on ethical health issues to departmental heads and their senior management teams and Assistant Commissioners.

ESD employs a Senior Ethical Health Initiatives Advisor who is responsible for knowledge management. Specifically, this role enables the identification of case studies and "lessons learnt" and the communication of that information to the Education Department, the Training and Communications Unit, and, more generally, across the organisation. This aids the learning of lessons from previous cases to be passed on to new recruits and other members during training.

Since the completion of a recent ARC (Australian Research Council) Linkage project on police integrity, training (particularly ethics training) has undergone significant changes at all levels. Subject matter experts now offer consistent training across all courses, such as recruits and detectives. Recruit training has also been completely restructured with a much larger focus on police ethics and integrity and including a period of field experience with a mentor that is then the subject of reflective learning at the academy.

ESD has a high level of engagement with the Centre for Investigations Training, which is responsible for detectives training, and also with Officer Safety Tactics Training (OSTT). VICPOL noted that a member of ESD had recently been released to the Education Department to head up the OSTT unit as a key way of driving culture change.

ESD conducts leadership training aimed to equip middle managers with an understanding of the goals in relation to ethical standards as well as providing the skills to effectively conduct workplace resolutions of complaints and undertake investigations. The training is designed to emphasise to managers that it is their responsibility to manage unethical behaviour in the workplace as well as providing the skills to do so.

VICPOL has recently launched information for employees on safe and ethical use of the "cyber world," including social media sites, such as Facebook, Internet dating sites, and e-mail. The information provides employees with an overview of potential risks for police and example case studies with stories from the international media, along with public comments in response to some of the stories. VICPOL has made available a number of fact sheets produced by the International Association of Chiefs of Police on a variety of social media. The fact sheets explain various positive, professional uses of social media for the police, including community engagement and communication as well as aids for recruitment and crime solving. A social networking forum was organised for early 2011 to further develop policy and management of social media use.

Office of Police Integrity

The Office of Police Integrity (OPI) was established in 2004 with amendments to the Police Regulation Act 1958, and then reestablished with additional objectives through the Police Integrity Act 2008. OPI has a jurisdiction over Victoria Police to ensure ethical and professional standards are upheld by the organisation and its members. The Police Integrity Act 2008 outlines OPI's functions as investigating, exposing, and preventing police corruption and serious misconduct through the analysis of intelligence as well as the analysis of Victoria Police systems. Further, OPI has a function to educate VICPOL about police corruption and serious misconduct and their consequences, and also inform the community regarding the performance of its functions. Since the introduction of Victoria's Charter of Human Rights and Responsibilities Act 2006, OPI also has an obligation to ensure that VICPOL's actions and policies comply with human rights, as outlined in the Act.

OPI is fully independent of VICPOL, although with legislative limitations in some areas. OPI reports directly to Parliament. OPI may take secondments (temporary transfers) of active members of VICPOL and, while taken less frequently in recent years, serving VICPOL members have police constable powers, as well as certain jurisdictional powers relevant to investigating some issues. However, while members on secondment retain their police constable powers, they are under the sole direction and control of the Director of OPI. OPI has direct access to a number of VICPOL's databases, including ESD's ROCSID. However, OPI's Annual Report for 2009–2010 (Office of Police Integrity, 2010b) notes that access to some necessary data has not been granted by VICPOL.

OPI is organised into four organisational areas. The Operations area includes the Investigations section and Specialist Support Group (including covert, tactical investigations, and high tech crime areas). The Enabling Services area includes sections of IT, finance, organisational performance, HR, information management, and policy. The Intelligence area includes professional standards assurance, electronic collections, intelligence, and security. Finally, the Strategic Projects, Education, and Legal Services area consists of sections for corruption prevention, strategic projects and publications, and legal and compliance.

Complaints Handling

Complaints about the conduct of (sworn) VICPOL members, former members, or VICPOL as an organisation can be made directly to OPI. OPI also receives notifications of complaints received by VICPOL. Complaints can be made to OPI via telephone, teletype, interpreter, mail, fax, or e-mail. However, typically complaints must be made in writing for action to be taken. OPI's Web site provides a complaint form as well as advice on what details should be included when making complaints, such as when and where the incident occurred; details of the police members involved and any witnesses; copies of any supporting documentation, such as medical reports or photographs; a description of what happened; any attempts already made to resolve the complaint; and details of the preferred action to resolve the complaint.

Complaints can be made anonymously, although OPI states in its online complaints information that anonymous complaints are difficult to investigate due to the lack of opportunity to request further information. OPI officers are able to discuss details of a complaint, as well as the complaint process, and provide advice to complainants before they formally lodge a complaint. Face-to-face appointments for such discussions are provided in some instances.

Complaints received by OPI are subject to an initial assessment by the Professional Standards Assurance Unit to check that the complaint falls within the OPI's jurisdiction and that a complaint warrants action. OPI has the discretion to take no further action on a complaint under certain circumstances, for example, if the complaint is considered frivolous, vexatious, or trivial. Matters initially assessed as being within OPI's jurisdiction and warranting OPI investigation are then considered by the Business Monitoring Committee (BMC) in relation to their fit with OPI's statutory obligations, the public interest, and finally the priority of the matter. OPI is required by the legislation to investigate any complaint that relates to the conduct of the Chief Commissioner or of a Deputy or Assistant Commissioner, but can also choose to investigate matters where (a) it considers it would be in the public interest for it to do so, or (b) where the complaint relates to practices or procedures that it believes should be reviewed. However, while OPI can conciliate or investigate complaints, the Police Integrity Act 2008 requires OPI to refer most complaints warranting investigation to VICPOL. For example, the 2009–2010 OPI Annual Report (Office of Police Integrity, 2010b) states that, during the reporting period, a total of 812 new complaints were received by OPI. Only 1.2% of these complaints were retained for investigation by OPI, with almost two thirds referred to VICPOL for action. Of the matters referred, about half were dealt with through local resolution with no subsequent review by OPI. Just over one quarter of all complaints were referred to VICPOL for investigation with OPI review, while one third of all matters did not warrant investigation or were outside of OPI's jurisdiction.

The BMC considers new matters on a biweekly basis, as well as ongoing matters, and prioritises the workload. OPI explained at interview that, further to the legislation requirements, the small size of its organisation prevents the investigation of all allegations against VICPOL and so resources must be directed toward the highest priority matters, with public interest and the potential for cultural change as major criteria in assessment.

Where a complaint is assessed as minor and not warranting formal investigation, matters are forwarded to VICPOL's Ethical Standards Department (ESD) for alternative dispute resolution (with the complainant's permission), typically without further involvement by OPI. Matters that are referred to ESD for investigation can be monitored by OPI and the investigation is reviewed to ensure thoroughness and appropriateness of the response. OPI can, when it receives a report from the Chief Commissioner of Police on an investigation, decide to request further investigation or take on the investigation itself. Requests for further investigation must be complied with by VICPOL or explanation offered as to why it is not warranted. OPI noted that, in the past, all matters handled by VICPOL were reviewed, including those referred for resolution rather than investigation. This moved to a model of reviewing all VICPOL internal investigations, but now currently only around one third of all complaints are selected for review. The number reviewed represents all complaints that OPI referred to ESD for investigation, as these reflect the more serious cases, plus a small number of additional matters. OPI stated that, typically, 10% of reviewed internal investigations are sent back to VICPOL for further work.

OPI is obliged to inform the complainant in writing of the outcome of the complaint, the results of the investigation, any further investigation, and any action proposed to be taken, unless provision of such details to the complainant is believed to be contrary to the public interest.

Investigations

Subject to the legislation and assessment processes described above, OPI can investigate matters relating to serious misconduct and corruption that arise from complaints by members of the public or VICPOL members. OPI also has the power to proactively conduct investigations on its own motion in the absence of a complaint. OPI stated that the majority of investigations conducted are done so under the own motion power rather than in response to particular complaints. This was believed to be largely due to OPI's jurisdiction of serious misconduct and corruption because "people don't complain about corruption or serious misconduct because most of those people have a criminal background or are people who are disadvantaged."

OPI is able to conduct own motion investigations into relevant matters that include the conduct of a member of VICPOL; police corruption or serious misconduct generally; or VICPOL policies, practices, or procedures.

Investigations can be conducted in the absence of any allegation or suspicion of misconduct against any particular member of Victoria Police or other person.

Powers

OPI investigators have a number of special powers delegated to them by the Director, including the authorisation to possess, carry, and use defensive equipment and firearms to enable investigators to perform functions and exercise powers of the Director in relation to investigations, or for their own defensive protection in the course of their duties. OPI can enter and search public authority premises, which include VICPOL premises, without a warrant, and inspect, copy, and/or seize documents and other things relevant to an investigation. However, seizure of documents or items may only take place if the document or item is relevant to the investigation and, if not immediately seized, may be concealed or destroyed or its forensic value diminished.

OPI can apply for and execute search warrants for particular premises that include both public authority premises and any other premises that are necessary for the purpose of an investigation. OPI can conduct examinations formally or informally, and in public or in private. OPI can summon witnesses to attend such examinations and give evidence on oath and/or produce documents or other items, and may apply to a magistrate for the issue of an arrest warrant to ensure attendance if a person fails to appear in response to a summons. OPI can also have a summonsed person charged with contempt if the person fails to produce documents or items, refuses to be sworn, or fails to answer a question.

Members of VICPOL can be directed by OPI to provide information and answer questions, including providing self-incriminatory evidence, when OPI is investigating a complaint into a possible breach of discipline. Where such a direction is given in an interview, failure to comply with it is considered a disciplinary offence. Evidence obtained through such a direction cannot be used in criminal or civil proceedings against the person with regard to that matter, but may be used for disciplinary matters. Where a direction is given to a member in the context of a hearing, evidence obtained can be used for some criminal charges against the person (in addition to use for disciplinary matters), such as charges of perjury or providing false information or misleading the OPI Director. OPI stated that the use of these powers is governed by a strict framework and that coercive questioning was typically an option of last resort. OPI noted that "the focus there is not so much to catch corrupt police, but to expose corruption, and one tool to expose this corruption is the use of these coercive powers."

Covert Operations

The year 2006 saw considerable enhancements to OPI's intelligence gathering capabilities with the granting of a number of powers, including the power to use assumed identities under the Crimes (Assumed Identities) Act 2004, and the authority to conduct telecommunication interceptions and receive intercept material, under the Telecommunications (Interception and Access) Act 1979. The Crimes (Controlled Operations) Act 2004 commenced operation in November 2009, allowing OPI to authorise, conduct, and monitor controlled operations for the purpose of obtaining evidence. However, the OPI Annual Report for 2009–2010 states that no controlled operations were conducted during the reporting period (Office of Police Integrity, 2010b).

Therefore, OPI can utilise a range of covert investigative techniques and can obtain warrants to use surveillance devices or intercept electronic telecommunications. An OPI report in 2007 noted that "OPI investigators have been able to obtain significant evidence through the execution of search warrants, use of surveillance devices, and use of assumed identities" (Office of Police Integrity, 2007a, p. 137) to both exonerate innocent police officers and expose those who are corrupt. At interview, OPI commented that "virtually every one of our proactive investigations utilises the covert area in some capacity or another."

The Covert and Electronic Collections sections work closely in support of OPI investigators. The Covert section is responsible for physical surveillance and employs personnel trained in surveillance techniques, including observation and covert filming, to obtain evidence to inform an investigation. The technical surveillance area is responsible for deployment of surveillance devices. All personnel in these areas are kept separate from the investigations section of OPI and from the OPI building, and are identified only by covert numbers. This is to preserve their covert identity so as not to compromise operations by identification of their affiliation with OPI. The Electronic Collections unit is responsible for monitoring and reviewing the surveillance and intercept material and reporting information products to OPI investigators.

Integrity Testing

OPI runs a dedicated integrity testing unit. OPI explained that the complexity and controversial nature of integrity testing as a strategy warrants a specialist unit with dedicated experts. OPI stated that integrity tests, "if handled appropriately, can bring significant benefits to Victoria Police," including both providing evidence for corruption and also producing a valuable deterrent effect. In order to preserve the deterrent effect, OPI stated that it does not publish the details of the number of integrity tests conducted. However, while the legislation does not dictate whether OPI conducts targeted or random integrity testing, OPI did note that the focus has been on targeted testing. OPI stated that, due to the strategy being "high risk and controversial," integrity tests go through a very rigid framework for approval. Targets for tests were described as selected on the basis of an intelligence assessment of the information, the credibility of its source, and availability (or lack thereof) of other evidence. A panel, including an independent person, is then formed and all must agree that an integrity test is a fair and reasonable strategy to deploy. The test is then signed off at the Deputy Director level before it can occur.

OPI noted that it does not measure the success of integrity tests by catching the target, but by the fact that the target remained unaware that he/she was the subject of a test. OPI does not advise targets that pass integrity tests that they have been subject to a test, but those who fail will face disciplinary or potentially criminal charges.

OPI also mentioned that integrity testing might be a beneficial tool for testing the effectiveness of policies and procedures rather than individual conduct. Such testing was highlighted as potentially useful for Quality Assurance testing of changes that may have been implemented in light of recommendations, thus testing their effectiveness. Further, testing could be a form of random audit of a process or procedure in light of complaints on a specific issue, such as property handling, in order to inform what changes might need to be made.

Outcomes

At the conclusion of its own investigation, OPI can make recommendations for an outcome. Findings may exonerate a person or lead to an outcome of no further action. Where there is evidence of wrongdoing, OPI can recommend that VICPOL take disciplinary action or make changes to policies, procedures, or training. Where evidence of criminal conduct is found, OPI can refer the matter to the Director of Public Prosecutions (DPP) for consideration of prosecution.

Recommendations are typically made in the form of a report, with OPI generally producing two types of reports where the test is one of public interest. Where a matter is considered to be of public interest, a report can be made in public to Parliament. These reports are generally the outcome of broad investigations and reviews of policies or systems (e.g., managing conflicts of interest). More specific investigatory reports may be provided only to the Chief Commissioner with recommendations for action, for example, in relation to a specific individual or case.

When OPI requests VICPOL to take action, the Chief Commissioner is obliged to provide a written response detailing whether action was taken or reasons for not taking action. OPI noted that VICPOL's acceptance of recommendations regarding policies or practices is generally very high, but that recommendations regarding disciplinary action in relation to individuals have a far lower acceptance rate. Problems cited included reinvestigation by VICPOL and differences in opinion regarding the standard of proof for disciplinary matters, as well as the length of time that disciplinary cases can take to reach an outcome and the possible overturning of decisions by the Police Appeals Board. Furthermore, OPI noted that VICPOL is sometimes constrained, for example, by employment conditions or enterprise bargaining agreements that prevent recommended action from being possible, even if it is accepted in principle. OPI keeps a database of its systemic recommendations and seeks status updates on their implementation through an audit process.

In relation to the discipline system of VICPOL, OPI conducted a review in 2007 and produced a report (Office of Police Integrity, 2007b) outlining a number of recommendations for reform. VICPOL has responded positively to many of these recommendations and it has led to a significant refocus of staff management processes. This has included the introduction of the Management Intervention Model and a focus on restorative justice and developmental rather than punitive strategies for managing staff performance.

Witness Support

OPI has a framework for supporting witnesses that are identified as needing protection. Effective witness protection and support was described as an important service to ensure the confidence of people who provide information to OPI. Witnesses at OPI examinations also have free legal assistance through an arrangement with the Department of Justice, and OPI can also perform psychological assessments and provide 24-hour availability of support. Aside from offering its own witness protection services, OPI also has a function in relation to the witness support offered by VICPOL. Under Section 17(5) of the Witness Protection Act 1991, OPI can receive appeals from any person whose participation in the VICPOL witness protection program is terminated. OPI has undertaken a review of VICPOL's witness protection.

Early Intervention

OPI explained that the early years of the organisation were spent predominantly focused on reactive investigations and building resources. More recently, OPI has been able to shift its attention to more proactive methods, particularly within the Professional Standards and Assurance Unit and the Prevention and Education area. OPI stated that they have both strategic and tactical intelligence staff and that strategic intelligence is used to locate hotspot areas of people with regard to recurring problems, particularly of a similar theme. The strategic intelligence is fed to the investigations section for proactive assessment. OPI stated that the establishment by VICPOL of its Professional Development Committees (PDCs) presented an important avenue for dissemination of this information to the appropriate region or division within VICPOL.

OPI noted that while its investigative work is typically independent of VICPOL, proactive work is increasingly collaborative to support VICPOL's own reform agenda. OPI stated that, while they may try to influence or support reform, ultimately VICPOL must own its solutions and so early collaboration was seen as fundamental. The PDCs were seen as a positive avenue for collaboration between OPI and VICPOL to work on solutions to identified problems.

Risk Management

OPI's current strategic plan covering 2010 to 2013 (Office of Police Integrity, n.d.) outlines its primary strategies as being to influence, prevent, deter, and detect. This includes strengthening and enhancing VICPOL's systems and culture and identifying systemic weaknesses. OPI utilises complaints and intelligence information to highlight areas that may be at risk of corruption within VICPOL, and to design tools for assessing and managing those risks. OPI noted that all its work areas are interconnected, allowing individual investigations or intelligence information to inform its education and prevention work as well as research.

Procedural Controls

OPI has provided a number of detailed reviews in relation to VICPOL with recommendations for procedural controls to minimise corruption and misconduct risks and enhance professionalism. Work has been conducted in the areas of property management, interviewing and obtaining confessional evidence, managing conflicts of interest, IT security, and conditions in police cells.

Staff Screening

OPI has made recommendations and provided resources to aid VICPOL in its staff screening procedures. This has included the provision of materials to aid assessing the integrity of applicants at recruit level as well as for promotions or special squads. OPI noted that effective recruitment is a strong prevention tool regarding corruption and serious misconduct. Further, a recent OPI discussion paper (Office of Police Integrity, 2010c) suggested the potential for psychological profiling tools to predict information-leaking behaviour of VICPOL members or applicants.

Ethics Education and Training

OPI has a dedicated Corruption Prevention and Education Unit that provides a range of educational and advisory services to VICPOL including training sessions, consultancy, and educational resources. OPI also provides presentations on the Probationary Constables course as well as at other events and special training days held by VICPOL. Sessions are delivered in metropolitan and rural regions and cover information about the role of OPI and its relationship to Victoria Police, and police members' rights and responsibilities in relation to OPI investigations. OPI also noted an increasing focus in education in relation to the Charter of Human Rights and Responsibilities. Other sessions may be given by request that focus on a specific identified issue or provide assistance for a particular workplace. OPI noted that, when going to present at particular stations in these circumstances, they utilise contemporaneous case studies (stemming from its investigative work) to tailor the presentation to issues that are currently being experienced. This was highlighted as an important engagement strategy for training.

Increasingly, OPI offers local managers assistance in dealing with specific issues on an ad hoc basis, whereby a member of the OPI can go to the region to help work on a strategy to address a particular problem. This was described as being well received, with managers keen to accept the offer of assistance and implement strategies. OPI has also provided advice and assistance to VICPOL in the content and redesign of its recruit curriculum and ethics training. OPI noted that its experience of complaint cases and lessons from investigations was helpful in identifying issues that VICPOL education programs are recommended to cover. OPI has also aided in the development of a Graduate Certificate in Integrity Studies, in conjunction with other Australian anticorruption agencies and the University of Wollongong. The course is aimed at those working throughout the integrity sector and commenced in 2010.

OPI produces a range of education products that are available online and in hardcopy. These include guidelines, checklists, toolkits, and papers about best practice. Recently, the OPI produced a decision wheel tool (available online*) for use in cases of potential conflicts of interest. The wheel covers areas of conflict in relation to employment, colleagues, family, influence, gifts, and associations. For each area, the wheel offers considerations in relation to, for example, policy, duty, or consequences, and a recommended action. The wheel was produced after a number of investigations had highlighted conflicts of interest.

OPI produces fact sheets on short topics, such as gifts and benefits, how to report misconduct, the role of OPI, and what police can do to reduce the

* Online at: http://www.opi.vic.gov.au/ethics_wheel.html

risk of complaints against them (including behaviour and conduct tips) and the complaints process and why it is important. More recently, OPI has announced the development of a National Law Enforcement Integrity Index, which is a self assessment tool for law enforcement agencies' integrity frameworks. The Index incorporates scores on seven factors: culture, recruitment, operations, professional standards, management and supervision, discipline, and complaints. Scores will highlight weaknesses in systems and aid improvement. It is hoped that the tool will aid comparison and benchmarking between similar agencies. The Index is reported to be in the pilot test phase (Office of Police Integrity, 2010b).

Audit

OPI noted that the Professional Standards Assurance Unit now undertakes more audits, particularly out on location. For example, a major piece of work was completed in relation to conditions in police cells. Reviews of particular systems also are conducted to identify any possible improvements that can impact on professionalism and effectiveness of VICPOL. Examples of reviews include the review of VICPOL's discipline system (Office of Police Integrity, 2011) as well as a review of the use of force by and against Victoria Police (Office of Police Integrity, 2009a).

OPI has a function in relation to the Charter of Human Rights and Responsibilities Act 2006 regarding monitoring VICPOL's compliance with the Charter as well as monitoring complaints that have a human rights component. OPI noted that VICPOL's complaints database had a field for recording human rights information and that OPI has live access to this database to review those complaints. OPI was, at the time of writing, also finalising a "Human Rights Monitoring Strategy" that covers all areas of operational policing.

Victoria Emerging Issues

During the interviews with VICPOL and OPI, emerging issues for Victoria in the field of police integrity were discussed, including new developments, successful strategies, and emerging ethical issues that may need attention.

Innovative Strategies

Victoria Police have introduced a new focus for the management of staff and, with it, a devolved model of responsibility for complaint handling. Minor complaints are now typically handled by local level managers who can directly manage subject officers and address the behaviour that led to the complaint. Thus, with local resolution has come a shift in focus from punishment of wrongdoing to correction of behaviour. To support the devolution of responsibility, Professional Development Committees (PDCs) have been established in each region. The PDCs help to decentralise the responsibility for minor matters, free up ESD for work on more serious issues, regulate the handling of minor matters, and aid knowledge transfer throughout the regions. The PDCs also provide strategic information to management groups within the region as well as assistance to the local resolution officers. OPI acknowledged the PDCs as a valuable position to aid communication of OPI intelligence regarding problems specific to its regions. The chairpersons of each PDC meet quarterly to discuss issues and trends affecting their regions and departments and to exchange best practice ideas and solutions to problems.

In a similar way, OPI spoke about the establishment of a Police Reform Advisory Group (PRAG) that establishes a link between various regions of VICPOL and OPI. The PRAG is described in the OPI's 2008–2009 Annual Report as "emerging leaders in Victoria Police with whom we engage in an ethical health dialogue" (Office of Police Integrity, 2009c, p. 14). The PRAG consists of approximately 25 members of VICPOL who have been identified by VICPOL's ESD and Chief Commissioner as natural leaders or ethical "champions." PRAG members provide OPI with knowledge of the issues affecting VICPOL so that OPI can ensure that its work is relevant, as well as practical advice on particular strategies, products, or projects. In turn, OPI supports PRAG members to communicate more widely with VICPOL on issues of integrity, with the use of OPI products, and members are formally recognised for their role by both the Chief Commissioner of VICPOL and Director of OPI. OPI stated that the PRAG continued to receive support from VICPOL at the executive level, and that it reflected a huge step forward, both for collaboration between VICPOL and OPI, and also for VICPOL involvement and investment in long-term sustainable reform.

VICPOL and OPI have been collaborating on efforts to improve the oversight of VICPOL internal investigations, particularly in relation to serious incidents, such as deaths related to custody, police pursuits, and police shootings. A checklist of principles has been developed to ensure management of issues, such as conflict of interest of investigators when carrying out such an investigation.

An emerging issue for both VICPOL and OPI was measurement of performance in relation to integrity at the organisational level. Both discussed the development of an index or checklist for aiding the assessment of VICPOL's ethical health (or commitment to integrity). OPI has announced the construction of a National Law Enforcement Integrity Index for use by all law enforcement agencies, which will help to assess and benchmark performance in a number of key areas of integrity management. At the time of writing, OPI was about to test the use of the Index with VICPOL. VICPOL is also engaged with the Australia New Zealand Police Advisory Agency (ANZPAA) in a number of projects, including one to examine ethical health indexes across Australia with a view to developing a nationally agreed performance measure.

OPI has launched its Sister Agency Knowledge Exchange (SAKE) project to aid communication and knowledge sharing between anticorruption organisations. SAKE utilises an online forum to allow participation of both national and international agencies to share information and enter into discussions.

Successful Strategies

Culture and Attitudes

Both VICPOL and OPI noted that ethics and integrity must be the responsibility of the entire organisation and that enhancing the attitudes of members to actively promote ethical behaviour and condemn misconduct is the crucial next step. OPI noted that the majority of VICPOL members are not unethical or will not behave inappropriately. However, it was noted that the problem is that many will turn a blind eye to the poor behaviour of others or will not push others to "do the right thing." VICPOL agreed, stating, "Our commitment needs to be towards creating an environment that is absolutely hostile to the emergence of corruption and misconduct … where people see it and it's dealt with rather than with silently protesting, which is the typical response."

Taking Responsibility

Both VICPOL and OPI stated that local ownership and accountability of complaints, particularly customer service issues, as well as professionalisation is vital. OPI noted that the PDCs provide good influence as well as senior "buy-in" and support. VICPOL noted that the model also needed an effective quality assurance framework.

From Discipline to Rehabilitation

VICPOL noted that the new model of discipline focusing on natural justice and rehabilitation, rather than punishment, will impact positively on behaviour. The benefits of the model regarding the learning that it provides were highlighted where behaviour is addressed and corrected through tailored, early interventions. VICPOL stated that "the principle of moving from retribution to forgiveness is a key theme, it's just the strongest pathway to greater effectiveness."

OPI Engagement With VICPOL

OPI noted that the contact they have had with VICPOL through education and training has had a variety of impacts. OPI mentioned that the sessions were excellent for promoting the organisation and dispelling many of the myths that may exist among VICPOL members. It was noted as well that it has encouraged some police to contact OPI for further engagement, advice, and consultancy.

Emerging Ethical Issues

Some issues were noted as ongoing concerns, for example, drug use by members, inappropriate associations, and informer management as well as work in certain crime-type areas. Further issues are covered in more depth below.

Removal of Discretionary Powers

VICPOL discussed that a critical ethical risk for policing was the removal of discretion and the introduction of mandatory responses. VICPOL noted that, while powers of discretion can, arguably, be unfairly applied, removal of police discretion would likely decrease ethical thinking and judgment in relation to interactions: "Police will treat people like objects and that will generate a whole range of adverse outcomes." VICPOL noted that the key was to engage members with the human rights issues and ethical issues in exercising powers of discretion and encourage critical thinking and judgment, rather than removing the power to exercise it.

Information Management and IT

Both VICPOL and OPI noted that the culture around information management presents a problem for VICPOL. OPI noted that inappropriate disclosures of information were one of OPI's highest concerns in terms of negative impact. While OPI highlighted that the majority of VICPOL members do not leak information, it was stated that consequences can include putting the lives of people at risk, seriously undermining the credibility of significant investigations, and presenting a reason for some to challenge the unity of VICPOL as an organisation.

OPI also noted that VICPOL's IT systems present a risk, for example, in terms of the ability to control access to information and protect technology from external threat. VICPOL members' use of IT was highlighted as a risk, including members' use of media, such as e-mail and social networks like Facebook. VICPOL has recently distributed information regarding the use of social media, and VICPOL noted that the area of information management and IT security was receiving investment. OPI has released a toolkit for assessing unauthorised and inappropriate e-mails for disciplinary purposes. This work was the result of collaboration between OPI and VICPOL and recently won the Institute of Public Administration Australia award for risk management.

Conflict of Interest and Associations

OPI noted that conflict of interest is an ongoing issue for VICPOL. While VICPOL has introduced a declarable associations policy, OPI noted that there was a continued problem with declaring associations in accordance with policy. VICPOL also noted that there had been cases where members had completed the declaration stating that they had no improper associations, but that such associations had come to light subsequently. OPI noted that it was important to encourage a culture of declaring and managing associations, and supporting members to manage risk, rather than members fearing there may be negative consequences to disclosure.

OPI also noted that conflicts of interest in investigations were an issue. As mentioned earlier, VICPOL and OPI have worked to improve the oversight of investigations into serious incidents, and conflicts of interest is one area that this work addresses. The work has produced a checklist of key areas that should be considered by those assigned to an investigation.

Use of Force

Monitoring VICPOL's use of force continues to be an area of high priority for OPI. A recent *Review of the Use of Force by and against Victoria Police* (Office of Police Integrity, 2009a) highlighted shortcomings in the education provided by VICPOL to its members on use of force. Previous reviews, by OPI on fatal shootings by Victoria Police (Office of Police Integrity, 2005) and internally by VICPOL on the "use of force" register, had highlighted areas for improvement and resulted in a number of recommendations. The recent OPI report (Office of Police Integrity, 2009a) noted a need for VICPOL officers to be trained in communication and negotiation skills, particularly with respect to interactions with people with mental health issues, a need for better information collection and use with regard to use of force incidents, and a need to implement recommendations that have been outstanding from previous reviews. OPI noted that, during 2010, VICPOL had made considerable efforts to reconcile recommendations that had been made in such reviews and had significantly improved use of force reporting capabilities as well as training.

Work Force Issues

OPI mentioned a number of workforce issues that might impact negatively on VICPOL. The need for professionalisation of policing, including competency-based development, was highlighted, as well as the need for VICPOL to be able to move staff in order to respond to priorities. OPI is currently undertaking a major project examining flexible work practices for police to ensure VICPOL will have a workforce able to respond to the changing needs of the public. After broad consultation with a range of stakeholders, OPI published an issues paper in April 2010 (Office of Police Integrity, 2010d). The issues paper has been used to guide discussions with a range of focus groups. A final report was tabled in Parliament in September 2011.

VICPOL also noted that a current heavy recruitment campaign set to see some 1,600 new officers employed over the next 3 years may bring challenges and potential problems to the organisation. It was noted that there is research to suggest that periods of heavy recruiting can cause a drop in standards that can later manifest in significant discipline and corruption issues for that police jurisdiction.

Western Australia

9

The Western Australia Police (WAPOL) integrity framework consists of the internal Professional Standards portfolio, with oversight and corruption investigations conducted by the independent Corruption and Crime Commission (CCC). A Joint Agency Steering Group (JASG) facilitates consultation between WAPOL and the CCC. The most significant event in policing in Western Australia, in relation to conduct issues, was the Kennedy Royal Commission, which ran from 2002 to 2004. It exposed police involvement in burglary, narcotics, assaults, procedural abuses, and fabrication of evidence. There have also been significant wrongful conviction cases involving police in Western Australia. The Kennedy Report led to the restructuring of the Western Australian Anti-Corruption Commission as the CCC, with the power to hold public hearings and conduct undercover operations (Kennedy, 2004). The work of the Commission has been focused more on public servants and politicians than police, but it has successfully investigated a number of police conduct issues (Corruption and Crime Commission, 2009a; Denholm & Salusinszky, 2008).

Western Australia Police

The Western Australia Police Professional Standards portfolio comprises divisions with responsibility for police complaint administration, ethical standards, and internal affairs. These functions focus on the prevention of corruption as well as internal investigations and complaint management.

Despite the central responsibility for professional standards mentioned above, WAPOL maintain a "whole of organisation" approach to ethics and behaviour, providing a Code of Conduct, complemented by a document describing the core values of the organisation and their relevance to members. The Code of Conduct, last revised April 2008 (Western Australian Police, 2008), outlines the values, legislative requirements, reporting requirements, and general standards of conduct expected of all members including volunteers, contractors, and subcontractors. The Code of Conduct also includes information on the various options for reporting unprofessional conduct and the support available. The code details a number of relevant areas in relation to expected standards of conduct, such as associations, secondary employment, and drugs and alcohol, among others.

Complaints Handling

WAPOL's Web site provides details on the process for making a complaint against the organisation or its members. Complaints can be made in writing, using an online complaints form, in person, or by telephone. Further, complaints can be taken at any station or district office, the Police Complaints Administration Centre, Internal Affairs Unit, or externally at the CCC. However, WAPOL encourages those with complaints to either use the online form or take the matter up with the nearest station or district office because it may be possible to resolve the issue rather than going to full investigation.

WAPOL's Web site outlines the information that complainants should aim to provide in relation to their complaint, including details of when and where the incident occurred, a brief description of the incident and complaint, any information from which a determination can be made as to the identity of involved officers, and details of any witnesses. The online complaints form also asks for details of the outcome sought, and states that the fields relating to complainant name and contact details are mandatory.

At interview, WAPOL discussed issues around increasing accessibility of the complaints system for indigenous people. WAPOL noted that there was a tendency among indigenous people to not bring their complaints to the police due to a belief that issues will not be dealt with or fear of reporting it to their local station. While complaints can be made directly to the Police Complaints Administration Centre (PCAC) or to the district rather than a local station, WAPOL has established a toll-free phone number for indigenous complainants, and regular meetings have occurred between the PCAC and the Aboriginal Legal Service to promote the phone number in indigenous communities.

Complaints and other incidents that are subject to internal investigation are recorded by the PCAC, which then assesses, allocates, and monitors these matters. Some matters can also be assessed at the district level. For example, where a matter does not allege misconduct or a breach of the Code of Conduct, or relates only to service delivery or procedures and policy, resolution may require only an explanation and will be responded to directly. Depending upon the information provided, these matters can be recorded either as a complaint with the subsequent submission of a Complaint Advice Notice (CAN) or into journals or occurrence books as information rather than complaints.

Where a matter cannot be resolved in this way, a CAN is completed electronically, which is received by the PCAC. If the PCAC receive complaints directly, it raises a complaint note after speaking to the complainant. The

PCAC can attempt to resolve complaints by a "complaint assessment and PCAC investigation" process where allegations are minor or procedural in nature, or where evidence is easily available to prove or disprove the allegation (e.g., where an audit trail is available). All matters, however, are recorded centrally and forwarded to the CCC by the PCAC. Where inappropriate behaviour or misconduct is alleged, matters are dealt with through a more formal process of either local complaint resolution or formal investigation for the more serious matters (after assessment by the CCC).

Local Complaint Resolution/Mediation

The majority of complaints received against members of WAPOL consistently relate to minor conduct matters, such as general inappropriate behaviour or demeanour. Minor matters relating to these customer service issues are dealt with through the Local Complaint Resolution (LCR) process. The process aims to resolve these issues quickly, within 30 days, thus benefiting both the subject officer and the complainant. To aid timeliness, the PCAC has developed system notifications to track the stages of investigations, whereby the PCAC is automatically notified when investigations are two thirds into their target time frame, and then it contacts the investigators to check on progress.

Complaints appropriate for LCR are assigned to a resolving officer at the local level. The resolving officer would typically be the subject officer's superior, thus allowing the subject officer's manager to identify and address any behaviour or performance issues through appropriate management action. Resolving officers discuss the complaint with both the complainant and subject officer to uncover the issues and expectations in terms of outcome. This may involve face-to-face mediation between all parties, but this was described as difficult in terms of the time constraints and logistics of physically getting everyone together at the same time. The CCC did comment that communication with complainants over minor issues had improved and that WAPOL was better at providing apologies and explanations for conduct.

On resolution of the issues, the complainant is notified in writing of the outcome. Where managerial action is determined to be warranted, this is delivered by the officer in charge of the member involved. The aim of the LCR process is to educate and modify behaviour rather than punish officers. Complaints that are resolved by local resolution, therefore, are not recorded in the subject officer's personnel file unless they are issued with a Managerial Notice. However, copies of the documentation are sent to the PCAC for quality assurance, recorded on the internal investigations database, and are made available to the CCC for review. This allows both central and external monitoring of patterns in minor matters that might need more than individual-level action.

Complaints Investigation

More serious misconduct matters are formally investigated. Those matters that concern criminal allegations or corruption, as well as matters arising from internal complaints, are investigated by the Internal Affairs Unit (or under their direction). Complaint investigations have a target 60-day time frame for completion, although more complex cases may take longer. WAPOL noted that quality of investigations should not be sacrificed at the expense of meeting timeline targets.

Formal investigations are conducted by appointed investigators. In 2006, the CCC highlighted a specific need for WAPOL to provide training on how to conduct internal investigations, particularly by middle management personnel (Corruption and Crime Commission, 2006). WAPOL developed an Internal Investigators Course, delivered at the academy, for developing skills and consistency in conducting and oversighting investigations carried out at the local level. Investigating officers are provided with a case officer at the CCC to discuss the approach to be taken with each investigation and have access to experienced Professional Standards staff as well as internal legal opinion should further assistance be required. These are all approaches to improve the consistency and defensibility with respect to the methods employed in investigations.

Quality assurance of investigations is provided by the PCAC. The PCAC monitors the progress and timeliness of complaint and investigation files as well as reviewing the standard of complaint investigations, providing feedback to the relevant district or division manager. The PCAC also specifically monitors complaint files concerning indigenous complainants with respect to equity. Complaints are reviewed externally by the CCC, with the PCAC providing the liaison between the CCC and WAPOL. Complainants are advised in writing of the outcome of the investigation at its conclusion. If complainants are unsatisfied with the outcome of their complaint as handled by WAPOL, they can report the matter to the CCC, which may require police to undertake further inquiry, or it can undertake its own investigation.

Powers and Covert Tactics

Investigators conducting internal and/or complaints investigations have powers to conduct formal recorded interviews, speak to witnesses, and take statements in the pursuit of gathering all evidence with the aim of proving or disproving the allegations. Where criminal behaviour is alleged, members will be interviewed under criminal caution, in line with standard investigative practice. However, where members give no comment, WAPOL can opt to pursue a directed disciplinary interview to compel the member to answer questions. Although, in general practice, evidence given under direction is not used in criminal proceedings, no specific legislation exists to prevent the Director of Public Prosecutions from furnishing this information to the court in particular circumstances. However, the use of such information was noted to potentially impact negatively on the trust of the internal investigative process.

The Internal Affairs Unit has capabilities, including equipment and resources, to utilise covert investigative techniques, such as undercover operatives, telephone interceptions, and surveillance. The Assistant Commissioner of Professional Standards can also authorise targeted integrity testing, and each test conducted has a formalised plan. In 2005, WAPOL and the CCC formed a joint Targeted Integrity Testing Unit that provided integrity testing with the benefits of the CCC's legislative powers and WAPOL's operational experience. Legislation to conduct integrity tests will also be strengthened with the introduction of the Police Administration Bill and/or through amendment to the existing Police Act 1892.

Outcomes and Discipline

Where a complaint is sustained after investigation, a number of outcomes can result, including action in relation to the subject officer or more general changes to policies, procedures, or training. Depending on the seriousness of the allegations, action against subject officers could involve remedial managerial action (behavioural modification), disciplinary or criminal charges, or dismissal through the Commissioner's Loss of Confidence process. Where serious criminal charges are preferred, the evidence is passed to the Director of Public Prosecutions (DPP) to assess and determine whether to pursue the case.

The Kennedy Royal Commission (2004) recommended that WAPOL's disciplinary system be reformed to move away from a punishment model and reflect a more managerial process with a remedial focus for any matters other than criminal allegations. WAPOL has since introduced a Managerial Intervention Model (MIM) for dealing with lower-level misconduct matters, which incorporates verbal guidance, management action plans, and managerial notices to correct members' behaviour. This system is based upon the Fisher model of discipline (Fisher, 2003). However, WAPOL has still retained disciplinary sanctions. WAPOL explained that the Fisher model lacked mid-range options for discipline, which were viewed as necessary where criminal charges may not be pursued by the DPP and a managerial notice was deemed inadequate. The CCC was also supportive of retaining disciplinary sanctions, providing the example of demotion where a member has substantiated misconduct or is not supervising staff adequately (demotion back to a position that does not involve supervision). WAPOL noted that, in the first 18 months after the introduction of the new disciplinary model, few disciplinary charges were sought, but that more recently some cases had warranted this response.

The managerial approach of the MIM is aimed at enhancing the responsibility of managers and supervisors, enhancing the accountability of subordinates to their managers, and modifying behaviour. MIM is designed to be developmental and recognises that members may make honest mistakes, but that performance can be enhanced through providing opportunities to learn and change behaviour with guidance rather than punishment. The model was subject to an external survey after its first year of operation. The survey found a lack of understanding by subject officers regarding the developmental focus, despite marketing attempts by WAPOL. It was noted that many officers ignored the information provided until they were subject to the process.

WAPOL introduced a brochure for officers subject to Management Action Plans (MAPs) that outlines their rights and responsibilities regarding the process. WAPOL noted that there was also evidence of a greater understanding at manager level of MAPs as a remedial strategy rather than punishment, but that MAPs were still not always used as intended. WAPOL suggested that the process required a change of thinking regarding the delivery of the action to the subject officers, by moving away from "ticking boxes" to explaining why the officers' behaviour was unacceptable and what is expected of them to get back on track and then move on. Furthermore, WAPOL discussed that outcomes could lack consistency due to the subjectivity of individual managers. The CCC also highlighted some inconsistencies with how the MIM was viewed by District Superintendents. While some were said to embrace the model as intended, others have viewed it as a further form of discipline, seeing the issuing of MAPs to their staff as reflecting badly on their district or their supervision. The CCC further stated that officers subject to MIM may not necessarily see it as nondisciplinary since some remedial actions are recorded and can be used in assessments for promotion. The CCC noted that the "straw test" for the MIM model was that the remedial approach did not seem to result in an increased likelihood of self-reporting or admissions of behaviour.

More serious matters are dealt with through a disciplinary process or removal under the Commissioner's Loss of Confidence provision. Both are the responsibility of the Ethical Standards Division. Under Section 23 of the Police Act 1892, where charges against a member for an offence against the discipline of the police force are brought, WAPOL has the power to conduct an investigative examination (heard by an Assistant Commissioner or Deputy Commissioner) and examine members under oath, where the officer appointed to examine is provided with "the same power to summon and examine witnesses and to administer oaths as a Justice" (Police Act 1892, s.23(3)). Officers can plead guilty prior to hearings. WAPOL has recently introduced directions hearings where officers can plead guilty and then discuss the issues and facts that are accepted as true by the parties involved.

Where a member is found to have committed a disciplinary offence, WAPOL can, in writing, caution or impose the following sanctions: reprimand, fine of not more than 3% of the annual base rate of pay of the member, demotion, reduction in salary, suspension, discharge, or dismissal. Members can appeal both the sanction and any decision upon which that sanction was based. Appeals are heard by the Police Appeal Board, which consists of a magistrate, an appointee of the Commissioner, and a member of WAPOL elected by members. While charges are pending, officers are typically stood aside (reassigned different duties) until the process is completed, but can be stood down from duty. The latter was noted to be more likely in cases where there is a notice of intention to remove the member.

Removal of a member from WAPOL can only be undertaken through application of the Commissioner's Loss of Confidence (LOC) provision of the Police Act 1892. Section 33L of the Act states that notice and details of the loss of confidence must be given to the member in writing, and the member provided the opportunity to respond. The member can choose to resign or appeal the Loss of Confidence removal within 28 days. Appeals are heard by the WA Industrial Relations Commission, but the onus is on the member to prove "that the decision to take removal action was harsh, oppressive, or unfair" (s.33Q). At interview, WAPOL stated that they did not have a problem with decisions being overturned at appeal, possibly due to the types of behaviour for which the provision tended to be used and that it is a well-documented process. The CCC also noted that the provision was typically only used as a "last resort" in serious cases. However, WAPOL did note that the LOC provision is also used for cases of medically unfit discharge, which was viewed as contentious, but potentially to be addressed in the new Police Administration Bill and/or amendments to the Police Act 1892.

All outcomes are assessed by the PCAC as part of its quality assurance of investigation files. The PCAC assesses whether outcomes are consistent with the evidence as well as previous cases. For example, where a MAP was delivered, district managers have the flexibility to consider mitigating circumstances and amend plans. The PCAC assesses the plan to ensure consistency across cases, members, and districts.

Witness Support

WAPOL members are required to report any unethical conduct of their colleagues. WAPOL's Code of Conduct clearly states that it is the duty of individual members to report unprofessional conduct. The Public Interest Disclosure Act 2003 supports such disclosures, offering protection whereby it is an offence to victimise any person for making a disclosure under the Act. To strengthen internal reporting, WAPOL introduced a dedicated telephone reporting line, the "Blue-line." and a Supported Internal Witness Program in 1999, run through the Risk Assessment Unit.

The Blue-line offers a confidential telephone line for members to report their concerns over unethical conduct of other WAPOL employees. The phone line offers callers the choice of anonymous reporting, although a recent evaluation of the Blue-line by the Sellenger Centre reported that this was viewed by management as hindering the effectiveness of the system by not allowing follow-up inquiries for information (Henry & Isaacson, 2010).

At interview, WAPOL stated that the Blue-line was not marketed well in its early days, which meant that few members used it, but that awareness has since improved. WAPOL's 2006–2007 Annual Report (Western Australia Police, 2007) detailed that, during the reporting period, marketing strategies included presentations to recruits, adverts on the computer network, and redistribution of advertising brochure material. During that same year, the Blue-line was reported to have received 15 calls regarding minor misconduct, a further two regarding corruption, and one requesting ethical advice.

The recent Sellenger Centre review (Henry & Isaacson, 2010) concluded that, while employees were aware of the Blue-line, they were less aware of the resulting complaints process or, particularly, the support offered. Thus, while the survey respondents were generally supportive of having an internal reporting system, they tended to lack trust in the Blue-line and its promise of confidentiality, preferring instead to report matters to their supervisors. Regardless of the channel of reporting internal conduct or ethical matters, employees who report are offered support and practical assistance through the Supported Internal Witness Program. This program can offer services ranging from monitoring for potential victimisation to facilitating action, including referral to Health and Welfare Services or physical protection and relocation in the most serious cases.

Early Intervention

The Kennedy Royal Commission (2004) recommended that WAPOL invest resources into a credible early warning system that would extend the roles of managers to prevention of unethical behaviour in the workplace rather than merely reacting to problems. When the CCC evaluated the first 2 years of the reform period that followed, they noted problems with the systems in place, but that a project was underway to implement a new case management system that would allow the use of behavioural indicators to develop thresholds for early advice and action. The new Professional Standards Information Management System (PSIMS), utilising early intervention software, was implemented fully in January 2007. The system provides support for an early intervention function for the Risk Assessment Unit as well as case management functions for internal investigations and administrative file management tasks for the PCAC. Particularly, the system allows identification of emerging trends through comparison or flagging of individuals, units, districts, and stations.

Part of the PCAC charter is to provide statistical information in relation to misconduct allegations, and the system allows the PCAC to obtain reports. The PCAC monitors the information for signs of emerging issues or hotspots and can provide the reports to educate the districts in question. This is a role that the PCAC is looking to expand.

The Early Intervention System also incorporates linked two-way access at the local level to allow districts to both read and input information directly in the form of Complaint Advice Notes. While this decentralised access allows for sharing of information to the relevant districts and an increase in responsibility for reporting, it was noted that there could be a danger of gaps in reporting of information to the system when relying on a decentralised model. The CCC also has networked read-only access to WAPOL's Early Intervention System to increase openness and accountability.

Preset thresholds of "at risk" behaviour are used within the Early Intervention System to identify officers who may require some form of intervention to rectify problem behaviour. When an officer is identified, his/her District or Divisional Superintendent is notified through an Early Intervention Notification. The Superintendent and his/her management team is then responsible for implementing actions to monitor or correct the behaviour and reduce the number, or seriousness, of future behavioural issues. In particular, WAPOL is moving toward a system of identifying the issues underlying officer behaviour. This can involve working with the subject officer through the Health and Welfare Branch, or encouraging the officer to seek support.

Risk Management

At the organisational level, WAPOL includes corruption prevention strategies within the agency's strategic and annual business plans. Each portfolio/district/division also has its own local business plan, and all managers are required to include corruption prevention planning and complaint management as part of their local action plans. Local risk management and corruption prevention strategies aim to build local-level corruption resilience by allowing officers in charge to address universal risks as well as tailor the plan to the risks of their specific area. The local risk plans are audited to ensure compliance, but also to manage and monitor the risks and allow districts to learn from each other. For example, where a problem is identified, the audit can examine what strategies have been successful in other areas for addressing that same problem. WAPOL also has an audit and risk management committee that provides a forum for discussing trends and issues from a corruption prevention and investigation perspective at a high level within the organisation.

Each area completes a risk summary based on the major areas outlined by the business plan. The risk summary documents risks and actions, and prioritises the risk, the consequences, and the likelihood of occurrence. High-risk areas and operations are also risk-managed, including policies for pursuits and public order events, and operational audits are conducted. The Risk Assessment Unit also audits members' driver's licenses regularly to check for validity, including the number of points and suspensions.

A further form of risk management, noted by the CCC, is that WAPOL has moved to outsource a variety of areas that were at risk of complaints, misconduct, or abuse, or where the powers of sworn members are not necessary to fulfil the role. Among these areas are firearms licensing and prisoner transport.

Procedural Controls

Since the Kennedy Royal Commission (2004), WAPOL has introduced stricter controls for a variety of operational areas and tasks, such as property management and video recording of searches (e.g., execution of warrants, drugs searches, organised crime), interviews, arrests, and watchhouse cells. Complaints-related interviews are audio recorded and can be videoed by the Internal Affairs Unit when deemed necessary. Many arrests are also videoed, although WAPOL stated that officers would not generally carry a camera out on the street for "ordinary arrests."

Video capabilities for Tasers® and also in-car video were discussed as potential improvements for WAPOL. The benefits of video were recognised in terms of its impact on complaints, protecting officers against false allegations as well as substantiating genuine complaints. However, resource and budget constraints have prevented adoption of these strategies. Costs in terms of acquiring the capabilities are compounded by additional resources needed to store and ensure the security of that information.

All frontline (operational) police vehicles, however, are fitted with a GPS Automatic Vehicle Location system that records data regarding the geographical position of vehicles and time and speed information. WAPOL noted that this provided a valuable investigative tool that has helped officers in relation to complaints, where complainants have been mistaken in a complaint regarding speeding of police vehicles.

A number of strategies are in place to track certain staff practices. There are policies regarding access to information that is not relevant to work, which are predominantly focused on access for personal benefit or to the detriment of others, but also include access for curiosity. Audi-Track is used to identify which members access sensitive data held within the WAPOL computer system. Audi-Track allows retrospective reports of access as well as live reporting to alert when certain information is accessed. A further system called K-Vault can be used to aid investigations into the use of WAPOL's e-mail system; it can scan the content of current and archived e-mails.

All detectives in WAPOL maintain a journal of their activities, which is bar coded to facilitate issuing and storage once completed. WAPOL has a gifts register and associated policy to record receipt of gifts or gratuities and any associated conflict of interest. WAPOL also has a detailed Informant Management Manual that outlines how police-informant relationships should be appropriately managed.

Drug and Alcohol Testing

Drug and alcohol use is referred to in the WAPOL Code of Conduct, which clearly states that use of any illicit drugs is always a criminal offence and therefore never acceptable, on or off duty. The Code also warns against abuse of prescribed drugs and states that any member on duty or on call/standby should not be impaired by any substance.

In December 2011, WAPOL introduced a new drug and alcohol testing program for members through amendments to the Police Force Regulations (*Police Force (Member Testing) Regulations 2011*). The new changes include provisions for drug and alcohol testing of all police, and to undertake random, targeted and mandatory testing of members. This includes mandated testing of officers involved in "critical incidents" both on and off duty, where critical incidents involve a death or serious injury or discharge of a firearm. Mandatory testing can also be applied to officers in areas considered to be high risk, including the Tactical Response Group, or where it is considered to be "appropriate for the member's health and safety, or is prudent to protect the member's credibility in any future court proceeding" (s.9.2(d)). The legislation also allows for targeted testing of officers where there is a credible suspicion of impairment by drugs or alcohol on duty, or having consumed a targeted (e.g. illegal) drug on or off duty. The legislation allows members to be recalled to duty to be tested, meaning that officers who use drugs in their off-duty time can still be tested and caught.

Members are obliged to comply with a direction for a test and can be required to provide a sample of breath, blood, urine, oral fluid or hair for testing. Failure to comply constitutes a disciplinary offence. If a member returns a positive result for a test, they can be referred to the WA Police Health and Welfare Unit for review, or be subject to managerial interventions, disciplinary action, or removal from the organisation.

Staff Screening

The Royal Commission recommended that WAPOL adopt a personnel security vetting program that conforms to national standards. WAPOL's Risk Assessment Unit provides the organisation with centralised integrity checking of recruits including local, national, and overseas criminal and traffic record checks as well as driver's license checks, traffic infringements, and any other police contact. Recruits also undergo a psychological inventory and formal psychological interview. Checks are conducted regarding Internal Affairs Unit (IAU) holdings for information on employees for promotions, exits, and awards. The promotions policy lists a number of integrity-related areas as preclusions to promotion that relate to an individual's conduct, complaint history, and internal investigation history (where a promotion is denied on the basis of such information, applicants are given an opportunity to respond). Applicants for positions with the Internal Affairs Unit are subject to a further integrity check.

The Personnel Security Vetting Unit (PSVU) was established within the Internal Affairs Unit in 2005 to provide high-level security clearances as well as initial vetting of all employees in WAPOL at the time of the unit's inception. Vetting of current employees was conducted in a stage process whereby all sworn officers as well as staff working in high-risk areas were vetted as a priority. Ongoing security clearances are now conducted in those high-risk areas as well as for personnel in specific operation roles that require access to national security classified information.

Ethics Education and Training

All recruits at the academy receive education on the expected standards of integrity and honesty. The IAU and the PCAC are involved in training at the academy, and corruption prevention presentations have been provided on recruit courses as well as management accountability courses and lateral entry courses (for entry from other jurisdictions or from overseas). These training sessions often incorporate information regarding current trends and issues that are evident in the complaints received. Moreover, to increase awareness of misconduct cases, details of disciplinary charges against members are disseminated in an internal publication.

Many of the management and supervisory courses have ethics components, which include information on managing complaints and administering the Local Complaints Resolution Process. Also, part of the PCAC charter is providing support and guidance to those involved in conducting internal investigations.

The Western Australia Police Academy has close links with Edith Cowan University (Perth) for provision of tertiary-level education to members. A range of courses available by e-learning as well, utilising the Blackboard system. This overcomes logistical, geographical, access problems to professional development for members.

Corruption and Crime Commission

The Corruption and Crime Commission (CCC) was established by the Corruption and Crime Commission Act 2003 after the Kennedy Royal Commission into whether there had been corrupt or criminal conduct by any Western Australia police officer (Kennedy, 2004). The CCC aims to improve the integrity of the whole public sector, including WAPOL. The CCC has three main functions. The first concerns prevention and education regarding corruption and misconduct in the public sector. Under this function, the CCC provides advice and assistance to agencies regarding how they can strengthen their capacity for dealing with misconduct. The second function relates to dealing with misconduct. Under this function, the CCC assesses matters, oversights matters dealt with by agencies, and also investigates cases itself that reach a particular threshold. The final function relates to organised crime, whereby the CCC, through powers provided to it by the Act, can assist WAPOL in combating organised crime by granting WAPOL members certain special powers. The CCC does not have a jurisdiction to investigate organised crime itself.

Complaints Handling

The CCC can receive complaints (or information) regarding the conduct of WAPOL members directly from members of the public. The CCC also receives matters referred by WAPOL under the Act. The threshold for matters within the CCC's jurisdiction over WAPOL is lower than for other public sector organisations. The CCC's jurisdiction includes corruption and serious conduct, but also Reviewable Police Action, which according to the Act means any action by an employee of the police service that is unlawful; unreasonable, unjust, oppressive, or improperly discriminatory (or in accordance with a law that may be); involves improper use of a power or discretion; or where reasons for the use of a power or discretion were not, but should have been, provided.

WAPOL is required under the Act to notify the CCC of any matters concerning (or potentially concerning) reviewable police action. Members of the public can also make complaints, report misconduct or corruption by WAPOL members, or provide information that may be of use to CCC investigations. The CCC can receive anonymous complaints and information, but is clear on its Web site that such matters can be difficult to investigate. Reports to the CCC can be made in writing (letter, fax, e-mail), by telephone or in person, and also online through the CCC Web site. The Web site provides an online complaint form (to submit electronically or print off) that asks for:

- contact details,
- details of the complaint (the only mandatory field),
- date, location, agency involved,
- officers involved,
- what happened,
- witnesses, and
- whether this matter has previously been reported to the CCC or another agency.

When the CCC receives complaints or reports, a Corruption Prevention Team assesses the matter regarding its appropriateness for the CCC's jurisdiction and decides what action should be taken in response. The CCC can also assess matters that do not arise in a specific allegation, for example, where a matter is highlighted through another investigation, consultation, or inquiry.

Assessment may result in the CCC taking no further action on a matter. This can be because the matter is outside the CCC's jurisdiction, in which case the complainant will be provided with guidance as to how to take alternative action, or because a matter has been previously investigated, occurred too long ago, or is deemed very minor.

Complaints Investigation

Where a matter is assessed as warranting investigation, the CCC can determine to refer the matter to another agency to investigate. In the majority of such cases, the matter is referred to the agency that is the subject of the complaint; thus complaints received about WAPOL are usually referred to WAPOL to investigate. Indeed, in 2009–2010, 78% of matters received by the CCC were referred to other agencies to deal with (Corruption and Crime Commission, 2010a). The CCC will then receive a report on the investigation for review. Thus, the CCC oversights how such matters are dealt with by WAPOL and aims to improve its handling of misconduct, ensuring that responsibility for such matters remains with WAPOL. As the CCC noted:

> Organisations, and the management in those organisations, must take responsibility for the conduct of their own staff … police internal investigations should, in the main, except perhaps in the very serious matters, be done in the workplaces in which they occur. That is, in police districts rather than some centralised body.

This model was proposed to maximise responsibility for staff conduct, whereby local managers must face complainants and answer for their staff. Internal investigations were also said to minimise the likelihood of effects of police culture on investigations, whereby an external investigation may result in reduced cooperation. Further, the workload for an external agency to deal with all police complaint matters was cited as far beyond the resources of the CCC and requiring manpower that would in effect constitute "a little police force in its own right and that doesn't even begin to make sense."

The CCC can decide to conduct its own investigation or investigate jointly with another agency. The CCC explained that joint investigations only occurred in relation to investigations of nonpolice matters, for example, where a public sector agency needed to utilise the CCC's investigatory powers. The CCC conducts few investigations itself, though, reserving this function for matters that relate to serious allegations or systemic issues. According to annual reports, only 1% of matters in both 2008–2009 and 2009–2010 were referred to the CCC investigations unit (Corruption and Crime Commission, 2009b; 2010a).

The CCC investigations are conducted by teams of civilian investigators, although most have a background in policing. The CCC explained that, while many of its investigators were former police officers, there are far fewer employees in the police oversight area who are former police, and those who are have typically been out of policing for a long time. The CCC does not second current WAPOL members, but can second members from other state/territory police or the Australia Federal Police (AFP). However, the CCC explained at interview that secondment of police officers was not a necessity in relation to powers, since the Act provides CCC investigators with the powers of special constables.

CCC investigators have the power to require (in writing) public sector members to produce a statement of information. However, the information cannot be used against that person for criminal proceedings. The Act specifies that such information is inadmissible for proceedings other than disciplinary action, or offences as specified within the Act, such as providing false information or contempt. The CCC can also summon witnesses, or other persons, to attend and produce specific items, such as evidence, documents, or records. The CCC may examine witnesses under oath, in private or in public. The 2009–2010 CCC Annual Report (Corruption and Crime Commission, 2010a) states that 10 hearings were conducted during that period, in comparison to 21 the previous year. All but one in each year were conducted in private rather than in public. CCC investigators can enter public sector premises without a warrant and inspect, and take copies of, documents found there. Searches can also be made of other premises upon issue of a search warrant from a judge. The CCC reports annually on the frequency of the use of its powers.

Covert Operations

The CCC can, and frequently does, use covert methods in investigations in order to obtain evidence. The Act allows the CCC to conduct controlled operations. While, the Act specifies that those acting within such operations "must not intentionally induce another person to engage in misconduct that there is no reason to suspect that person has previously engaged in," it does allow for controlled operations to be conducted in the absence of a specific allegation of misconduct. CCC investigators can also use assumed identities and are granted immunity from criminal responsibility for acts committed in relation to acquiring or using that identity in the course of duty. The CCC can apply to use surveillance devices and telecommunications interceptions. The CCC Annual Report 2009–2010 (Corruption and Crime Commission, 2010a) specifies that information obtained through such methods was shared with WAPOL to aid in investigations of criminal matters as well as disciplinary action against members.

Integrity Testing

The Corruption and Crime Commission Act 2003 allows the CCC to conduct integrity tests on WAPOL members on both a random and targeted basis; thus integrity tests can be conducted in the absence of any specific allegation of misconduct. The Australian Federal Police (AFP) assisted the CCC in developing integrity testing training, drawing on AFP training in undercover competencies. Individuals acting within an authorised integrity testing program are not held criminally responsible for authorised activity during the course of an operation that may constitute an offence. The CCC explained that decisions regarding integrity testing are affected by available resources. The CCC reports annually on the number of integrity testing programs conducted; CCC Annual Reports show that nine were conducted in 2006–2007, five in 2007–2008, and four in each subsequent year (Corruption and Crime Commission, 2007; 2008).

Outcomes

Where the CCC has referred matters to WAPOL to investigate, WAPOL is obliged to provide a report on the action taken. The CCC can then review how WAPOL has dealt with misconduct matters, and seek an explanation if WAPOL has not taken action as recommended by the CCC. After such reviews, or the conclusion of the CCC's own investigations of matters, the CCC can make recommendations to WAPOL. The CCC explained that there are generally two forms of recommendations made: those that are very prescriptive and specific in contrast to those that are more philosophical (or general). The latter was viewed to be more appropriate for the CCC to make to WAPOL but was said to be more difficult to track in terms of following its implementation. Specific recommendations can include recommendations for WAPOL to institute disciplinary action or prosecution of particular individuals. The CCC can also bring criminal prosecutions itself. Prosecutions of police officers were, however, described at interview as difficult with regard to achieving convictions from juries.

Other forms of recommendations that the CCC make to WAPOL include amendments to procedures or policies, for example, regarding interactions with citizens or use of discretionary powers (such as the use of summons rather than arrest). The CCC monitors the recommendations that it makes and reports on the numbers made and accepted and implemented annually. However, the monitoring of implementation of recommendations for WAPOL was described by the CCC as "hopefully more about a dialogue in which we could comment in the end about whether the outcome of that dialogue was a positive or negative one" rather than a specific process of directing change. As the CCC stated:

> The more detailed the recommendations, the more you engage with the police service in telling them how to run the police service ... just because we are the oversight body doesn't mean that we're always right or have the higher moral ground, nor do we have the practical experience to be able to implement all these things in the way they should be implemented.

Thus, the relationship between the CCC and WAPOL was viewed more as an advisory service, to suggest improvements to the organisation that WAPOL can then implement in a way that works in a practical way.

Witness Support

The CCC Act has provisions for offering protection from victimisation to individuals who provide information or evidence to the CCC, appear as a witness, or assist the CCC in any way. The Act outlines a number of offences in relation to harassment, detrimental action, damage, or disadvantage by individuals or employers. Where it appears that such behaviour is, or will be, directed toward an individual due to his/her aiding of the CCC, the CCC can make arrangements to protect that person or avoid prejudice. Such arrangements can involve other agencies, such as police services (WAPOL, any other state or territory police, or the AFP) or the Police Minister.

Early Intervention

The CCC has access to WAPOL's Early Intervention System, enabling it to monitor the information recorded and trends within complaints. The CCC also gathers intelligence proactively and can conduct investigations in the absence of complaints. Intelligence is collected on individual police officers as well as particular areas. As WAPOL explained, "That intelligence would enable us, from time-to-time, to make the decision to investigate the conduct of individual police officers without necessarily having a complaint."

Risk Management

The CCC has a misconduct and corruption prevention function. Activities under this function include research, inquiries, and reviews that lead to recommendations to WAPOL regarding potential risks and responses. This can mean highlighting particular issues, for example, the use of Tasers or misuse of information, and recommending improvements to systems or policies. For example, during 2009–2010, the CCC produced a research report on WAPOL's use of Tasers (Corruption and Crime Commission, 2010b). The report concluded that the majority of Taser use by WAPOL is reasonable, but made 10 recommendations for improvement, 4 of which were supported (at least in part) by WAPOL.

The CCC has also developed and marketed a Misconduct Resistance framework guide and toolkit. The framework focuses on the key areas of culture, operational strategies, and management environment, and provides focus questions, signs of success, and ideas for building capacity in each of these areas. The framework is supported by a toolkit that comprises a "health check," poster, and suggested references and resources. The health check is a short questionnaire aimed toward staff completion to inform managers as to the current staff perceptions relevant to misconduct resistance. The questionnaire is supported by a spreadsheet to enter staff responses, which calculates and generates a report (this as available on the CCC's Web site) and an "agency implementation status mapping tool" that can be used to visually represent areas of strength and weakness that may need a response or ongoing monitoring.

Ethics Education and Training

The CCC, as part of its corruption prevention and education function, delivers a number of presentations and workshops to agencies. This includes sessions for WAPOL recruit training as well as seminars to other areas of WAPOL on an ad hoc basis. Sessions cover information regarding the role of the CCC, and some may be on specific systemic issues that are highlighted through the work of the CCC. However, the latter was said to be less frequent than the former, although seen as very important and a potential area for increased attention. The CCC remarked on the view that education regarding misconduct was key to prevention: "One needs to adopt the general proposition that more information is better than less and that if you provide people with the information and tools, at some point they will actually start to use them."

The CCC Annual Report (Corruption and Crime Commission, 2010a) states that new workshops covering misconduct risks for managers and misconduct awareness were developed and run in the 2009–2010 reporting period. The CCC also raises awareness of issues through publication of a *Corruption*

Prevention newsletter. Three such newsletters were published in 2009–2010 and included educational information on activities and developments in the field of misconduct resistance as well as case studies of investigations.

Audit

The CCC carries out an audit function in relation to WAPOL's handling of complaints. Audits, or systems-based evaluations, are now conducted on the way that police districts deal with misconduct by examining a sample of the complaints investigation files. This process entails members of the CCC going out to the districts to view files, which also provides them the opportunity to speak to District Superintendents and other officers as well as potential complainants and consumers of police services about issues. The CCC described the audit process as a prevention strategy in that it is designed to build the capacity of agencies to adequately deal with misconduct by providing feedback on this process.

These audits occur alongside the standard oversight process of misconduct handling that may involve the monitoring of a referred investigation and/or outcome on a case-by-case basis. The CCC oversees investigations through the receipt of investigation reports at the conclusion of WAPOL complaints and misconduct investigations. The CCC reviews the investigation reports to ensure that investigations are conducted to the Australian Complaint Handling Standard. Investigations that fail to meet this standard are returned with advice for conducting further work.

Western Australia Emerging Issues

Since the Kennedy Royal Commission (2004), WAPOL has received an increased budget enabling implementation of a number of strategies to combat misconduct. Most notably, WAPOL has implemented a process of security vetting for personnel, a new Managerial Intervention Model for behaviour modification, and associated changes to the disciplinary system. WAPOL is currently reviewing this approach with a view to having a new and/or amended disciplinary approach in place in 2011. The introduction of the new Police Administration Bill, when it is approved, or, in the interim, amendments to the Police Act 1892 and/or Police Force Regulations 1974, will produce further changes with hopes for enhancing more advanced strategies regarding drug and alcohol testing and integrity testing.

Post-Kennedy Royal Commission also saw the establishment of the CCC to oversee WAPOL's complaint investigations as well as provide an investigatory capacity for cases of serious misconduct or corruption. In practice, WAPOL still investigates the majority of matters, but the CCC does provide independent review or oversight of that process and/or its outcomes. The CCC has also provided a monitoring service for the implementation of the Kennedy Royal Commission recommendations, reporting publicly on the first 2 years of activity, thus enhancing the accountability of WAPOL regarding its response.

One particularly promising strategy that WAPOL has had in place since before the Kennedy Royal Commission is the provision of support for internal reporting of misconduct and unethical behaviour. The Blue-line dedicated telephone reporting line and the Supported Internal Witness Program were established in 1999 as a result of an internal survey that recognised reluctance among members regarding internal reporting. However, while the provision of such services is commendable and important in enhancing the ethical culture of the organisation, the recent report by the Sellenger Centre (Henry & Isaacson, 2010) shows that, even after 10 years of operation, the services still have not gained the acceptance and trust of the workforce, despite a general recognised need and support in principle.

Innovative Strategies

Recent changes to WAPOL practices have focused on a variety of policies reflecting associations, or public perceptions of associations. This includes a tighter gifts policy that has decreased the value of allowable gifts to $100 and a gifts register for each division and portfolio. Public perceptions over potential conflicts of interest and events in other states were noted as a driver for these developments. Policy changes have also been made regarding WAPOL's register of associations, including that criminal associations in relation to family and friends must be declared in order to be risk managed. The new policy was also noted to impact positively on the potential for inappropriate access to information as the Risk Assessment Unit (RAU) can now conduct checks on associations on behalf of employees. As WAPOL stated:

> Previously, if an agency expected you not to associate with someone, you might look them up to see why, or if you were renting a house to someone you weren't sure of, you might look them up. Now you register that association with RAU and they will conduct that check on your behalf.

The CCC's new systems-based evaluation model of auditing WAPOL's complaint handling was mentioned (by WAPOL) as a positive change and a good innovation. This was because it involves both CCC officers and officers from WAPOL's Police Complaints Administration Centre travelling to the districts to communicate with those responsible for complaint handling. This helps to build WAPOL's capacity at the local level as well as build relationships between the CCC and WAPOL in their work. As the CCC stated, the approach enables them to "enter into a dialogue with police to tell them where the systemic or cultural issues exist that are undermining their capacity."

Successful Strategies

Entire Agency Approach

The entire approach to corruption prevention provides responsibility to districts and individuals to report misconduct as well as district activities in relation to risk management and corruption-prevention plans. WAPOL noted that the propensity for officers to report the complaints that they receive from the public has increased. WAPOL further discussed the positive impact of the mandatory reporting requirement for individual officers, where officers must report to their supervisor if they are charged with an offence. WAPOL expressed a desire to strengthen this requirement further to include a reporting requirement for infringement notices received and overseas incidents that may "bring the organisation into disrepute."

Identifying Systemic Issues

The CCC noted that a successful strategy in its work is using the individual case investigations (and reviews of investigations) to identify possible systemic issues rather than just focusing on individual complaints. The case-by-case approach of assessment, investigation, and review was still said to be "a very useful tool in encouraging police to take police conduct issues seriously, to accept the need for and embrace the concept of external oversight of their organisation, and improve the overall standard of police misconduct handling." However, the case-by-case approach was viewed to be less effective at dealing with some of the more entrenched and systemic cultural issues that were said to exist in the police service. In order to tackle these issues, the CCC stated that it was necessary to identify the reasons behind complaints and "join the dots" between complaints to highlight patterns and trends.

Police Internal Investigations

The CCC noted the importance of devolution of police internal investigations back to the police. The devolution of responsibility for investigations was noted to be central to the police taking responsibility for their organisation and the work of their members. As the CCC stated, "Anything that we can do to make the responsibility as close to the misconduct as possible and as immediate as possible is powerful."

Providing the Right Tools

The CCC noted that providing police with operational support to its work has resulted in a positive impact on reducing misconduct in the form of breaking rules to achieve results (often termed noble-cause corruption). The CCC stated that provision of improved practices, technology, and powers had directly affected the ability of police to perform their job. "If you give them (police) the tools to do the job, they will use the lawfully available tools every time before they use illegal ones. They tend to use the illegal ones because there aren't any lawful tools to do it." Provision of technology for collecting DNA, video taping of searches, and the power to detain people for questioning were cited as examples of capabilities that had reduced specific types of allegations against police, such as planting of evidence or improperly detaining suspects.

Disbanding Police Squads

The CCC noted that, historically, the disbanding of many police special squads had impacted significantly on systemic problems within WAPOL. However, while this move has been positive in that regard, it was noted that the effect was counterbalanced by a negative effect of rotating out experienced staff. "The areas where you have serious cultural problems are very often those that are involved with the more serious crime and then the cost involved is quite significant because then you have a whole lot of novices, you don't build up experience."

Emerging Ethical Issues

While some issues were highlighted to be ongoing, such as the high proportion of complaints regarding customer service issues as well as excessive force, some emerging issues were also noted. These are discussed below.

Domestic Violence by Police

Domestic violence by police officers was identified by WAPOL to be increasing. The CCC also noted that domestic violence by police is an identified issue, as well as other forms of problematic behaviour associated with relationships and relationship breakups, with stalking cited as an example.

Social Networking Sites

Social networking Web sites, such as Facebook, were highlighted by WAPOL as an area of concern in terms of WAPOL members' use of such sites. Members identifying themselves as police officers on sites, including posting photographs of them wearing their police uniform, was said to be a problem in that members seem to be unaware of how this information about them can be used. Particularly, WAPOL noted that such information is now being used by the defence as character information to potentially discredit officers who may be required to provide evidence in court.

Tasers

At the time of our interview, both the CCC and WAPOL noted that Taser use by WAPOL was an area that needed monitoring. WAPOL noted that there had been relatively few complaints concerning Tasers (compared to how many Taser uses had occurred in Western Australia) and that few of the complaints made had been sustained. However, WAPOL did note that there was a potential issue around using Tasers for gaining compliance that warranted exploration. WAPOL also noted that initial Taser policy wording had been problematic in that there was a disconnect between the policy and the legislation in terms of when Tasers could be used. However, the policy was described as providing specific additional restrictions on Taser use (that they can only be used to prevent injury to a person) within the legislation that provides officers with the right to use reasonable force. WAPOL noted that cameras for Tasers were an option being considered, but that this has a range of resources issues.

As mentioned previously, the CCC conducted a review of *The Use of Taser Weapons by WA Police* (Corruption and Crime Commission, 2010b). The report concluded that, while the majority of Taser use was appropriate, some incidents of misuse were identified, and, further, the WAPOL policy threshold for Taser use was the lowest in Australia. Since the report, the CCC has launched an investigation into an incident of WAPOL Taser use in a police watchhouse, and WAPOL has changed its Taser use threshold.

Confessional Evidence

WAPOL noted some recent problems arising in court cases around confessional evidence, with instances of evidence being made inadmissible due to feelings that it was not gained lawfully or under correct procedure. WAPOL stated that this showed a need for changes to policy or training with respect to interviewing to fit the standards and address the problems arising in court. As WAPOL stated, "At the end of the day, if that is the way the judiciary are ruling, then it's a problem we need to address, whether or not we agree directly." WAPOL has conducted project Anticus to improve detective practices and, in 2009, rolled out new standardised investigative training programs.

Critique and Recommendations 10

This chapter reviews the strategies and issues identified in Chapter 2 through Chapter 9 with a view to making practical recommendations for maintaining and improving police integrity. Chapter 1 reported that Australian jurisdictions have made an enormous investment in police integrity systems. While it appears that many of the more organised and systemic forms of corruption and misconduct have been substantially reduced, there are still ongoing conduct problems evidenced by periodic scandals, high volumes of complaints, and convictions of police on a range of disciplinary and criminal charges. A close examination of contemporary practice in Australia suggests that there is room for improvement in order to bring systems closer in line with available information about best practice.

This chapter is organised around key themes of the national stocktake study of police integrity strategies. The first section sets the general framework in terms of the shared responsibilities of external and internal agencies for police integrity. Subsequent sections cover customer service, complaints management, early intervention, staff development, staff support and organisational culture, random and targeted surveillance strategies, knowledge management and learning, and emerging ethical issues. The chapter includes clear recommendations to refine strategies and improve outcomes. It is envisaged that these recommendations will be directly relevant to Australian policing and to many other countries that face similar challenges in police integrity management.

Shared Responsibility for Police Integrity

Police oversight models for each Australian jurisdiction involve at least one external agency with the power to review police complaint handling, including an investigative role, although resources and powers and/or remit for this role differ. For example, some agencies may be limited to conducting investigations of only administrative matters, or on-duty actions of sworn officers, while others may have the power to conduct an investigation into any matter of public interest, including high-level corruption. Resources also differ in that, while some agencies are large, with well-resourced specialised support for investigations (e.g., dedicated covert tactics and intelligence-gathering units), others are small, with low staff numbers and low levels of funding, meaning that certain powers or functions are unable to be exercised. In many cases, legislation dictates what matters are to be handled by which agency and, in some cases, legislation provides the oversight agency with the power to make such decisions. In practice, some agencies have developed a memorandum of understanding regarding agency jurisdiction over matters, and legislation often allows oversight agencies the power to investigate or oversee any matter that it decides is appropriate or necessary. This may leave grey areas of responsibility, misunderstandings of roles, or feelings of powerlessness for police, particularly where multiple external agencies are involved. However, most jurisdictions appear to have reached a workable model in regard to assignment of responsibility for cases. The development of clearer standards for assigning cases between internal and external agencies is likely to be beneficial, though, particularly in enhancing the transparency of complaints management models.

The decision to bring criminal charges against a police officer is typically at the discretion of the Director of Public Prosecutions, while police forces hold the power to discipline their members. All oversight agencies have the power to make recommendations for disciplinary action against police members or for changes to police practices. However, no oversight agency has the power to enforce the acceptance or implementation of recommendations. Thus, reform is a process of discussion, persuasion, and negotiation, but oversight agencies can resort to pressure through exposure by public reports or reports to government.

This provides an interesting duality to oversight functions. Much as police internal investigations departments have taken on wider roles to enhance the professional standards of police, so oversight agencies are increasingly being tasked with educational and advisory roles in addition to their oversight and investigatory work. The difference between the coercive, intrusive investigatory role and the collaborative advisory role was described by one agency as the difference of "using sticks or carrots." Whilst both functions are necessary, these different dynamics could create tensions that negatively impact both areas, or each function could complement and inform the other.

The present research identified a number of strategies in use by police and oversight agencies that are relevant to reducing misconduct. Table 10.1 shows some examples of strategies found that address the different organisational and social influences on corruption that were outlined in Chapter 1. Table 10.2, at the end of this chapter, concentrates on some of the major strategies in use in Australia, as discovered through this research, and compares agencies with respect to these strategies.

Table 10.1 Police Integrity-Related Strategies in Use by Police and Oversight Agencies in Australia at the Time of This Research

Organisational Strategies				
Organisational Culture	Policy/Rules	Leadership	Limiting Opportunities	Investigation/Consequences
• Statement of values • Alternative dispute resolution • Inter-agency advice/ research • Customer Service Charter • Community Liaison • Ethical/professional standards performance indicators	• Code of conduct • Legislation • Education/training (in rules and risks) • Safe driving/pursuit management • Use of force • Taser use	• Devolution to local managers • Management models of discipline • Leadership in high rank recruitment specs • Leadership training • Integrity criteria for promotions	• Audit • Staff screening • Risk management • Procedural controls • Officer rotation • Record keeping • Financial checks • Controlling and recording access to data • Video/audio recording	• Investigations • Integrity testing • Intelligence analysis/research • Drug/alcohol testing • Complaints management • Local complaint management • Controlled ops • Covert methods • Early intervention system • Investigative powers • Discipline • Remedial interventions • Prosecutions experts/advice

Social Strategies		
Social Culture	Colleague Influence	External Influence
• Harassment offence • Reporting hotlines • Witness protection • Awards for integrity & good performance	• Staff support • Mandatory reporting of own and others' misconduct	• Registers and policies for: –Criminal associations –Secondary employment –Gifts & benefits –Human source handling

Customer Service

All jurisdictions spoke of large and/or increasing numbers of customer service-level complaints against the police, in comparison to numbers of serious matters. As noted in Chapter 1, this appears to be a common problem. These complaints typically involve unhappiness with the service offered, such as complaints of inaction or poor communication regarding action, and also demeanour-related complaints of rudeness and incivility. While such complaints may be considered low level and less important than serious integrity-related allegations, they still reflect a significant area of concern. The volume of complaints means that considerable resources are spent on handling matters that might be easily avoidable. Furthermore, the dissatisfaction represented by these complaints could impact upon general public confidence in police and public efforts to come forward with information or cooperate with the police in more serious matters.

Some police jurisdictions have begun to recognise the problem and respond directly. While all the police services have codes of ethics or conduct, some jurisdictions have introduced specific Customer Service Charters that outline the quality of service that members of the public can expect in their contact with police. In some cases, specific training has also been provided to frontline officers addressing the new customer service charter. Further, some agencies (e.g., NSW Police Force) spoke of "mystery shopper" techniques for randomly testing levels of service given, to evaluate problems and/or the training and policies provided.

Cleary an important aspect to such programs is buy-in at all levels of the organisation, but particularly frontline officers who have increased contact with the public. Understanding not just the policy but the rationale for, and importance of, improved customer service is key. Many agencies highlighted the importance of an organisational perspective on valuing complaints as a tool for improvement and organisational learning, replacing negative attitudes toward complainants as vexatious troublemakers. Access for making complaints has been a focus for many jurisdictions, with the utilisation of online resources as well as dedicated complaints reporting telephone lines, particularly for encouraging access by indigenous complainants. However, while complaint handling efforts are endorsed centrally, there tends to be more mixed support at the local level.

It is interesting to note, though, that the national surveys of satisfaction with the police, conducted by the Productivity Commission (2010), show that the satisfaction of those surveyed who have had personal contact with the police is generally higher than the satisfaction of the general public (many of whom will not have had contact with the police themselves, and so are likely influenced by secondary sources, e.g., media, etc.). This suggests that increased positive contact, for example, through community policing, might increase confidence in the police by overcoming second-hand perceptions.

In trialing interventions to improve police–community interactions, complaints can provide one measure of improvement, especially in light of the fact—as noted in Chapter 1—that complaints generally represent the tip of the iceberg of public dissatisfaction. Addressing the factors that give rise to complaints and reducing the number of complaints should have significant flow-on effects to all police–citizen interactions. Adopting an explicit policy and program of complaint reduction, therefore, is one way to seek to improve police service delivery and community satisfaction. However, those attempting to reduce complaints face a number of risks, including police avoiding doing their job, deflecting complainants, or disguising the true number of complaints. Nonetheless, there is research showing that complaints can be reduced without evidence of these problems, although system improvements may initially attract increased complaints as public confidence in the complaints and discipline system increases (Criminal Justice Commission, 1997a). Improved policing practices, such as improved negotiating skills and minimising the use of force, appear to be among the best methods for reducing complaints in tandem with the use of early intervention systems that profile potential problem behaviour by individual officers and police organisational units (Davis, Mateu-Gelabert, & Miller, 2005; Force Task Force, 2009; Porter, Prenzler, & Fleming, 2011; Walker, Alpert, & Kenney, 2000; see below for a more developed analysis).

Communication with the public is clearly important in terms of the general levels of service offered and members' conduct during citizen encounters as well as when handling complaints. Tasmania Police, aided by low numbers of complaints, are able to provide a consistent and personal service to complainants, including the opportunity to make complaints in person to Internal Investigations staff at headquarters without an appointment. Other agencies can also arrange to take complaints in person, or they encourage complainants to go to their local police station. The benefits of communicating with complainants, particularly providing regular updates (even when there may be no progress), were highlighted as important for complainant satisfaction. Dealing with minor complaints satisfactorily, and speedily, was pointed out to help prevent matters from escalating to persistent complaints or more serious complaints.

Better handling of complaints can also prevent the compounding of dissatisfaction when complainants are further alienated as a result of their experience with the complaints and discipline system. Better communication and more timely action are likely to be key elements in a system that is more favourably received by complainants (Prenzler, Allard, Curry, & Macintyre, 2010). A standard survey attached to the final correspondence with complainants (when they are notified of the outcome of their complaint) would provide a systematic method for collecting feedback to improve practice. Similarly, such surveys could be provided to the subject officers, as their experiences of the complaints process is clearly also important for the organisations and interagency relations.

Recommendation 1: Increase understanding of complaints as a learning and improvement tool.
Recommendation 2: Police to utilise the training and/or resources for complaint handling and investigating available through oversight agencies.
Recommendation 3: Stakeholder surveys to be provided to complainants and subject officers at the conclusion of a complaint case.

Complaints Management

The majority of Australian jurisdictions now have a form of triage system in place for complaint handling, in recognition that different complaints may require different resources and levels of oversight. While threshold levels differ by agency, there is a general consistency in separating customer service complaints of minor matters from those that allege more serious misconduct and corruption. Increasingly, minor matters are dealt with by police at a regional, or local, level rather than through a central department, and increasingly they are dealt with through a process of dispute resolution rather than full investigation. However, while dispute resolution is likely to involve communication with complainants to come to an agreed outcome, it rarely involves face-to-face mediation between the complainant and the subject officer. Typically, the complainant will not be provided an opportunity to meet with or speak to the subject officer. The matter will instead be resolved by the local manager of the subject officer, who will communicate to the complainant and subject officer separately. Conciliation, therefore, may involve an explanation offered by the subject officer's manager, or an assurance that the subject officer will be counselled about his/her conduct.

While not traditional mediation, local resolution serves two important functions: it focuses on resolution, and, therefore, complainant satisfaction and customer service; and, it empowers local managers to be responsible for the conduct and performance of their staff. Local managers are in the best position to observe and recognise staff performance, enact interventions quickly where needed, as well as communicate and provide an example, or model, for expected performance (Ede & Barnes, 1992). Complainants are more likely to be satisfied with the complaint handling process when their complaints are dealt with through mediation rather than an investigate and prosecute model—with complainants often simply wanting an assurance that the subject officer understands the complaint and will not repeat the same conduct in the future. However, research also shows that face-to-face mediation between the subject officer and complainant is the preferred option for complainants (Ede & Barnes, 2002; Prenzler, 2009b, pp. 97–112).

There has long been a debate over the most appropriate agency to investigate complaints against police, with public criticism of police investigating their own complaints typically spurring external agency involvement. This, again, is a process that has occurred in many countries, as outlined in Chapter 1. However, the Australian research showed that most oversight agencies are supportive of police investigating themselves (at least for less serious matters), noting the skills and experience of internal investigators and improvements in the quality and professionalism of investigations as well as the need for police to take responsibility for the conduct of members. Several oversight agencies saw their role as a "safety net" that allowed scrutiny of cases in certain circumstances (where complainants are unhappy with the police internal investigation, or where the matter is of significant seriousness or public interest) to enhance public confidence. Indeed, anticorruption agencies are typically only resourced to investigate the most serious of matters or those that hold public interest.

"Devolution" (both from an external agency to police and from a central police department to the local level), in theory, enables better use of resources through more appropriate responses (rather than subjecting all matters to a full investigation). Devolution also aids timeliness of dealing with matters, which impacts not only complainant satisfaction, but also the effectiveness of responses and the experience of the subject officer. However, devolution relies on decentralisation of roles and responsibility and, therefore, the effectiveness of the people who occupy those roles. Thus, in order to ensure the effectiveness of devolution, appropriate support and training needs to be provided to local managers as well as monitoring of cases to ensure consistency of action. While strict rules and policies may aid in consistency, the ability to exercise discretion will enable local ownership of decision making. Several jurisdictions have introduced an additional layer of accountability and support through the adoption of regional teams to assist the local managers with these functions and increase the consistency of staff management and complaint handling standards. It should be kept in mind, nonetheless, that surveys indicate strongly that a greater degree of independent input into the complaints process—whether it be investigations or mediation—is likely to generate a better experience for complainants (Prenzler et al., 2010).

Recommendation 4: Provision of leadership and management training to local managers, and support for aiding the consistency of complaint handling and addressing staff performance (or under performance).

Recommendation 5: Greater consideration given to the preferences of complainants regarding which agency investigates and adjudicates their complaint.

Early Intervention

While complaint handling and investigations have largely been core business for both police internal departments and oversight agencies, there has been a widening of this function to encompass ethical and professional standards more generally, encouraging a shift to more proactive strategies. Analysis of complaints data held by agencies allows for profiling of problems at the individual or area level. Identification of patterns in complaints can aid the tailoring of interventions to address the problem, but also to prevent further, escalating problems. Complaints, thus, typically form the basis of Early Intervention Systems (EISs), which inform localised prevention efforts. EISs are, therefore, systems of identification of problems based on objective data and thresholds, but also require a process in place to address the problem and monitor its development in light of any action taken. EISs are increasingly evolving to encompass a broader range of indicators, beyond complaint numbers. Indictors of individual stressors and behavioural problems are being incorporated into systems. Thus, systems are increasingly relying on information collected and held by a variety of different departments and databases within police organisations, such as health and welfare (e.g., sick leave or absences), performance, duties and work area, use of force deployments, arrest-release and resist-arrest incidents, as well as complaints. Thus, such systems put a strain on many organisations' existing IT capabilities, or require expensive upgrades.

An EIS also relies on the dissemination of the knowledge captured (e.g., when an officer reaches a determined threshold), an appropriate response, and monitoring of the effects of that response. Local resolution of issues, as well as performance management frameworks, can support these elements of the Early Intervention process. Many jurisdictions are opting for the same software package that allows flexibility in the indicators specified, the thresholds required to "flag" problems as well as levels of access to the system. With regard to the latter, the software can be used as a central repository, but also can allow access by other areas of the organisation to view and/or input data. This allows for sharing of information, both gathering information to aid analysis and disseminating information to those responsible for the areas and individuals identified as needing a response.

Responses to problem behaviour and poor performance have shifted to complement the Early Intervention process—from punishment to remedial approaches that recognise honest mistakes and seek to rectify behaviour through learning. Approaches such as counselling, training, mentoring, and increased supervision are replacing punishments such as fines. The remedial responses focus less on individual blame for behaviour and more on supporting the individual to achieve communicated standards. Such approaches are also hoped to allow speedier responses to poor performance, rather than a formal disciplinary process, the length of which was the subject of much criticism by agencies. In order to respond to the intervention needs of staff, supervisors require the skills and support to effectively identify and manage problems.

Recommendation 6: Implementation of an Early Intervention System, preferably integrated with data beyond just numbers of complaints, and a framework for following through the intervention, including support and training for local managers.

Staff Development

As well as intervening in poor staff performance, staff development should be positively encouraged. Most police organisations now have a variety of codes and charters to reflect required standards of behaviour. However, there are fewer examples of highlighting or rewarding good practice, performance, or conduct. Performance-based promotion is now more common, with recognition that promotion typically means more responsibility for managing others, and that this requires managerial and leadership skills. One jurisdiction noted that promotion applicants are often motivated more by the financial implications of promotion rather than the role itself, which was problematic. The use of integrity as a specific promotion criterion is emerging, with applicants asked to address and demonstrate this in applications.

Many of the jurisdictions offer a good conduct medal to members in recognition of performance, although such medals are typically only achieved after many years of service. The New South Wales Police Force offers an internal integrity award for members of its Professional Standards Command (PSC) and was contemplating broadening this to members outside of PSC. NSW Police Force also runs stories commending good work in their *Police Weekly* publication.

Frequent and varied recognition of good conduct, as well as strong ethical leadership, would support an ethical culture and provide more incentive for engaging with the organisation's ethical values. Victoria Police and Office of Police Integrity (OPI) in Victoria spoke about identifying police members for their ethical leadership to fulfil roles in the integrity framework, including acting on the Police Reform Advisory Group to aid interaction between Victoria Police and OPI as well as being selected for the Professional Development Committees that provide dissemination and support services to aid the decentralisation of responsibility for integrity throughout the police. Given the necessity to support the development of staff and encourage ethical leadership, as well as comments from agencies regarding establishing professional competencies for development within the police (to increase professionalisation of the police), use might be made of these positions as more formal career pathways to promotion.

Recommendation 7: Performance-based management and/or promotion, and recognition of integrity, and ethics, particularly in leadership.

Staff Support and Organisational Culture

Some agencies spoke of measuring the ethical climate or ethical health of police forces. For example, the Corruption and Crime Commission in Western Australia conducts surveys on public officers' perceptions of misconduct risks. Further, the Crime and Misconduct Commission in Queensland has surveyed police recruits and first-year constables since 1995 to compare their understanding of misconduct scenarios. These techniques are similar to Klockars, Ivkovich, Harver, & Haberfeld's (2000) survey of police officers in the United States, which has been replicated in several countries, including the United Kingdom and Sweden. The Australian Federal Police spoke about considering similar internal ethics surveys of members.

An indicator of a healthy ethical culture is likely to be seen in the unwillingness of members of an organisation to tolerate unethical behaviour or misconduct. Willingness to report misconduct, support for those who do report, as well as an absence of harassment of "whistleblowers" are all positive indicators of an ethical culture. Some jurisdictions offer anonymous reporting telephone lines to encourage members to report unethical behaviour. However, many police forces now require mandatory reporting of misconduct; thus members must identify themselves when reporting misconduct in order to document that they have fulfilled their obligation.

The Australian Federal Police has a sophisticated support system in place for members to report misconduct. Their Confidant Network offers 24-hour support in the form of trained individuals to record reports of misconduct, offer advice, and coordinate welfare services or witness protection if necessary. However, generally, while support services undoubtedly encourage members to report misconduct, there often still exists mistrust of such services; generally, mistrust of, and on occasion hostility toward, oversight agencies investigating misconduct; and a laissez-faire attitude among many with regard to integrity, either in turning a blind eye or shifting responsibility. Fundamentally, it is important to have an organisational culture that is actively intolerant of unethical conduct and harassment of members. Police organisations are well-known for solidarity among members. This solidarity has been criticised and blamed for harbouring and encouraging misconduct. However, this solidarity could be a positive and powerful mechanism for the organisation. Good leadership throughout the organisation is an important part of the process of engaging honest and conscientious officers, particularly as visible ethical role models, as well as organisational recognition for active ethical conduct. Furthermore, the system that deals with the minority of officers who do not behave appropriately must be seen to be fair and consistent, in order for members to have confidence in supporting that system. The managerial models of discipline that focus on the process of natural justice and procedural fairness, which many jurisdictions are adopting, should aid this.

Recommendation 8: Police to adopt more "social support" strategies and improve an active culture against misconduct and harassment.

Random and Targeted Surveillance Strategies

Member morale and trust in the organisation are important aspects of the processes described above and were recognised by many jurisdictions. Most police forces agreed that strategies such as random integrity testing can undermine this trust and, therefore, should not be used by police. The NSW Police Force has, however, introduced a form of random integrity testing in its mystery shopper program to test customer service. Victoria's OPI also suggested that a similar technique could have potential for testing systems, or the effectiveness and impact of implemented recommendations. Thus, while random integrity testing might be viewed as inappropriate and ineffective as an integrity strategy for some forms of conduct, there is the potential for the use of similar practices in some areas.

Random alcohol and/or drug testing has also been adopted by some agencies. Agencies endorsed the deterrent effect of random drug and alcohol testing, but emphasised that numbers of tests conducted had to be high enough to produce a perceived risk of being tested. The ability to recall officers to duty for testing was highlighted as important in order to capture potential recreational off-duty drug use, while hair testing remains controversial. A highly publicised "zero tolerance" for drugs is endorsed by some agencies because this also serves to deter unsuitable applicants. Some agencies communicate this in their application process, including requiring signed statements that applicants are aware that they will likely be tested for drugs both at the academy and as a sworn officer. Some agencies, however, showed concern that a zero-tolerance approach to drugs did not allow self-disclosure of drug abuse problems or access to appropriate support services within the organisation.

General covert investigative techniques, such as surveillance, listening devices, and telecommunications interception, were all valued by police and oversight agencies for investigating corruption or serious misconduct. Such powers are increasingly being given to anticorruption agencies, with mandatory annual reporting of the use of these powers (e.g., the number of warrants applied for and granted under each piece of legislation). Overt audio and video recording practices are also being adopted and are endorsed for their positive impacts on police-citizen encounters—regulating the behaviour of both police and citizens as well as providing valuable evidence in complaint cases. Anecdotally, the use of recording devices by officers was cited as reducing numbers of complaints.

Recommendation 9: There appears to be the opportunity for agencies to make greater use of the deterrent effect of random drug testing and random "integrity testing" for specific issues (such as customer service), systems, or evaluating change.

Recommendation 10: Consideration of new technological advances, such as body-worn video, and their deterrent effects on police and citizen behaviour.

Knowledge Management/Learning

Many of Australia's oversight agencies are in a powerful position to potentially enhance the knowledge of the agencies that they oversee. Most hold comprehensive databases of complaints that can be strategically analysed, and many also have specific research capabilities. Oversight agencies also commonly stated that it is important to use investigations to enhance knowledge: to uncover *why* an officer has engaged in unethical behaviour, not just to prove *what* that officer did. This reflects the rise in calls for "evidence-based practice." However, all agencies noted that there are difficulties with evaluating the impact of anticorruption efforts and that, while individual strategies may be easier to evaluate, resources often prevented in-depth evaluations from being conducted.

Some oversight agencies are legislated to perform an educational function with respect to the police, while others are only tasked with reviewing complaints and complaint systems. Thus, some oversight agencies are not involved in police training at all, or may only be involved in police training to educate about their own organisation and role in the complaints system. However, knowledge management, knowledge sharing, and "learning the lessons" will aid improvement, and various examples of this were found among the agencies. Some oversight agencies utilise their knowledge of commonly received complaints to educate police members, particularly new recruits, as to potential risks and how to avoid them. Police agencies themselves are also beginning to disseminate this information among members, typically via professional standards departments. Dissemination methods include presentations and publications. For example, South Australia Police produce current issues papers that incorporate case studies to illustrate acceptable and unacceptable behaviour and the consequences. Victoria Police have also undertaken the Ceja Knowledge Management Project to specifically develop learning materials, including case studies, from the information arising out of the Ceja Task Force's successful investigation and prosecution of members of the former drug squad—as well as appointing a Senior Ethical Health Initiatives Advisor who is responsible for knowledge management.

Recommendation 11: More effort to evaluate strategies and share evaluation outcomes.
Recommendation 12: Oversight agencies could provide training sessions on risks (complaint trend analysis and case studies).
Recommendation 13: Extracting and communicating the lessons from misconduct investigations and cases to aid organisational learning.
Recommendation 14: Oversight agencies could help with systemic risk identification and mitigation strategies (through research, literature searches, and data analysis).

Emerging Ethical Issues

Agencies noted that, while some new issues were emerging as warranting concern, many issues affecting police integrity are either ongoing or rotational, thus requiring continued attention to guard against complacency. Issues that have been, and are still, of particular concern included drugs, use of force, inappropriate associations, misuse (or unauthorised access and release) of information, and (real or perceived) conflicts of interest.

Some of these issues were proposed to be linked to the recruitment context. The values and experiences of young people of the current generation (Gen Y), who form the bulk of the applicant pool, were said to pose certain risks, including current or historic recreational drug use (or attitudes supporting drug use) and use of technology, particularly social networking sites, but also social media more generally. The risks of police officers using social networking sites included creating vulnerabilities that could be exploited by criminals; identification of officers who may later want to engage in covert work; and bringing the police service into disrepute, as well as undermining their own credibility in court, through inappropriate content of material posted on sites. Inappropriate use of e-mail was also cited as a problem, not just for new officers, as was misuse of the Internet, such as accessing nonwork-related sites at work; harassment of, or distributing inappropriate content to, colleagues; unauthorised access and release of information; and some (rarer) cases of access to illegal content including child pornography. Information sheets with guidelines provide one way of communicating the risks involved with the use of social media. Information can include case studies to illustrate consequences.

Citizen interactions were highlighted in a number of ways as an area of concern. Inappropriate use of force and complaints regarding use of force remain an issue, and the introduction of Tasers as an additional use of force option presents further challenges. Strategies for increased accountability include a mandatory reporting system for use of force deployments (use of force forms), subject to audit and analysis in order to track problems or patterns. Some jurisdictions have introduced, or tested, the use of video and audio equipment, such as body-worn video as well as Taser cameras. While Taser cameras are automatically activated, they were critiqued as providing only footage of the actual Tasering incident and not the interaction that led to the deployment of the Taser. Therefore, body-worn video was said to be preferable to capture the full circumstances of the incident. Clear policies and adequate training are also important, for example, many jurisdictions do not allow Tasers to be used in dry-stun mode (where the Taser is held directly against the body), only by firing of the projectiles (cf., Alpert & Dunham, 2010).

Adequate training for use of force, or operational skills and tactics, can clearly impact upon police–citizen encounters and the potential for complaints. Particularly, some jurisdictions have seen benefits in verbal communication training for recruits, including techniques of deescalating potentially hostile situations. Simulation-based training looks to have been a successful mode for recruit learning in these areas. Tasmania Police have seen large reductions in assault and excessive use of force complaints since introducing training that emphasises deescalation as well as utilising realistic simulation scenarios (Porter et al., 2011; see also Davis et al., 2005; Force Task Force, 2009). For example, training scenarios allow recruits to experience stressful, potentially threatening simulated encounters (stress inoculation) and apply operational tactics with a range of realistic corresponding outcomes (from physical violence to deescalation). Video recording of the simulations adds another layer to the learning, allowing self-analysis as well as accountability training.

On a more general level, police–citizen interactions were thought by agencies to be improved through communication in the form of providing information. Many complaints are received that concern citizens' misunderstanding of the powers of police and can be resolved by an explanation of the legislation. Agencies suggested that many of these complaints could be avoided if frontline officers provided that information at the time of the interaction, for example, explaining or writing down the legislation (the Act/part) that enabled the officer to stop and search the person.

Minority communities were also raised as presenting several potential challenges to policing, for example, due to differences in culture, language, and experiences or expectations of police. Particularly, Australia's increasing population of immigrants was noted to potentially bring with them a mistrust of police that can be difficult to overcome. Australia's own indigenous populations are often underrepresented in complaint statistics showing an unwillingness to complain or difficulties accessing the complaints system. Several jurisdictions have launched initiatives to increase the accessibility of services, for example, introducing and advertising dedicated complaints telephone lines for indigenous communities, working with community groups, and employing community liaison officers. With the increasing diversity of Australia's population, care needs to be taken in assigning liaison officers to communities, and keeping up-to-date with international events that might affect home communities (and relationships between different communities).

Since the 9/11 terrorist attacks, community engagement has become high on the agenda of police agencies for a variety of reasons. Increased police powers in response to terrorism threats have provided increased potential for abuse, or public perception of abuse. Agencies were asked to comment specifically on new ethical issues in the context of antiterrorism powers as well as human rights legislation that has been enacted in some states. Many jurisdictions felt that they had not experienced any problems in these areas, and that more traditional ethical concerns were still at the forefront of their agenda. Where jurisdictions did comment on these issues, it was typically in relation to the need for public reassurance and communication in the use of police powers, and concerns over future changes that could bring about more extreme powers, or remove police discretion in the use of powers.

In the case of many identified risks, such as those above, the response is often to enact policies, rules, or guidelines that constrain actions or highlight the appropriate or required action. This response undoubtedly has its advantages, for example, constraining the use of Tasers in certain ways, such as prohibiting dry-stun mode or use on vulnerable people, is likely to significantly reduce the risk of adverse outcomes. However, enacting too many prescriptive policies for police action was highlighted to potentially create problems. Several agencies noted that general, simple codes of conduct that can be applied to all areas of policing were more workable than detailed policies for specific aspects of work. Understanding general ethical principles was highlighted as enabling discretion and ethical decision making, which allows ownership and accountability rather than mechanically following rules. Additionally, rules that are unworkable or too complex can cause individuals to circumvent the process, which could lead to believed justification for corner cutting and ignoring the rules, or the development of one's own working practices that are then inconsistent across the organisation and difficult to monitor and oversee. All of this aids a culture that justifies misconduct. Further, while ethics training and codes of ethics can communicate expected standards of behaviour (and activity in both these areas has increased in police forces), there is a difference between compliance and cultural change. While rules and sanctions may create compliance, cultural change needs to be fostered through ethics training that encourages thought in applying general principles to decision making, and teaches the practical reasons why ethics are important, including the consequences for the organisation, the members, and the work that they do.

Recommendation 15: Consider introducing a use of force report form to improve accountability in this area and aid policy-oriented analysis.

Recommendation 16: Agencies should engage in regular environmental scans to identify current and emerging ethical risks that need to be addressed.

Conclusions

This study has shown that numerous strategies are employed within increasingly complex integrity frameworks across the different jurisdictions in Australia. At the same time, there are certain key themes important to all agencies in their fight against misconduct. Leadership is of central importance to the success of many strategies. Organisational values will not be accepted by members of an organisation unless they are demonstrated by those who occupy key roles. Ethical leaders who provide positive role models for more junior staff will encourage ethical behaviour to be the organisational norm. Thus, leadership is important at all levels of the organisation, and in various forms. Leaders must be visible, consistent and fair in their behaviour, and be empowered to performance manage their staff as necessary.

A second key theme is communication. Communication within agencies aids in knowledge sharing to support and address localised problems. Interagency communication and collaboration is also important, and agencies can engage their different perspectives to address common problems and share or develop best practice. Currently, a forum run by the Australia New Zealand Police Advisory Agency allows this to happen between police agencies, with attendance by representatives from all the state/territory police (from the central departments responsible for ethical standards and complaints). This encourages communication and collaboration between police agencies over emerging issues. Further, 2010 saw the establishment of a similar forum for anticorruption agencies—the Australia–New Zealand Police Integrity Leadership Forum. However, a similar vehicle for

Table 10.2 Agency Comparison of the Use of Integrity-Related Strategies at the Time of This Research

Jurisdiction	Fed/ACT			NSW			NT		QLD		SA		TAS		VIC		WA	
Strategy / Agency	AFP	ACLEI	Com Omb	NSWPF	PIC	NSW Omb	NT Police	NT Omb	QPS	CMC	SAPol	PCA	TAS Pol	TAS Omb	VIC Pol	OPI	WA Pol	CCC
Early **I**ntervention **S**ystem/ **C**omplaints **P**rofiling/ **T**rend **A**nalysis	CP	TA	TA	EIS*	TA	CP	CP	CP	CP	CP	EIS	CP	EIS		EIS	CP	EIS	CP
Risk management	✓	✓		✓	✓	✓	✓		✓	✓	✓				✓	✓	✓	✓
Drug and alcohol testing (**R**andom, **T**argeted, & **M**andatory)	✓			✓					R (Alcohol); T & M drug & alcohol		R (drug) covert officers only		✓-		T, M		T, R*	
Integrity testing (**R**andom, **T**argeted)	T*			T					T-	T	T		T-		T	T	T	T, R
Complaints investigation	✓	✓	✓	✓	✓	✓	✓	✓-	✓	✓	✓	✓	✓	✓	✓	✓	✓	✓
Covert operations in complaints/misconduct investigations	✓	✓		✓	✓		✓-		✓	✓	✓	J	✓-		✓	✓	✓	✓
Local management intervention	✓			✓			✓		✓		✓		✓		✓		✓	
Complaints mediation						✓	✓-	✓	✓				✓-		✓	✓-	✓-	
Ethics education/training	✓	✓		✓	✓		✓		✓	✓	✓	✓	✓		✓	✓	✓	✓
Staff screening	✓	✓		✓	✓		✓		✓	✓	✓		✓		✓		✓	✓
Witness support	✓	✓		✓	✓				✓	✓	✓		✓-		✓	✓	✓	✓

Note: ✓ = strategy in use by agency.
✓- = can, but never or rarely used in practice (e.g., because unnecessary, unsuccessful, or not resourced).
* = being developed at time of interview.
J = does jointly with another agency by leveraging their powers or resource.

encouraging collaboration between police *and* oversight agencies would be beneficial. Currently, annual conferences provide some opportunities, and the Australian Federal Police's Inter-Agency Integrity Investigators Program also brings together investigators from national and international integrity agencies. However, the latter is a training course for select participants. A more stable and committed group arrangement (committee or forum) for representatives from national agencies (both police and oversight and anti-corruption) with long-term goals would be valuable for building relationships and sharing learning.

Communication with the public, and particularly complainants, can help to prevent complaints or escalation of complaints. The majority of police complaints arise out of conduct of officers in citizen encounters, whether that is minor issues of demeanour, lack of action or explanation, or more serious forms of contact, such as complaints of wrongful arrest, excessive use of force, or assault. Techniques to improve police–public interactions, including enhanced communication (whether that is enhanced personal skills or organisational procedures), are likely to improve citizen satisfaction and confidence in police and, in turn, reduce complaints.

Leadership, communication, and knowledge provide the framework of an integrity system that supports and enables more focused individual strategies. However, it is also important to ensure the right mix of regulatory strategies. In other words, a "one size fits all" strategy is unlikely to be appropriate, and consideration of the types of misconduct and where certain problems may lie, both nationally and regionally, is vital. A rounded integrity system will have both proactive strategies (e.g., education, research and analysis, and risk assessment) and reactive strategies (e.g., complaints receipt and investigation, and performance management). Strategies should also address key underlying risk areas of both the organisation (its structures, systems, policies, and procedures) and the members within the organisation (including individuals and the collective culture).

Given jurisdictional differences in experience and needs, a national integrity system may not be appropriate for Australia, nor, indeed, for other countries. However, a national integrity *framework* that guides decision making over the adoption of strategies might be possible. Such a framework could be as simple as providing national minimum standards, or it could offer a more sophisticated model that suggests specific areas of importance, strategies to address those areas, and criteria for evaluation. Furthermore, moves toward interoperability and interagency information sharing, as well as national performance measures, might call for consistency in recording and storing professional standards and complaints information that could allow a national shared database. However, such advances will rely on technological capabilities as well as the support and investment of agencies.

Many of the stakeholders interviewed expressed the sentiment that sustainable reform needs both the right tools and the right use of those tools; whilst agencies external to the police may aid the provision of such tools, ultimately it is the police culture that will determine their success through supporting and driving their appropriate use.

References

ABC News. (2005, February 16). Police transportation case may cause procedure changes. Retrieved from http//global.factiva.com

Alpert, G. P. & Dunham, R. G. (2010). Policy and training recommendations related to police use of CEDs: Overview of findings from a comprehensive national study. *Police Quarterly, 13*(3), 235–259.

Attorney General. (2009). *Commonwealth organized crime strategic framework*. Canberra: Attorney General's Department.

Australian Commission for Law Enforcement Integrity. (2008). *Annual report of the integrity commissioner 2007–2008*. Canberra: Australian Commission for Law Enforcement Integrity.

Australian Commission for Law Enforcement Integrity. (2009a). *Resistance to corruption*. Canberra: Australian Commission for Law Enforcement Integrity.

Australian Commission for Law Enforcement Integrity. (2009b). *Annual report of the integrity commissioner 2008–2009*. Canberra: Australian Commission for Law Enforcement Integrity.

Australian Commission for Law Enforcement Integrity. (2010). *Annual report of the integrity commissioner 2009–2010*. Canberra: Australian Commission for Law Enforcement Integrity.

Australian Crime Commission. (2009). *Annual report 08–09*. Canberra: ACC.

Australian Federal Police. (2007). *Annual report for 2006–7*. Canberra: AFP.

Australian Federal Police. (2008). *Annual report for 2007–8*. Canberra: AFP.

Australian Federal Police. (2009). *Annual report for 2008–9*. Canberra: AFP.

Australian Federal Police. (2010). *Annual report for 2009–10*. Canberra: AFP.

Australian Law Reform Commission. (1995). *Under the spotlight: Complaints against the AFP and NCA*. Sydney: ALRC.

BBC News (2002, July 10). Flashback: Rodney King and the LA riots. Retrieved from http://news.bbc.co.uk/1/hi/world/Americas/2119943.stm

Beck, A., & Robertson, A. (2009). The challenges to developing democratic policing in post-Soviet societies: The Russian experience. *Police Practice and Research: An International Journal, 10*(4), 285–293.

Board of Inquiry. (2000). *Board of inquiry into the rampart corruption incident: Final report*. Los Angeles: Los Angeles Police Department.

Brown, D. (1987). *The police complaints procedure: A survey of complainants' views*. London: Home Office.

Brumby, J. (2010). Government adopts Proust integrity model. Retrieved from www.premier.vic.gov.au/component/content/article/10643.html

Bryett, K., Harrison, A., & Shaw, J. (1997). *The role and function of police in Australia*. Sydney: Butterworths.

Christopher, W. (1991). *Report of the Independent Commission on the Los Angeles Police Department*. Los Angeles: Independent Commission on the LAPD.

Civilian Complaint Review Board. (2010). *Annual report*. New York, NY.
Commonwealth Human Rights Initiative. (2005) *Police accountability: Too important to neglect, too urgent to delay*. New Delhi: Commonwealth Human Rights Initiative.
Commonwealth Ombudsman. (2007a). *Annual report for 2006–2007*. Canberra: Commonwealth Ombudsman.
Commonwealth Ombudsman. (2007b). *Review of ACT policing's watchhouse operations: Joint report by the Australian Federal Police and the Commonwealth Ombudsman*. Canberra: Commonwealth Ombudsman.
Commonwealth Ombudsman. (2008a). *Annual report for 2007–2008*. Canberra: Commonwealth Ombudsman.
Commonwealth Ombudsman. (2008b). *Report on the Ombudsman's activities under Part V of the Australian Federal Police Act 1979*. Canberra: Commonwealth Ombudsman.
Commonwealth Ombudsman. (2009). *Annual report for 2008–2009*. Canberra: Commonwealth Ombudsman.
Commonwealth Ombudsman. (2010). *Annual report for 2009–2010*. Canberra: Commonwealth Ombudsman.
Corruption and Crime Commission. (2009a). *Public perceptions survey*. Perth: CCC.
Corruption and Crime Commission. (2006). *'Two years out'—A report of the first two years of the Western Australia Police. Reform program*. Perth: CCC. Retrieved from http://www.ccc.wa.gov.au/Publications/Reports/Documents/Published%20Reports/2006/report_2006-police-reform-program.pdf
Corruption and Crime Commission. (2007). *Corruption and Crime Commission annual report 2006–2007*. Perth: CCC.
Corruption and Crime Commission. (2008). *Corruption and Crime Commission annual report 2007–2008*. Perth: CCC.
Corruption and Crime Commission. (2009). *Corruption and Crime Commission annual report 2008–2009*. Perth: CCC.
Corruption and Crime Commission. (2010a). *Corruption and Crime Commission annual report 2009–2010*. Perth: CCC.
Corruption and Crime Commission. (2010b). *The use of Taser weapons by Western Australia police*. Perth: CCC. Retrieved from http://www.ccc.wa.gov.au/Publications/Reports/Published%20Reports%202010/Full%20Report%20-%20Use%20of%20Taser%20Weapons%20by%20WAPOL.pdf
Crime and Misconduct Commission. (2008). *Annual report 2007–08*. Brisbane: CMC.
Crime and Misconduct Commission. (2009a). *Public perceptions of the Queensland Police Service: Findings from the 2008 public attitudes survey*. Brisbane: CMC.
Crime and Misconduct Commission. (2009b). *Dangerous liaisons: A report arising from a CMC investigation into allegations of police misconduct (Operation Capri)*. Brisbane: CMC. Retrieved from http://www.cmc.qld.gov.au/data/portal/00000005/content/05464001248164585939.pdf
Crime and Misconduct Commission. (2009c). *Annual report 2008–09*. Brisbane: CMC.
Crime and Misconduct Commission. (2010a). *Setting the Standard: A review of current processes for the management of police discipline and misconduct matters*. Brisbane: CMC. Retrieved from http://www.cmc.qld.gov.au/data/portal/00000005/content/13136001292219485158.pdf
Crime and Misconduct Commission. (2010b). CMC review of Queensland Police Service's *Palm Island Review*. Brisbane: CMC. Retrieved from http://www.cmc.qld.gov.au/data/portal/00000005/content/13053001276649217949.pdf

Criminal Justice Commission. (1997a). *Integrity in the Queensland Police Service: Implementation and impact of the Fitzgerald Inquiry Reforms*. Brisbane: CJC. Retrieved from http://www.cmc.qld.gov.au/data/portal/00000005/content/17318001131412435681.pdf

Criminal Justice Commission. (1997b). *Reducing police-civilian conflict*. Brisbane: CJC. Retrieved from http://www.cmc.qld.gov.au/data/portal/00000005/content/15410001200279162656.pdf

Criminal Justice Commission. (2000). *Public attitudes towards the QPS*. Brisbane: CJC.

Criminal Justice Commission. (2001). *Integrity in the Queensland Police Service: QPS reform update* (Vol. 1). Brisbane: CJC. Retrieved from http://www.cmc.qld.gov.au/data/portal/00000005/content/61788001141698731096.pdf

Critchley, T. (1967). *A history of police in England and Wales 900–1966*. London: Constable & Company.

Daley, R. (1978). *Prince of the city*. Boston: Houghton Mifflin.

Davis, R., Mateu-Gelabert, P., & Miller, J. (2005). Can effective policing also be respectful? Two examples in the South Bronx. *Police Quarterly, 8*(2), 229–247.

Denholm, M., & Salusinszky, I. (2008, May 24). A watchdog for every house. *The Australian*. Retrieved from http://www.theaustralian.com.au/national-affairs/state-politics/a-watchdog-for-every-house/story-e6frgczx-1111116427545

Dixon, D. (2006). A window into the interviewing process? The audio-visual recording of police interrogation in New South Wales, Australia. *Policing & Society, 16*(4), 323–348.

Dwyer, J. (2009, December 2) Fewer officers, attracting more lawsuits. *New York Times*, p. 28.

Ede, A., & Barnes, M. (2002). Alternative strategies for resolving complaints. In T. Prenzler & J. Ransley (Eds.), *Police reform: Building integrity* (pp. 115–130). Sydney: Federation Press.

Finn, P. (2001) *Citizen review of police: Approaches and implementation*. Washington, D.C.: National Institute of Justice.

Finnane, M. (1999). From police force to police service? Aspects of the recent history of the New South Wales Police. In D. Dixon (Ed.), *A culture of corruption* (pp. 6–35). Sydney: Hawkins Press.

Fisher, W. (2003). A review of professional standards in the Australian Federal Police. Canberra: Australian Federal Police.

Fitzgerald, T. (1989). *Report of a Commission of Inquiry pursuant to orders in council*. Brisbane: Government Printer.

Force Task Force. (2009). *Use of force by the Portland police bureau follow-up*. Portland, OR: Office of the City Auditor.

Gilinskiy, Y. (2011). Torture by the Russian police: An empirical study. *Police Practice and Research: An International Journal, 12*(2), 163–171.

Girodo, M. (2003, January). *A global view of police integrity management*. Paper presented at ICAC-Interpol "Partnership Against Corruption" Conference. Retrieved March 19, 2008 from http://www.icac.org.hk/symposium/2003/Presentation/Day2/IGEC%20-%20Mission%20and%20Vision%20(Michel%20Girodo,%20Speech).pdf

Hatty, S. (1989). Policing male violence in Australia. In J. Hanmer, J. Radford, & E. A. Stanko (Eds.), *Women, policing and male violence: International perspectives* (pp. 70–89). London: Routledge.

Hayes, M. (1997). *A police ombudsman for Northern Ireland?* Belfast: Home Office Stationery Office.

HayGroup. (2002). *Qualitative and strategic audit of the reform process (QSARP) of the NSW Police*. Sydney: HayGroup.

Henry, P., & Isaacson, N. (2010). *Evaluation of the Blueline*. Joondalup, Australia: Edith Cowan University.

Henry, V. (1994). Police corruption: Tradition and evolution. In K. Bryett & C. Lewis (Eds.), *Un-Peeling tradition: Contemporary policing* (pp. 160–176). Melbourne: Macmillan.

Hind, R. (2010, June 15). Ombudsman lacks firepower to probe police. Retrieved from www.abc.net.au/news/stories/2010/06/15/2927564.htm.

Home Office. (2010). *Police officer strength in England and Wales by police force area on 31 March 2010*. Retrieved from www.homeoffice.gov.uk/publications/science-research-statistics/research-statistics/police-research/hosb1410/apo0910-tabs?view=Binary; and http://www.parliament.nsw.gov.au/Prod/parlment/committee.nsf/0/d865cf4e34ecad91ca25722d001b35e6/$FILE/10%20Year%20Review%20of%20Police%20Oversight%20NSW.pdf

Independent Police Complaints Commission. (2010). *Police complaints: Statistics for England and Wales 2009–10*. London: IPCC.

Johnston, E. (1991). *Royal commission into aboriginal deaths in custody: National report*, (Vol. 3). Canberra: Australian Government Publishing Service.

Judge, T. A. & Piccolo, R. F. (2004). Transformational and transactional leadership: A meta-analytic test of their relative validity. *Journal of Applied Psychology, 89*(5): 755–768.

Kaariainen, J. (2007). Trust in the police in 16 European countries: A multilevel analysis. *European Journal of Criminology, 4*(4), 409–435.

Kappeler, V., Sluder, R., & Alpert, G. (1998). *Forces of deviance: Understanding the dark side of policing*. Prospect Heights, IL: Waveland Press.

Kennedy, G. A. (2004). *Royal commission into whether there has been corrupt or criminal conduct by any Western Australian police officer, Final Report* (Vol. 2). Perth: Government of Western Australia.

Klockars, C. B., Ivkovich, S. K., Harver, W. E., & Haberfeld, M. R. (2000). *The measurement of police integrity.* A National Institute of Justice Research in Brief. Washington, D.C.: National Institute of Justice.

Knapp, W. (1972). *Report of a commission to investigate allegations of police corruption and the city's anti-corruption procedures*. New York: The City of New York.

Lewis, C. (1999). *Complaints against the police: The politics of reform*. Sydney: Hawkins Press.

Lewis, C., & Prenzler, T. (1999). Civilian oversight of police in Australia. *Trends and Issues in Crime and Criminal Justice, 141*, 1–6.

MacPherson, W. (1999). *The Stephen Lawrence Inquiry: Report of an inquiry by Sir William MacPherson of Cluny*. London: Her Majesty's Stationery Office.

Maguire, M., & Corbett, C. (1991). *A study of the police complaints system*. London: Her Majesty's Stationery Office.

Marx, G. (1992). When the guards guard themselves: Undercover tactics turned inward. *Policing and Society, 2*(3): 151–172.

Matthews, K. (2007, October 8). Abner Louima remembers New York police torture case on 10th anniversary. *Brooklyn Daily Express*. Retrieved from www.brooklyneagle.com/categories/category.php?category_id=4&id=14753

McCarthy, B. (2011, September 16). 2 N.O. cops sentenced in fatal beating. *The Times-Picayune*, p. A 01.

McKinney, M., & Mitchell, C. (2011, August 1). Cost of Minneapolis police payouts could hit record this year. *Star Tribune*, p. 1A.

Mieczkowski, T., & Lersch, K. (2002). Drug-testing police officers and police recruits. *Policing: An International Journal of Police Strategies and Management, 25*(3): 581–601.

Moss, P. (2009). Corruption: Matching measures to risks. Address to the Corruption Prevention Network Seminar hosted by the Australian Taxation Office. Retrieved from http://www.aclei.gov.au/www/aclei/rwpattach.nsf/VAP/%284CA02151F94FFB778ADAEC2E6EA8653D%29~Matching+Measures+to+Risks+-+CPN+-+12+June+2009.pdf/$file/Matching+Measures+to+Risks+-+CPN+-+12+June+2009.pdf

Muir, H., & Taylor, D. (2011, September 10). National: Mark Duggan funeral. *The Guardian*, p. 14.

Murray, J. (2005). Policing terrorism: A threat to community policing or just a shift in priorities? *Police Practice and Research: An International Journal, 6*(4), 347–361.

New South Wales Ombudsman. (2006). *Domestic violence: improving police practice*. Sydney: NSW Ombudsman. Retrieved from http://www.ombo.nsw.gov.au/publication/PDF/specialreport/DV%20Improving%20police%20practice%20dec%202006.pdf

New South Wales Ombudsman. (2007). *Annual report 2006–2007*. Sydney: NSW Ombudsman.

New South Wales Ombudsman. (2008). *Annual report 2007–2008*. Sydney: NSW Ombudsman.

New South Wales Ombudsman. (2009). *Annual report 2008–2009*. Sydney: NSW Ombudsman.

New South Wales Ombudsman. (2010). *Annual report 2009–2010*. Sydney: NSW Ombudsman.

New South Wales Police Force. (2007). *NSW Police Force drug and alcohol policy*. Sydney: NSW Police Force Safety Command. Retrieved from http://www.police.nsw.gov.au/__data/assets/file/0010/4321/Drug_and_Alcohol_Policy.pdf

New South Wales Police Force. (2008). *Annual report 2007–2008*. Sydney: New South Wales Police.

New South Wales Police Force. (2009). *Annual report 2008–2009*. Sydney: New South Wales Police.

New York Police Department. (2011). Frequently asked questions. Retrieved from http://www.nyc.gov/html/nypd/html/faq/faq_police.shtml#1

Northern Territory Ombudsman. (2009). *Thirty first annual report 2008–09*. Darwin: Northern Territory Ombudsman.

Northern Territory Police. (2007a). *Performance management and internal investigations general order*. Darwin: Northern Territory Police.

Northern Territory Police. (2007b). *NT police, fire and emergency services annual report 2007*. Darwin: NT Police, Fire and Emergency Services.

Northern Territory Police. (2009). *NT police, fire and emergency services annual report 2009*. Darwin: NT Police, Fire and Emergency Services.

O'Connell, R. (2010, November 8). Police face drug tests but heads won't roll. *The West Australian*. Retrieved from http://au.news.yahoo.com/thewest/a/-/breaking/8275248/police-face-drug-tests-but-heads-wont-roll/

Office of Police Integrity. (2005). *Review of fatal shootings by Victoria Police*. Melbourne: OPI. Retrieved from http://www.opi.vic.gov.au/file.php?73

Office of Police Integrity. (2007a). *Past patterns—Future directions: Victoria Police and the problem of corruption and serious misconduct*. Melbourne: OPI. Retrieved from http://www.opi.vic.gov.au/file.php?61

Office of Police Integrity. (2007b). *A fair and effective Victoria Police discipline system*. Melbourne: OPI. Retrieved from http://www.opi.vic.gov.au/file.php?3

Office of Police Integrity. (2009a). *The Victorian armed offenders squad: A case study*. Melbourne: OPI.

Office of Police Integrity. (2009b). Review of the use of force by and against Victorian police. Melbourne: OPI. Retrieved from http://www.opi.vic.gov.au/file.php?176

Office of Police Integrity. (2009c). *Annual report financial year ending 30 June 2009*. Melbourne: OPI.

Office of Police Integrity. (2010a). *Office of Police Integrity submission to the Integrity and anti-corruption system review*. Melbourne: OPI.

Office of Police Integrity. (2010b). Annual report financial year ending 30 June 2010. Melbourne: OPI.

Office of Police Integrity. (2010c). *Sensitive and confidential information in a police environment*. (OPI discussion paper no. 2). Melbourne: OPI. Retrieved from http://www.opi.vic.gov.au/file.php?216

Office of Police Integrity. (2010d). *Flexible work practices for policing*. Melbourne: OPI. Retrieved from http://www.opi.vic.gov.au/file.php?202

Office of Police Integrity. (2011). *Improving Victoria Police discipline and complaint handling systems: A progress report*. Melbourne: OPI. Retrieved from http://www.opi.vic.gov.au/file.php?247

Office of Police Integrity. (n.d.). *Strategic plan 2010–2013*. Melbourne: OPI. Retrieved from http://www.opi.vic.gov.au/file.php?219

O'Malley, P. (1979). Class conflict, land and social banditry: Bushranging in nineteenth century Australia. *Social Problems, 26*(3), 271–283.

Ombudsman of Victoria. (1998). *Operation BART: Investigation of allegations against police in relation to the shutter allocation system, final report*. Melbourne: Victorian Government Printer.

Parliamentary Crime and Misconduct Committee. (2006). *Three year review of the Crime and Misconduct Commission*. (Report no. 71). Brisbane: Queensland Parliament. Retrieved from http://www.parliament.qld.gov.au/documents/committees/PCMC/2006/three-year-review-06/Report71-3yrReview.pdf

Parliamentary Crime and Misconduct Committee. (2009). *Three yearly review of the Crime and Misconduct Commission*. (Report no. 79). Brisbane: Queensland Parliament. Retrieved from http://www.parliament.qld.gov.au/documents/committees/PCMC/2009/three-year-review-09/Report79-3yrReview.pdf

People, J. (2009). *Project Marrella: Is misconduct by NSW police officers affected by the number of students in a training intake at the NSW Police College?* (Research and Issues Paper 3). Sydney: Police Integrity Commission. Retrieved from http://www.pic.nsw.gov.au/files/reports/Project%20Marrella%2027%20October%20 2009.pdf

Perez, A., Berg, K., & Myers, D. (2003). Police and riots, 1967–1969. *Journal of Black Studies, 34*(2), 153–182.

Perrott, S. B., & Kelloway, E .K. (2011). Scandals, sagging morale, and role ambiguity in the Royal Canadian Mounted Police: The end of a Canadian institution as we know it? *Police Practice and Research: An International Journal, 12*(2), 120–135.

Police Complaints Authority (2008). *23rd Annual Report*. Adelaide, Australia: Police Complaints Authority.

Police Complaints Authority (2010). *Origins of the Police Complaints Authority*. Retrieved from www.pca.sa.gov.au/PCAmain.htm

Police Integrity Commission. (2000). *Project Dresden: An audit of the quality of NSW police service internal investigations*. Sydney: PIC. Retrieved from http://www.pic.nsw.gov.au/files/reports/Dresden.pdf

Police Integrity Commission. (2005). Operation Abelia: Research and investigations into illegal drug use by NSW police officers. (Vol. 1–4). Sydney: PIC.

Police Integrity Commission. (2009a). *Annual report 2008–2009*. Sydney: PIC.

Police Integrity Commission. (2009b). *Project Manta report 1 identification and communication of command misconduct risks*. Sydney: PIC. Retrieved from http://www.pic.nsw.gov.au/files/reports/Manta%202009.pdf

Police Integrity Commission. (2009c). *Project Odin: Identifying and managing high risk officers in the NSW Police Force*. Sydney: PIC. Retrieved from http://www.pic.nsw.gov.au/files/reports/Project%20Odin%20Report.pdf

Porter, L. E. (2005). Policing the police service: Psychological contributions to the study and prevention of police corruption. In L. J. Alison (Ed.), *Offender profiling and criminal investigation: A forensic psychologist's casebook*, (pp. 143–169). Cullompton: Willan.

Porter, L. E., Prenzler, T., & Fleming, J. (2011). Complaint reduction in the Tasmania Police. *Policing & Society*.

Prados, J. (1986). *Presidents' secret wars: CIA and Pentagon covert operations since World War II*. New York: William Morrow.

Prenzler, T. (2009a). *Ethics and accountability in criminal justice*. Brisbane: Australian Academic Press.

Prenzler, T. (2009b) *Police corruption: Preventing misconduct and maintaining integrity*. Boca Raton FL: CRC Press/Taylor & Francis.

Prenzler, T. (2010). Change and continuity in Australian policing. In R. Lincoln & S. Robinson (Eds.), *Crime over time: Temporal perspectives on crime and punishment in Australia* (pp. 171–186). Newcastle upon Tyne: Cambridge Scholars Publishing.

Prenzler, T. (2011). The evolution of police oversight in Australia. *Policing and Society, 21*(3), 284–303.

Prenzler, T., Allard, T., Curry, S., and Macintyre, S. (2010). Complaints against police: The complainants' experience. *Journal of Criminal Justice Research*, 1(1): 1-18

Prenzler, T., & Ronken, C. (2001). Police integrity testing in Australia. *Criminal Justice: The International Journal of Policy and Practice, 1*(3), 319–342.

Prenzler, T., & Ronken, C. (2003). A survey of innovations in the development and maintenance of ethical standards by Australian police departments. *Police Practice and Research: An International Journal, 4*(2), 163–178.

Productivity Commission. (2010). *Report on government services.* Canberra: Productivity Commission.

Punch, M. (2003). Rotten orchards: "Pestilence," police misconduct and system failure. *Policing and Society, 13*(2), 171–196.

Queensland Council for Civil Liberties. (2010). *Call for judicial inquiry into police complaints process.* Retrieved from http://www.qccl.org.au/documents/Media_TOG_17June10_Call_JudicialInquiry_PoliceComplaints.pdf

Queensland Police Service. (2007). *Corruption Prevention Plan 2009–2013.* Brisbane: QPS. Retrieved from http://www.police.qld.gov.au/Resources/Internet/services/reportsPublications/corrupt/document/CorruptionPreventionPlan%20_WEB.pdf

Queensland Police Service. (2009). *Annual report 2008–9.* Brisbane: QPS.

Queensland Police Service. (2010). *Annual report 2009–10.* Brisbane: QPS.

Queensland Police Service and Crime and Misconduct Commission. (2009). *Review of Taser policy, training, and monitoring and review practices.* Brisbane: QPS–CMC. Retrieved from http://www.cmc.qld.gov.au/data/portal/00000005/content/16225001252029372054.pdf

Richards, J. (2008). *The secret war: A true history of Queensland's native police.* Brisbane: University of Queensland Press.

Ross, G. (2007). Police oversight: Help or hindrance? In M. Mitchell & J. Casey (Eds.), *Police leadership and management* (pp. 150–166). Sydney: Federation Press.

Royal Commission. (1981). *Second report—Freedom and security under the law.* Ottawa: Commission of Inquiry Concerning Certain Activities of the RCMP, Canadian Government Publishing Centre.

Rudd, K. (2008). *The first national security statement to the Parliament.* Address by the Prime Minister of Australia, The Hon. Kevin Rudd MP. Retrieved from http://pmrudd.archive.dpmc.gov.au/sites/default/files/file/documents/20081204_national_security_statement.pdf

Sandy, A., & Baskin, B. (2011, August 16) Dirty little secrets uncovered. *Courier Mail,* pp. 1, 19.

Sarre, R. (1989). Towards the notion of policing "by consent" and its implications for police accountability. In D. Chappell & P. Wilson (Eds.), *Australian policing: Contemporary issues* (pp. 102–119). Sydney: Butterworths.

Savage, C., & Alvarez, L. (2011, September 11). Police in Puerto Rico are accused of abuses. Justice Department report. Retrieved from http://www.nytimes.com/2011/09/08/us/08police.html?_r=2

Scarman, L. G. (1986). *Scarman report.* London: Penguin.

Seneviratne, M. (2004). Policing the police in the United Kingdom. *Policing and Society, 14*(4), 329.

South Australia Police. (2008). *Annual report 2007/2008.* Adelaide. SAP.

South Australia Police. (2009). *Annual report 2008/2009.* Adelaide. SAP.

Stewart, C. (2011, June 23). Overland faces new probe on statistics. *The Australian,* p. 1.

Tasmania Ombudsman. (2004). *Review of Ombudsman Act, 1978: Position paper.* Hobart: Office of the Ombudsman. Retrieved from http://www.ombudsman.tas.gov.au/__data/assets/pdf_file/0006/145383/Review_of_Omb_Act_Position_Paper_May2004.pdf

Tasmania Police. (2004). *Internal investigations annual report 2003/4.* Hobart: Tasmania Police.

Tasmania Police. (2009). *Annual report 2008/09.* Hobart: Department of Police and Public Safety.

Tasmania Police. (2010). *Annual report 2009/10.* Hobart: Department of Police and Public Safety.

The Committee. (2002). *Research report on trends in police corruption.* Sydney: Committee on the Office of the Ombudsman and the Police Integrity Commission, NSW Parliament. Retrieved from http://www.parliament.nsw.gov.au/prod/parlment/committee.nsf/0/a467316feb212c4cca256cfb0013c1d2/$FILE/Research%20Report%20on%20Trends%20in%20Police%20Corruption.PDF

The Committee. (2006). *Report on ten year review of the police oversight system in New South Wales.* Sydney: Committee on the Office of the Ombudsman and the Police Integrity Commission, NSW Parliament. Retrieved from http://www.parliament.nsw.gov.au/Prod/parlment/committee.nsf/0/d865cf4e34ecad91ca25722d001b35e6/$FILE/10%20Year%20Review%20of%20Police%20Oversight%20NSW.pdf

Transparency International UK. (2011a). *Corruption in the UK, Part Two, Assessment of sectors.* London: Transparency International.

Transparency International UK. (2011b). *National integrity system assessment United Kingdom, corruption in the UK.* (Part 3). London: Transparency International.

U.S. Department of Justice/Civil Rights Division. (2011a). *Investigation of the New Orleans Police Department.* Washington, D.C.: Government Printing Office.

U.S. Department of Justice/Civil Rights Division. (2011b). *Investigation of the Puerto Rico Police Department.* Washington, D.C.: Government Printing Office.

Usborne, D. (2011, August 6). Officers guilty over shootings that shamed New Orleans. *The Independent,* pp. 22, 23.

van Natta Jr., D. (2011, July 18). Scotland Yard failed to act. *International Herald Tribune,* p. 4.

Vejnovic, D., & Lalic, V. (2005). Community policing in a changing world: A case study in Bosnia and Herzegovina. *Police Practice and Research: An International Journal, 6*(4), 363–373.

Victoria Police. (2008). *Victoria Police community service charter.* Melbourne: Victoria Police. Retrieved from http://www.police.vic.gov.au/content.asp?a=internetBridgingPage&Media_ID=28806

Victoria Police. (2009). *Ethical Standards Department annual information report for 2008/09.* Melbourne: Victoria Police.

Walker, S. (2001). *Police accountability: The role of citizen oversight.* Belmont, CA: Wadsworth.

Walker, S. (2003). *Early intervention systems for law enforcement agencies: A planning and management guide.* Washington, D.C.: U.S. Department of Justice, Government Printing Office.

Walker, S. (2007). Police accountability: Current issues and research needs. Paper presented at the *Policing Research Workshop: Planning for the Future*, National Institute of Justice, Washington, D.C., November 28–29.

Walker, S., Alpert, G. P., and Kenney, D. J. (2000). Early warning systems for police: Concept, history, and issues. *Police Quarterly, 3*(2): 132.

Weitzer, R. (2002). Incidents of police misconduct and public opinion, *Journal of Criminal Justice, 30*, 397–408.

Weitzer, R. (2004). Public perceptions of police misconduct and reform. In M. Hickman, A. Piquero, & J. Greene (Eds.), *Police integrity and ethics* (pp. 190–208). Belmont, CA: Wadsworth.

Western Australia Police. (2007). *Annual report 2007*. Perth: WAP.

Western Australia Police. (2008). *Code of conduct*. Perth: WAP. Retrieved from http://www.police.wa.gov.au/LinkClick.aspx?link=PDFs%2FWAPolice_Code_of_Conduct_Sept08.pdf&tabid=1295

Wilson, J. M., & Grammich, C. A. (2011). Reconstructing internal security in post-conflict societies: The challenge and successfulness of developing democratic police and justice institutions. *Security Journal, 12*(1), 52–68.

Wong, K. C. (2011). *Police reform in China*. Boca Raton, FL: CRC Press/Taylor & Francis.

Wood, J. R. T. (1996). *Royal commission into the New South Wales police service interim report, February 1996*. Sydney: New South Wales Government Printer.

Wood, J. R. T. (1997). *Final report of the Royal Commission into the New South Wales police service*. Sydney: New South Wales Government Printer.

Legislation

Commonwealth
AFP Act 1979
Complaints (Australian Federal Police) Act 1981
Law Enforcement Integrity Commissioner Act 2006
Ombudsman Act 1976 (Cth.)
Surveillance Devices Act 2004
Telecommunications (Interception and Access) Act 1979

New South Wales
Police Act 1990
Police Integrity Commission Act 1996
Protected Disclosures Act 1994
Witness Protection Act 1995

Northern Territory
Northern Territory of Australia Ombudsman Act, 2009
Ombudsman (Northern Territory) Act
Ombudsman Act 2009
Police Administration Act
Surveillance Devices Act 2007
Telecommunications (Interception) Northern Territory Act 2001

Queensland
Crime and Misconduct Act 2001
Police Service Administration Act 1990
Public Service Act (Qld) 2008
Telecommunications Interception Act 2009 (Qld)

South Australia
Freedom of Information Act 1991 (SA)
Listening and Surveillance Devices Act, 1972
Police (Complaints and Disciplinary Proceedings) Act 1985
Police Act 1998
Police Regulations Act 1999
Summary Offences Act 1953
Telecommunications (Interception) Act 1988

Tasmania
Freedom of Information Act 1991 (Tas)
Integrity Commission Act 2009
Police Powers (Controlled Operations) Act 2006
Police Powers (Surveillance Devices) Act 2006
Police Services Act 2003
Telecommunications (Interception) Tasmania Act 1999
Witness Protection Act 2000

Victoria
Charter of Human Rights and Responsibilities Act, 2006
Crimes (Assumed Identities) Act 2004
Crimes (Controlled Operations) Act 2004
Police Integrity Act 2008
Police Regulation Act 1958
Witness Protection Act 1991

Western Australia
Corruption and Crime Commission Act 2003
Police Act 1892
Police Force Regulations 1974
Public Interest Disclosure Act 2003

A Call for Authors

Advances in Police Theory and Practice

AIMS AND SCOPE:

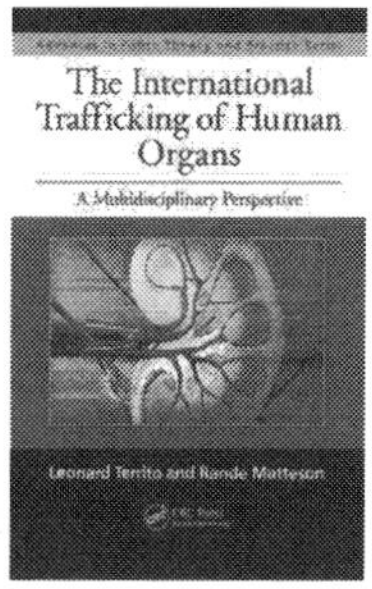

This cutting-edge series is designed to promote publication of books on contemporary advances in police theory and practice. We are especially interested in volumes that focus on the nexus between research and practice, with the end goal of disseminating innovations in policing. We will consider collections of expert contributions as well as individually authored works. Books in this series will be marketed internationally to both academic and professional audiences. This series also seeks to —

- Bridge the gap in knowledge about advances in theory and practice regarding who the police are, what they do, and how they maintain order, administer laws, and serve their communities
- Improve cooperation between those who are active in the field and those who are involved in academic research so as to facilitate the application of innovative advances in theory and practice

The series especially encourages the contribution of works coauthored by police practitioners and researchers. We are also interested in works comparing policing approaches and methods globally, examining such areas as the policing of transitional states, democratic policing, policing and minorities, preventive policing, investigation, patrolling and response, terrorism, organized crime and drug enforcement. In fact, every aspect of policing,public safety, and security, as well as public order is relevant for the series. Manuscripts should be between 300 and 600 printed pages. If you have a proposal for an original work or for a contributed volume, please be in touch.

Series Editor
Dilip Das, Ph.D., Ph: 802-598-3680
E-mail: dilipkd@aol.com

Dr. Das is a professor of criminal justice and Human Rights Consultant to the United Nations. He is a former chief of police and, founding president of the International Police Executive Symposium, IPES, www.ipes.info. He is also founding editor-in-chief of *Police Practice and Research: An International Journal* (PPR), (Routledge/Taylor & Francis), www.tandf.co.uk/journals. In addition to editing the *World Police Encyclopedia* (Taylor & Francis, 2006), Dr. Das has published numerous books and articles during his many years of involve-ment in police practice, research, writing, and education.

Proposals for the series may be submitted to the series editor or directly to –

Carolyn Spence
Senior Editor • CRC Press / Taylor & Francis Group
561-998-2515 • 561-997-7249 (fax)
carolyn.spence@taylorandfrancis.com • www.crcpress.com
6000 Broken Sound Parkway NW, Suite 300, Boca Raton, FL 33487

Index

I

J

K

L

O

P

Q

R

T

Y

Z